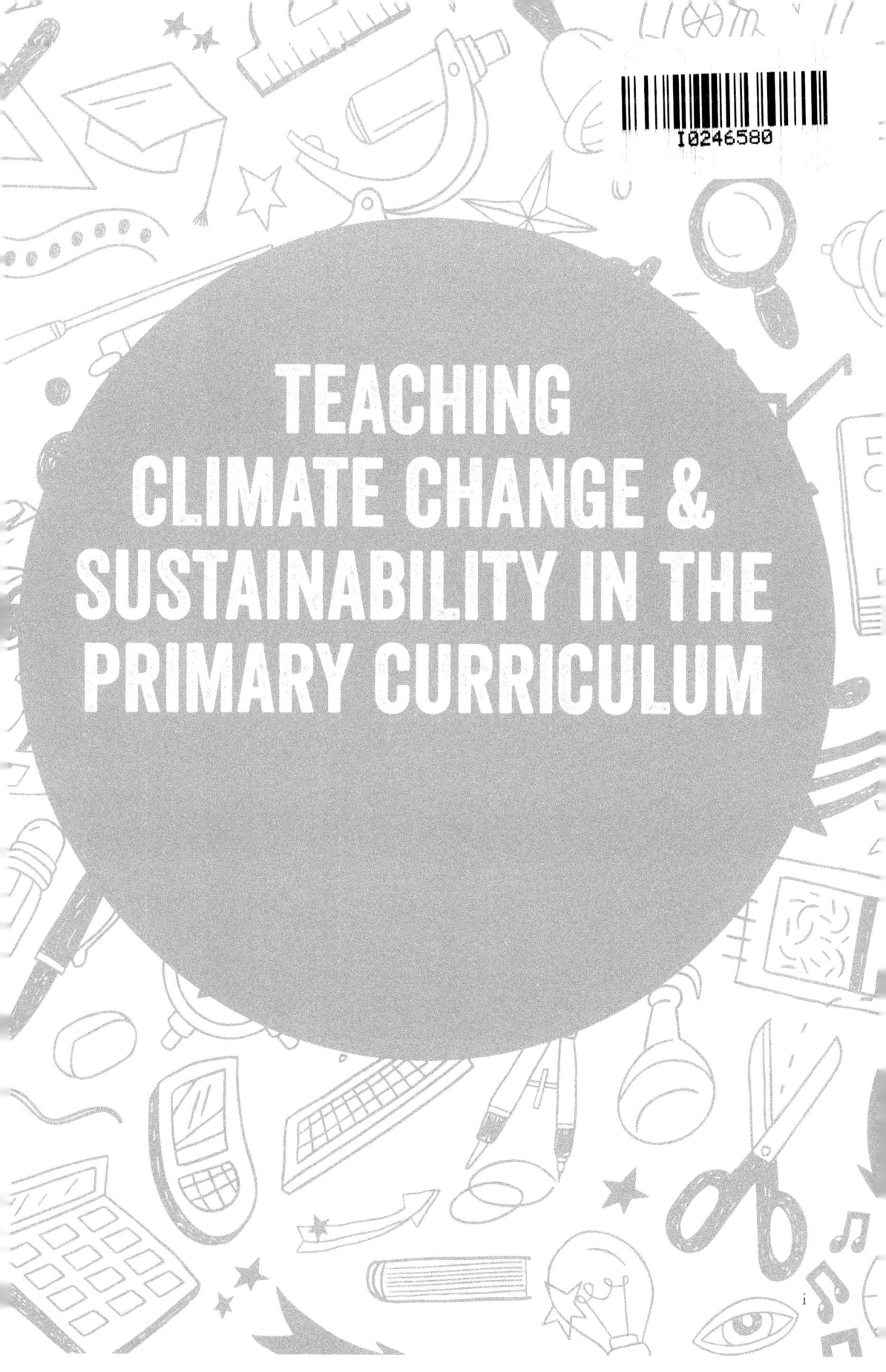

TEACHING CLIMATE CHANGE & SUSTAINABILITY IN THE PRIMARY CURRICULUM

Sara Miller McCune founded Sage Publishing in 1965 to support the dissemination of usable knowledge and educate a global community. Sage publishes more than 1000 journals and over 800 new books each year, spanning a wide range of subject areas. Our growing selection of library products includes archives, data, case studies and video. Sage remains majority owned by our founder and after her lifetime will become owned by a charitable trust that secures the company's continued independence.

Los Angeles | London | New Delhi | Singapore | Washington DC | Melbourne

TEACHING CLIMATE CHANGE & SUSTAINABILITY IN THE PRIMARY CURRICULUM

EDITED BY

KARIN DOULL
SUSAN OGIER

Learning Matters

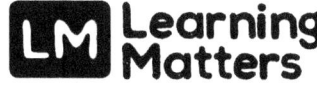

Learning Matters
A Sage Publishing Company
1 Oliver's Yard
55 City Road
London EC1Y 1SP

Sage Publications Inc.
2455 Teller Road
Thousand Oaks, California 91320

Sage Publications India Pvt Ltd
B 1/I 1 Mohan Cooperative Industrial Area
Mathura Road
New Delhi 110 044

Sage Publications Asia-Pacific Pte Ltd
3 Church Street
#10-04 Samsung Hub
Singapore 049483

Editor: Amy Thornton
Senior project editor: Chris Marke
Project management: TNQ Technologies
Cover design: Wendy Scott
Typeset by: TNQ Technologies

© 2024 Editorial arrangement Karin Doull and Susan Ogier.

Chapter 1 Sarah Leonard; Chapter 2 Richard Dunne and Emilie Martin; Chapter 3 Sarah Sprake and Emily Rotchell; Chapter 4 Deborah Pop; Chapter 5 Susan Ogier and Lynda Chinaka; Chapter 6 Anthony Barlow; Chapter 7 Karin Doull; Chapter 8 Verity Jones. Chapter 9 Emese Hall; Chapter 10 Susie Townsend; Chapter 11 Karin Doull and Susan Ogier with Tanya Bastian; Chapter 12 Alastair Greig, Helen Mead, Sarah Lloyd, and Jon Audain; Chapter 13 Alison Murray, Sarah Adams, Jo Nugent.

Apart from any fair dealing for the purposes of research or private study, or criticism or review, as permitted under the Copyright, Design and Patents Act, 1988, this publication may be reproduced, stored or transmitted in any form, or by any means, only with the prior permission in writing of the publishers, or in the case of reprographic reproduction, in accordance with the terms of licences issued by the Copyright Licensing Agency. Enquiries concerning reproduction outside these terms should be sent to the publishers.

Library of Congress Control Number: 2023944502

British Library Cataloguing in Publication Data

A catalogue record for this book is available from the British Library.

ISBN 978-1-5296-2841-8
ISBN 978-1-5296-2840-1 (pbk)

At Sage we take sustainability seriously. Most of our products are printed in the UK using responsibly sourced papers and boards. When we print overseas we ensure sustainable papers are used as measured by the Paper Chain Project grading system. We undertake an annual audit to monitor our sustainability.

CONTENTS

About the editors and contributors	vii
Foreword	xi
The earth	xiii

	Introduction: Teaching for Sustainable Futures Karin Doull and Susan Ogier	1
1	The Personal, Social, Emotional and Citizenship Dimensions of Sustainability Education Sarah Leonard	11
2	Creating Harmony Through Curriculum Design Richard Dunne and Emilie Martin	21
3	Learning to Care About Our World in the Early Years Sarah Sprake and Emily Rotchell	33
4	Becoming Conservation Champions Through Science Learning Deborah Pope	45
5	Teaching for Sustainability Within Design and Computing Education Susan Ogier and Lynda Chinaka	62
6	Exploring the Climate in Context Through Geography Anthony Barlow	77
7	Exploring the History of Humans and Their Environment Karin Doull	91
8	Learning to Care About the Environment Through Picturebooks Verity Jones	107
9	Education for Sustainable Development Through Art: Project CARE Emese Hall	117
10	Religious Education and Sustainable Living Susie Townsend	129
11	Understanding Our World Challenges Through Mathematics Karin Doull and Susan Ogier with Tanya Bastian	140
12	Exploring Our World Through Music and Sound *Alastair Greig* (Part 1) *and Helen Mead, Sarah Lloyd and Jon Audain* (Part 2)	153

13 Physical Education for Sustainability and Well-Being   174
    Alison Murray, Sarah Adams and Jo Nugent

Appendix 1: A Small Research Project: Investigating Climate Change and Sustainability
    With Ichthys Class   187
Appendix 2: The 17 Sustainable Development Goals (SDGs) to Transform Our World   190
Appendix 3: Initial Teacher Training (ITT) Core Content Framework (CCF)   192
Index   195

ABOUT THE EDITORS AND CONTRIBUTORS

Karin Doull is a freelance consultant and writer in primary history. Until recently she was a Principal Lecturer at the University of Roehampton leading the primary history team. She remains an honorary research fellow for the university. Karin is active within History Teacher Education Network (HTEN) and presented at History Educators International Research Network (HEIRNET). Karin is a fellow of the Historical Association (HA) and member of the primary committee. She is lead editor for *Primary History Journal*, to which she frequently contributes. Karin has also published several books relating to teaching primary history. Karin is fascinated by all history and keen to share her enthusiasm. Her main area of interest is women's history and she has written two historical short stories featuring female protagonists.

Susan Ogier is a Senior Lecturer in Primary Education, specialising in Art and Design at the University of Roehampton, London. She is author of Teaching Primary Art and Design (2017), Teaching Arts in the Primary Curriculum (2021) published by Sage, as well as a series of books for children, professional and peer-reviewed journal articles, and book chapters. She holds a variety of consultancy roles, including Associate Consultant for Primary Art and Design for NASBTT, and works closely with learned society, NSEAD. Susan's most recent book in the Learning Matters series is the revised second publication of *A Broad and Balanced Curriculum: Educating the Whole Child* (2022), and has written the chapter, Subject Knowledge in Art, Craft and Design (2023) in Majid, N. *Essential Subject Knowledge for Primary Teachers* published by Sage.

Jon Audain is a Senior Lecturer in Education and Co-Lead of the Primary PGCE at the Institute of Education, University of Winchester. Jon is the author and collaborator of over 20 books, chapters, peer-reviewed journal articles and papers, is an Apple Distinguished Educator (ADE) and Past-Chair of the Technology, Pedagogy in Education Association (TPEA).

Sarah Adams worked at the University of Roehampton as a Senior Lecturer in Primary Physical Education, before emigrating back to Canada where she is currently working as a PE teacher. Having taught in the primary sector in both Canada and the United Kingdom, Sarah has invested time to educate and inspire children and student teachers alike. She is interested in supporting student well-being through inclusive curriculum design and collaborating with stakeholders across the PE sector both in Canada and the United Kingdom.

Anthony Barlow is a Principal Lecturer, Programme Convenor and subject leader for Geography Education at the University of Roehampton. He taught in London and Bolton for 12 years before entering Higher Education. He is Trustee of the Early Years and Primary Committee (EYPPC) of the Geographical Association. He is a member of the GeogLive! Geography collective as part of the EYPPC and they have produced more than 15 hours of free CPD, available free on YouTube. He is a consultant for local authorities, academy groups and schools through the GA and has authored resources and acted as consultant on various projects for TTS, Rising Stars/Hodder, Findel, Scholastic, the BBC and GridClub/Channel 4. Anthony co-wrote the book *Mastering Primary Geography* (Bloomsbury, 2019) and has chapters in books as diverse as on effective primary displays and on diversity in education and the danger of 'single stories'. He tweets @totalgeography and @EYPPC_GA.

Tanya Bastian is an Assistant Headteacher with a BA in Primary Education and Mathematics Specialism from the University of Reading, brings seven years of teaching experience across KS1 and KS2. She is devoted to fostering academic growth, creating an inclusive environment and supporting fellow teachers' professional development. Tanya's true passion lies in nurturing students' confidence as problem solvers and igniting their love for mathematics.

Lynda Chinaka is a Senior Lecturer in Computing Education leading in primary computing at the University of Roehampton. She has led the development of computing in schools in various roles as well as Teacher Leader for a local London Authority's School Improvement Service, as an Associate Facilitator of the National Centre of Computing Education and a Hub Leader for Computing At Schools (CAS) the subject association and community for computing. She is keen to promote access to computing for everyone. Lynda recently co-authored the chapter, Diversity Matters: Perspectives for teaching in Design and Technology, Science and Equity Focused Computing in *Teaching in the Diverse Classroom* edited by Karin Doull and published by Sage.

Richard Dunne is the Founder and Director of The Harmony Project (www.theharmonyproject.org.uk) and has a career in education spanning 30 years. Formerly, he was Headteacher of an Ofsted-rated outstanding school in Surrey, where he successfully implemented Harmony principles across the curriculum as well as within and beyond the school community.

Alastair Greig has been involved in Music Education for over 30 years, running parallel with his compositional output. As a Senior Fellow of the University of Roehampton, Associate Lecturer at UCL and a Fellow of the Higher Education Academy, his work focusses in on musical creativity: composition. His work involves training teachers to understand how music works by breaking complex material down, demonstrating how children can explore this material and discover how to manipulate sound for themselves. He has worked with many schools on developing subject knowledge for teachers and how to apply this in their classrooms, contributed several chapters for educational books and organised a conference to develop how to establish sustainable links between composers and schools.

Emese Hall is a Senior Lecturer in art and design education at the School of Education, University of Exeter, UK. Previously a primary and early years teacher, she has worked within teacher education since 2005. Her research interests include teachers' professional learning and art education for the environment and climate emergency. She is a member of the International Society for Education through Art (InSEA) and the (UK) National Society for Education in Art and Design (NSEAD), where she held the position of NSEAD Vice President (January 2018–December 2021).

Verity Jones is an Associate Professor in the School of Education and Childhood at the University of the West of England, Bristol. With over 20 years' experience in sustainable education and research, her interests range from food to fashion, plants to pollution and drought to dung beetles. She has worked with national and international organisations to promote and develop climate change and sustainable education with the BBC, Friends of the Earth, the Royal Entomological Society and Fashion Revolution.

Sarah Leonard is Head of primary initial teacher education at the University of Roehampton where she also leads the professional studies programmes for undergraduate and postgraduate students. Her doctoral studies explored how context influences learning which supported cross-school work on behaviour and social and emotional aspects of learning. She has led primary and through schools and has extensive experience in school improvement work, with a focus on improving leadership and management and outcomes for pupils vulnerable to underachievement in the school system. She is involved in school-based CPD on multilingualism with the Bell Foundation.

Sarah Lloyd is a primary music specialist with over 20 years experience. She coaches and mentors leaders and non-specialist teachers to embed music within their schools and works with local music hubs. Sarah collaborates to create learning resources and co-author chapters around primary music. She teaches EYFS, primary and leads CPD sessions for teachers and ITT students.

Alison Murray has taught primary and secondary Physical Education in the United States and United Kingdom, specialising in motor development and learning in the United States and Mexico. She has supported and led Physical Education teacher education in US and UK HE and has thrived as PE Primary Lead with the University of Roehampton. Alison is a proud member of the PE National Task Force, the All-Party Parliamentary Group on a Fit and Healthy Childhood and is an ambassador for the Children's Alliance. Alison enjoys collaborating with her amazing colleagues through knowledge exchange, research opportunities and policy-related advocacy. As extended from her doctoral studies, Alison is keen to better understand and facilitate learner autonomy as regards health and well-being.

Emilie Martin is a journalist, former teacher and long-standing contributor to The Harmony Project. The Harmony Project itself was borne from the school curriculum developed by Richard Dunned, which was inspired by the vision of harmony set out by King Charles III in his 2010 book, *Harmony: A New Way of Looking at Our World*. The Harmony Project works to transform education so that it prepares young people to engage with the environmental challenges we face, equipping them with the skills and understanding they need to co-create a future that enables all life to flourish.

Helen Mead is a freelance music educator, supporting music in hubs, schools and communities. She leads sessions in mainstream, EYFS and SEND settings and for ITT students. She has worked as a specialist primary music teacher in schools and hubs in the South East for over 20 years. Helen now creates content and supports national organisations to develop their music education provision.

Jo Nugent has enjoyed a long and exciting career in education, having taught in UK primary schools for over 20 years before moving into higher education. Jo is currently working at the University of Roehampton as a Senior Lecturer in Primary Education and is the Assistant Programme Convenor for the BA Primary Programme. Jo dedicates time to train, coach and mentor student teachers across both undergraduate and postgraduate programmes and is interested in the development of professional practices that support students across their early careers.

Deborah Pope has many years of teaching experience in both primary schools and universities. Currently a Senior Lecturer in Education at the University of Chester, Deborah teaches on a range of undergraduate and postgraduate courses, specialising in science education and teachers' professional learning. Deborah edited the text for trainee teachers, *Understanding Subject Knowledge for Primary Teaching*. In a previous life she studied Zoology and researched in the field of Evolutionary Ecology.

Emily Rotchell is a Senior Lecturer in Primary Initial Teacher Education (Geography) at The University of Roehampton, and prior to this was a Deputy Headteacher at an Infant School. Emily is currently the joint secretary of The Early Years and Primary Phase Committee for The Geographical Association and a member of The Royal Geographical Society's (with IBG) Education Committee. Emily is a member of the Geographical Association primary and early years committee. She has written articles for the *Primary Geography Journal* produced by The Geographical Association

Sarah Sprake is an early years adviser and prior to this was a teacher across the early years and primary age range. Before becoming a teacher Sarah studied Geography at the University of Bristol and worked on regeneration and urban design projects with European partner cities, including projects to develop spaces co-produced with children. Sarah is a member of the Geographical Association primary and early years committee. She has written articles for the *Primary Geography Journal* produced by The Geographical Association.

Susie Townsend is a Senior Lecturer at the University of Roehampton and is the History subject lead, teaching on the undergraduate BA Ed course and PGCE programmes. She has an MA in Education and is also a Senior Fellow of the Higher Education Academy. She has been in teaching since 1986 with 25 years experience teaching History in a range of comprehensive schools and was Head of History and Head of Humanities, teaching RE, Geography and Social Science. Susie moved into primary teaching with a special interest in transition from Year 6–7 which formed the basis of her MA dissertation. She is an Honorary Fellow for the Historical Association and makes regular contributions to the *Primary History Journal* and to workshops at the Annual Conferences.

FOREWORD

Creating a Vision for the Future

Climate change affects us all, but especially young children who have their lives stretching out before them. It is part of a web of complex inter-related environmental problems confronting humanity, any one of which has the potential to cause devastating consequences.

Climate change is unlike other problems in that it is particularly hard to see the links between cause and effect. Pollution that was emitted in one place in the past can linger in the atmosphere for many decades, affecting people elsewhere in the world far into the future. There is also a psychological dimension. Evolution has equipped us to deal with immediate and tangible threats but has left us vulnerable to dangers that are delayed and distributed. Climate change is such a pervasive and bewildering problem that it is easy to feel overwhelmed by it. It raises questions about power relations, intergenerational justice and the responsibilities one group of people has to another. The poor and disadvantaged are particularly vulnerable because they do not have the capacity to cope with significant disruption. Our institutional structures are singularly badly placed to deal with such issues. In these circumstances, socially constructed silence becomes a convenient response.

But silence is not an option. We know from multiple scientific studies that the decisions we make in the next few decades are liable to have implications for thousands of years to come. Although it is difficult to be certain, there is every indication that we are living at a pivotal moment in human history when the choices and good judgement have never been more important. How can we best respond, individually, nationally and internationally to climate change and other environmental challenges? And what do we need to do to steer towards a safe place where humanity has the best chance of flourishing within planetary limits?

There is no single answer, but it is widely acknowledged that education has a significant part to play in reframing economic, social and cultural values and in helping to fashion more sustainable ways of living. This is not just the opinion of educational experts. It was affirmed, for example, by UNESCO in the Berlin Declaration on Education for Sustainable Development (2021) which unequivocally states that 'education is a powerful enabler of positive mindsets' that enables learners to develop both the 'cognitive and non-cognitive skills' to confront current challenges. All areas of the curriculum will need to be harnessed in this endeavour. The importance of new narratives, the value of the wisdom embodied in traditional belief systems and deep questions about meaning and purpose of life are also coming to the fore. At the same time, a respect for nature and a commitment to human rights, democracy and international understanding are seen as fundamental.

This book assembles the collective experiences and wisdom of a range of well-respected practitioners and teacher educators, all of whom have a deep understanding of sustainability education and curriculum issues. The focus is on the primary years – the time when the life message which children will take with them into adulthood is so often formed. It is heartening to find expert advice about so many different curriculum areas gathered together in a single volume. The balance between theory and practice will be particularly welcomed by many readers.

This is a time of great peril and great opportunities. There are literally hundreds of groups and organisations in the United Kingdom and other countries that are dedicated to promoting sustainability education. The pedagogies and practices to support sustainability awareness are widely established and respected in schools. Forest schools have shown the value of first-hand outdoor experience in nature and have many advocates. Regenerative and transformative learning are ideas that are gaining traction. The chapters presented here add further weight to the argument for educational reform. With so many of the key pieces in place there is potential for transformative change.

Climate change isn't simply a problem waiting for a solution or a technical fix. Rather, as climate scientist Mike Hulme (2009) points out, it's an environmental, cultural and political phenomenon which is reshaping the way we think about ourselves, our societies and our relationship with the natural world. We now know all too clearly that the notions of conquest, exploitation and progress which underpinned the fossil fuel age cannot be sustained. Finding a new direction – devising a new story of what it means to live well – is the challenge of our age. There is an urgent need to empower young people so they can play their part in shaping the future. At the moment, we can only glimpse the possibilities that lie ahead but if we want to create a positive future, we have to imagine it first. One of the key tasks of the progressive educator, Paulo Freire (1994, p3) reminds us, is 'to unveil opportunities for hope, whatever the obstacles might be'. We can all play a part in this process, however big or small our role might be.

Dr Stephen Scoffham
Visiting Reader in Sustainability and Education,
Canterbury Christ Church University, UK

THE EARTH

The earth shaped us, defined us, protected us

Once we lived in harmony with our world

We heard its voice, danced to its song

But

We lost our way

We upset the balance

We would not listen to what it was telling us

We created, changed, invented,

For the better, for the future

But

We thought only of ourselves

Trusting that the bountiful resources were endless

We did not try to ruin things

We did not think

We did not listen

So,

We have shaped the Earth,

Defined its future

Now we must learn to protect it

To listen to its song of harmony

Karin J. Doull, 2023

INTRODUCTION: TEACHING FOR SUSTAINABLE FUTURES

KARIN DOULL AND SUSAN OGIER

SUSTAINABLE DEVELOPMENT GOALS

GOAL 4: Quality Education
GOAL 13: Climate Action

As we got further and further away, it [the Earth] diminished in size. Finally, it shrank to the size of a marble, the most beautiful you can imagine. That beautiful, warm, living object looked so fragile, so delicate, that if you touched it with a finger it would crumble and fall apart.

James Irwin, Astronaut

A growing recognition of the effects of climate change developed in 1960s as man travelled into space and saw, for the first time, the home planet in all its beauty and fragility. At the same time, an understanding of the impact that man was having on the planet began to register alarm bells with some scientific communities. For those born in the 1960s, it was a time of innovation, change and 'progress'. It was also then, however, that the realisation grew that this profligate use of resources, particularly by rich developed nations, could have grave consequences for the planet. The intervening 60 years have seen this knowledge and continuing crisis develop to the stage that it has become imperative to act.

Over the years key issues were identified such as global warming and climate change, resource depletion, waste disposal, extinction of species and degradation of ecosystems. Climate fluctuations are now more intense than in the past. Lost ecosystems cannot be replaced. Scientists have calculated that we are nearing the point when it will be impossible to return the climate to a more sustainable level for both humans and the natural world (Dolan, 2021; Leger-Goodes et al., 2022; Taylor et al., 2015). Governments have come to recognise the imminent danger that the planet is warning us of. Conferences have been held, scientists and activists have talked, and pledges have been given. These are not always easy to uphold, however, even with the urgency of the agenda (Scoffham and Rawlinson, 2022). The differing needs of individual countries require different responses and regulators.

Global climate summits were held and, finally at COP 21 in 2015, the Paris Accords were signed with governments recognising and pledging to take effective action to reduce global warming. This was the first universal global agreement (Dolan, 2021). From this also came the United Nations Sustainable Development Goals (SDGs). Nevertheless, the world has continued to warm creating increasingly destructive phenomena such as intense wildfires, drought, rising sea temperatures and extreme weather patterns. COP 26, in Glasgow (2021), reviewed the effectiveness of those measures and the achievements of the SDGs (see further https://unstats.un.org/sdgs/report/2022/). The Dasgupta Review on Economic Biodiversity was a key document.

The Dasgupta Review (HM Treasury, 2021) definitively detailed the interrelationship of humans with the natural world, identifying the economic case for decisive action to consolidate natural resources. It recognised nature as our most precious asset that has been both underacknowledged and overused. It notes how the rise in human prosperity has led to corresponding ecological disaster. It highlighted the economic importance of considering the biospheres and human effect upon them. This powerful economic case has begun to lead governments to consider how to effect the transformative change that would be necessary to secure this resource for future generations.

Furthermore, this report suggests that individual and community actions can be transformative and will become an essential part of the solution for many of the issues that we are expected to face as a species. Teachers need to consider ways to empower the next generation so that they understand how they can develop ecologically sound ways of living. They need to influence a positive outlook for the future through their attitudes and everyday teaching – as it is the children in our schools today who will be picking up the pieces emanating from current global policies.

How does the natural world and human world intersect?

The myriad systems that regulate the earth are interlocked and multifaceted. Although Lovelock's theory of the Gaia hypothesis (1972) has been criticised, the view of planet as a web of symbiotic and interdependent relationships (Scoffham and Rawlinson, 2022) cannot be dismissed entirely. Within this, the connections between humans and the natural world are also complex and can be considered through a range of lenses. The different imperatives of those lenses shape our interactions (Flynn, 2017; Hicks, 2018; Scoffham and Rawlinson, 2022; Taylor et al., 2015).

Introduction: teaching for sustainable futures

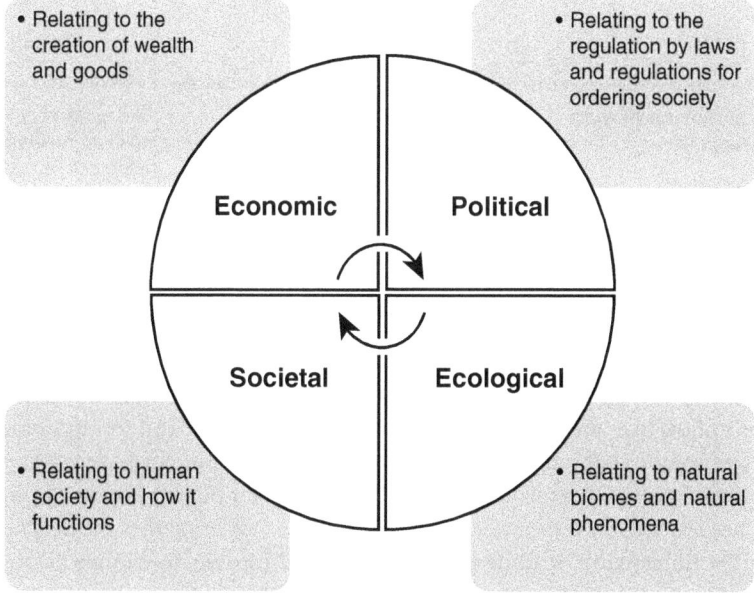

Figure 1   Co-dependency of systems (Source: Adapted from Taylor et al., 2015).

These systems are interrelated, with health of one dependant on the others (Taylor et al., 2015) as we can see in Figure 1. What is clear is the centrality of economic influence in determining how we use the planet's resources. This is further shaped by political aims, although these too are inordinately shaped by economics (Hicks, 2018). It is hard to determine political actions that run contrary to this, although this was achieved with the Paris Accords 2015.

PAUSE FOR THOUGHT

Soya is increasingly important as an ingredient for animal feed in the dairy and meat industries. It is grown mainly in Brazil and Argentina. In Brazil, this has led to deforestation.

Look at what the effects may be from an economic, political, societal and ecological point of view. What is the defining lever?

The supremacy of humanity's control and use of planetary resources has led scientists to designate that we are entering new geological period, the Anthropocene (Hicks, 2018; Kidd, 2020; Scoffham and Rawlinson, 2022). Dolan define this as 'an epoch influenced by humans, where atmospheric, geologic, hydrologic and biospheric systems are altered by humans' (2021, p15).

The challenge for world governments is to move the focus from the economic sphere into that of the ecological. It is important to realise that 'growth and economic progress were damaging the global environment and that the earth was an enclosed system with finite resources' (Scoffham and Rawlinson, 2022, p1). Acceptance of this view, of course, presents problems, such as how to react and what to do. In seeking solutions, there are perhaps three potential responses as suggested by Dolan (2021) (see Figure 2).

Denial	Adaptation	Mitigation
• Refuse to accept results from scientists, 'experts' • Dispute research	• Use science and technology to find ways to live with the situation	• Find ways to limit the effects focus on renewable resources, eco technology

Figure 2 Three potential responses to the climate crisis

Different nations and stakeholders will focus on different reactions. Those who are most affected, however, will be those with least opportunity for change. It is tempting to consider that, as human beings are inventive, new technology will be able to provide all the answers without having to make radical changes to how lives are led. Taylor et al. (2015) refer to weak and strong sustainability. Weak sustainability sees solutions through the development of new technologies or *adaptation* in Dolan's view. This is still anthropogenic as nature continues to be used for human benefit. Strong sustainability recognises the need to become eco-centric, creating a balance that recognises the needs of the planet as equal to those on humankind. It understands that natural ecosystems cannot be replicated if they collapse too far. This suggests *mitigation* as a solution. *Denial* is no longer an option.

There are changes afoot to redraw perspectives. In 2008, Ecuador enshrined the legal rights of nature into its constitution. In 2017, the river Te Awa Tupua was declared a living entity and ancestor of the Whanganui people. It was provided with two guardians to uphold its rights, not to be polluted or degraded or for its waters to be overdrawn. Other countries such as India and Bangladesh have followed this example. There are moves to provide legal status for areas of land or particular species. The Strengthening Welfare in Marine Settings Act, or SWIMS Act of 2022, seeks to make it illegal to capture or breed whales for display (see further https://www.nonhumanrights.org/).

PAUSE FOR THOUGHT

Do you think it is a good idea to grant legal status to non-human entities such as land, rivers or species? What issues might arise if the river Nile was accorded this living entity status. While this would strengthen the ecological aspect how would it create political, economic or social issues?

Should we be teaching climate change and sustainability in schools and if so, why?

Studying climate change and sustainability is complicated. It makes use of complex data and uses a range of specific vocabulary. Some ideas such as the ozone layer or global warming are difficult to understand. Scoffham and Rawlinson suggest that even 'if its impacts are clearly visible, the causes can be hard to comprehend' (2022, p58). The area requires a level of substantive subject knowledge that many adults do not feel comfortable with. Fortner identifies 'scales of time and space that are not well understood by the adult public' (2001, p19). Certainly, there was at least one world leader who was unable to distinguish between weather patterns and climate changes. Notwithstanding both Fortner, Scoffham and Rawlinson accept the need to engage in climate change education.

In a recent survey with undergraduate teachers on a primary education programme, 45% lacked confidence in their ability to teach this area. Approximately 98% felt that it should be taught in schools although 49% felt they needed specific training in how to teach it. In New Zealand, where education for sustainable development is an aspect of the curriculum, 92% felt it was an important focus but 91% had not implemented the programme. These teachers too showed a lack of confidence in their abilities and felt ill equipped because of a lack of initial teacher education (ITE) and poor understanding of concepts (Taylor et al., 2015). Fortner (2021) too found that teachers felt ill-prepared having only superficial subject knowledge.

Prospective teachers training, now and in the future, will be entering the profession, perhaps having obtained much of their information from social media sites, where misconceptions can be found. Delgado identifies the lack of appropriate and effective textbooks needed to support and develop relevant subject knowledge. This was also a need identified by prospective teachers alongside professional training. It is vital that teachers are able to be reliably informed and present a positive and hopeful outlook of the world to children they will be teaching.

As teachers, we need to be clear about why we want to include this within an already overcrowded curriculum. While academics (Dolan, 2021; Hicks, 2018; Scoffham and Rawlinson, 2022; Taylor et al., 2015; Warden, 2022) produce powerful arguments to support its inclusion in school, we must also seek to provide class teachers with a good understanding of its place. While many may recognise the importance of teaching climate change, they may identify different reasons for doing so (see Figure 3 below). Those differing opinions will, in all probability, suggest different angles of investigation. It is important for teachers and schools to discuss and clarify what they hope to achieve through teaching about climate change.

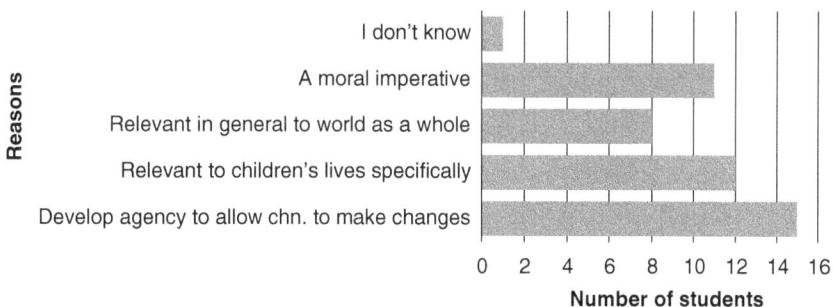

Figure 3   Survey of teaching students' confidence to teach about climate and sustainability

Teachers need to be provided with the tools to develop their own confidence in and understanding of the area. Continuing professional development (CPD) is woefully lacking and the priorities of SLTs in schools remain focussed on core area of English and Maths due to external pressures. However - these are not going to help prepare children for their futures in a holistic and thoughtful way. Suggestions for practical activities embedded with relevant research and curriculum design that is age appropriate, are essential to support and develop teachers' understanding of this current issue. This is a developing area that is urgently needed, which is where we hope you will find the chapters in this book a useful tool to help you tackle the issues of climate change and sustainable living across the whole curriculum.

The new Natural History GCSE points to developing recognition of the importance of teaching climate change and sustainability. There is clearly a developing focus on the importance of understanding the natural world at KS3/4. The focus on this will be to 'to explore the world by learning about organisms and environments, environmental and sustainability issues' (DfE, 2022a). While this is clearly focussed at KS4, there is already a trickle-down effect to other phases of education. As such primary teachers will need to be prepared to explore some of the key principles and ideas. We shall all need to make changes in the way we live our lives, and this needs to be embedded in all we teach so that we can demonstrate green and ecologically sound practices as part of our classroom day to day experiences.

In many ways this has already begun. The importance of forest schools, with the focus on learning within and about the natural world, and the possible renaissance of 'nature study' activities demonstrate how primary teachers are working to reconnect children with their environment. This builds on the work of Rachel Carson (1962) and other early activists of 1960s who first began to identify problems between the relationship humans have with their world. Strengthening connections between children and the natural world through various forms of outdoor and sustainable learning will help prepare them for their future (DfE, 2022b). It can also provide them with a voice and strengthen their sense of agency. Warden develops this when discussing nature pedagogy, seeing this a creating 'a relational power balance between humans and rest of their natural world' (2022, p19). She highlights the importance of learning about, in and with the natural world or inside, outside and beyond. There is clear evidence of climate change that is now affecting our lives, and children will need the tools to make sense of this in a safe and supported way.

Interconnectedness

As we enter the Anthropocene epoch, identifying and cataloguing the effects that humans have had on their world highlights the need to give teachers tools to help them investigate this area with children and to create conversations. This is too important to confine to one or two areas of the curriculum and this should be a feature across the full range of the primary curriculum in order to embed understanding (Delgado, 2022; Jenson, 2002; SOS, 2022; Tynan, 2021). The interconnected systems of the natural world should be mirrored in our teaching and in what we teach (Delgado, 2022; Scoffham and Rawlinson, 2022). In Harmony, the then Prince of Wales, agrees suggesting that 'all of these subjects are completely interrelated and that we need to look at the whole picture to understand the problems that we face' (HRH the Prince of Wales et al., 2010, p5). Jenson (2002) highlights the need to ensure that any knowledge accrued must also be internalised through active enquiry. He identifies the importance of ensuring the environmental education is not bound to only one or two dimensions as this limits identifying potential causes and solutions possible. It is also important to ensure that teaching should be age appropriate, translating issues to allow even the youngest in the school to respond. A whole school, whole curriculum approach allows teachers and children to identify interconnectedness and pathways that will facilitate non-linear solutions (O'Donnell and Higginson, 2011; SOS, 2022).

The pandemic clearly demonstrated the importance of building relationships with nature and the environment and the effect that this had on mental well-being (Warden, 2022). Recent research has demonstrated 'consistently high levels of concern about climate change' (DeMocker, 2022; Hicks, 2018) and eco-anxiety (a chronic fear of ecological doom). While Leger-Goodes et al. (2022, p3) found that 'general knowledge about climate change amongst younger people seems low, but their level of concern and anxiety is high', there remains little research related to primary age children. Teachers need to be able to create safe learning spaces that will allow children to articulate concerns and then, importantly, develop confidence to take action (Hicks, 2018; Kidd, 2020). Taylor et al. (2015) highlight the need to recognise that an over-emphasis on the problems that exist can disempower children as they see no solution or possibility of action. Thunberg (2021) strongly links hope with action, 'Hope doesn't come from words. Hope only comes from actions'. It is important therefore to create agency and empowerment for children even if those actions are small scale. It is vital to create optimism rather than succumb to eco-anxiety (Alcock, 2019; Tynan, 2021).

There is much emphasis on environmental issues, and growing concern in the general population. There is also a growing sense of activism amongst young people, this has been demonstrated through Black Lives Matter and Extinction Rebellion. Greta Thunberg has become a powerful advocate for children's concerns highlighting the need to listen and then act. She highlights the importance of providing hope through action. Her calls to action are passionate and immediate. Who can forget when she told world leaders 'If you choose to fail us we will never forgive you!'? (Thunberg, 2019). She dares not just politicians but everyone to act.

> **PAUSE FOR THOUGHT**
>
> Consider this quote from the then Secretary for State for Education, Gavin Williamson in reference to a children's climate strike in 2019:
>
> *They should be learning; they shouldn't be bunking off and it's very irresponsible for people to encourage them to do so.*
>
> What do you think about this? What is learning? What responsibility do we have to promote or depress children's desire for action?

In order to make judgements however, we need to develop critical thinking providing children with the skills to identify the essentials (Scoffham and Rawson, 2022; Waters, 2013). It is important that children are able to formulate questions about what may have caused the problem (Taylor et al., 2015). Jenson (2002) suggests a cause and change approach that identifies the problem but also encourages the children to think about how to find solutions. Flynn (2017) highlights the need to recognise the affective dimension within environmental teaching, considering respect and a commitment to social justice. Action and emotion can be strongly linked to promote agency, looking at facts with emotions (DeMocker, 2022; Tynan, 2021).

How to use this book

In this book we provide a structure for learning about the environment and climate change, linked to relevant and authentic research within subject specific foci relevant to primary education. This will enable you to consider how you might embed sound ecological principles across the entire primary curriculum and, ideally to take a whole school approach. Every teacher is ultimately responsible for the curriculum in their own class, so even if your school is not taking this up yet as policy, each small adaptation you can make, whether it is through modelling changing behaviours, or using some of the ideas and resources from these chapters, you will be making the change that is needed.

We have attempted to be as all-encompassing as possible by covering the key areas of learning in the primary curriculum, and have included chapters on PHSE (Chapter 1), Early Years (Chapter 3) and curriculum design through Principles of Harmony (Chapter 2). In addition, we have chosen to promote the contribution that the arts subjects can provide, and we are pleased to be able to present two visual art chapter, and two views of music education. This is also top reinforce our belief that teaching about the climate and the environment should not be limited to the subjects of geography and science.

The chapters are structured to provide essential background information and subject specific knowledge. The second part of each chapter is dedicated to practical ideas that you can use **In the Classroom**. Chapters are linked to the UN SDGs (United Nations, 2015), and these are documented as a reference in the Appendix, as are links from each chapter to Teachers Standards/Core Curriculum Framework.

Of course, we would hope that you will read the book from cover to cover, but it is equally accessible by dipping in, and choosing an area of interest, as each individual chapter stands independently in terms of subject specificity.

As primary teachers we have a great deal of power and influence in building children's attitudes and dispositions, which is why this is such an important book at this time. The messages in these chapters are founded on a pedagogy that promotes hope and action – both for you, as the teacher - so that you are inspired to innovate for a modern and relevant curriculum - and especially for the children, so that they can take a love and care of nature, and ways of sustainable living forward into their future lives.

References

Alcock, D. (2019) An optimistic education: rebalancing the curriculum to more accurately convey human progress. Impact. Available at: https://my.chartered.college/impact_article/an-optimistic-education-rebalancing-the-curriculum-to-more-accurately-convey-human-progress/

Carson, R. (1962) *Silent Spring*. Boston: Houghton Mifflin Harcourt.

Delgado, C. (2022) College text books aren't keeping up with the severity of the global climate crisis Popular Science. Available at: https://www.popsci.com/environment/climate-change-textbooks/

De Mocker, M. (2022) The best ways to teach and talk about climate change with kids Popular Science. Available at: https://www.popsci.com/environment/climate-education-kids-us/

DfE (2022a) The new Natural History GCSE and how we're leading the way in climate and sustainability education – your questions answered. Available at: https://educationhub.blog.gov.uk/2022/04/25/the-new-natural-history-gcse-and-how-were-leading-the-way-in-climate-and-sustainability-education-your-questions-answered/

DfE (2022b) *Sustainability and Climate Change: A Strategy for the Education and Children's Services Systems*. Available at: https://www.gov.uk/government/publications/sustainability-and-climate-change-strategy/sustainability-and-climate-change-a-strategy-for-the-education-and-childrens-services-systems

Dolan, A. (ed.) (2021) *Teaching Climate Change in Primary Schools: An Interdisciplinary Approach*. Abingdon: Routledge.

Fortner, R. (2021) Climate change in schools: where does it fit and are we ready for it? *Canadian Journal of Environmental Education*, 6(1): 18–31.

Flynn, T. (2017) *Teaching about Climate Change in Irish Primary Schools*. Kildare: Trócaire.

HM Treasury (2021) *The Economics of Biodiversity: The Dasgupta Review: Headline Messages*. Available at: https://assets.publishing.service.gov.uk/government/uploads/system/uploads/attachment_data/file/957629/Dasgupta_Review_-_Headline_Messages.pdf

Hicks, D. (2018) Why we still need a geography of hope. *Geography*, 103(2): 78–85.

HRH the Prince of Wales et al. (2010) *Harmony: A New Way of Looking at Our World*. London: Harper Collins.

Jenson, B. (2002) Knowledge, action and pro-environmental behaviour. *Environmental Education Research*, 8(3): 325–334.

Kidd, D. (2020) *A Curriculum of Hope: As Rich in Humanity as in Knowledge*. Carmarthen: Independent Thinking Press.

Leger-Goodes, T. et al. (2022) Eco-anxiety in children: a scoping review of the mental health impacts of the awareness of climate change. *Frontiers in Psychology*, 13: 872544.

O'Donnell, S. and Higginson, C. (2021) *Education for Sustainable Development: International Curriculum Audit National Council for Curriculum and Assessment*. Available at: https://ncca.ie/media/5342/ncca_esd_curriculum_audit_2022.pdf

Scoffham, S. and Rawlinson, S. (2022) *Sustainability Education: A Classroom Guide*. London: Bloomsbury.

SOS (2022) *Curriculum for Changed Climate: Executive Summary*. Available at: https://www.sos-uk.org/resources/teach-the-future-report-a-track-changes-review-of-the-national-curriculum-for-england

SOS (2022) *Climate Change Tracker*. Available at: https://www.sos-uk.org/research/climate-change-tracker

Taylor, N., Quinn, F. and Eames, C. (2015) *Educating for Sustainability in Primary Schools*. Rotterdam: Sense Publications.

Thunberg, G. (2019) Speech at UN Climate Summit. New York, 23 September 2019.

Thunberg, G. (2021) A year to change the world. BBCI Player. April 6.

Tynan, F. (2021) A thematic approach to teaching climate change. In A. Dolan (ed.), *Teaching Climate Change in Primary Schools: An Interdisciplinary Approach*. Abingdon: Routledge.

United Nations (UN) (2015) *Sustainable Development Goals*. Available at: https://sdgs.un.org/goals

Warden, C. (2022) *Green Teaching*. London: Sage.

Waters, M. (2013) *Thinking Allowed on Schooling*. Carmarthen: Independent Thinking Press.

GLOSSARY OF TERMS

Term	Definition
Anthropocene	A geological era where the earth is shaped by the actions of humans
Biodiversity	A variety of plant and animal life within an ecosystem. A rich biodiversity is usually desirable
Brundtland's principal of sustainability	Meeting the needs of the present without compromising the ability of future generations to meet their own needs
Climate change	An event or process that unbalances the natural systems of the Earth representing changes in climate and temperatures that detrimentally affect life on the planet
COP	(Conference of the Parties) UN Framework Convention on Climate Change (UNFCCC) decision-making board
Eco-centric	A nature-centred, as opposed to human-centred, system of values where the needs of other living things are considered equally important to those of humans
Exceptionalism (Human)	The belief that humans are exceptional compared to other lifeforms and that their needs supersede those of these other lifeforms
Gaia	The Gaia hypothesis, proposes that living organisms interact with their inorganic surroundings on Earth to form a synergistic and self-regulating, complex system that helps to maintain and perpetuate the conditions for life on the planet
Greenwashing	Greenwashing involves making an unsubstantiated claim to deceive consumers into believing that a company's products are environmentally friendly or have a greater positive environmental impact than they actually do
Ozone Layer	The *ozone layer* or ozone shield is a region of Earth's stratosphere that absorbs most of the Sun's ultraviolet radiation
Sustainable Development Goals	On 1 January 2016, the 17 Sustainable Development Goals (SDGs) of the 2030 Agenda for Sustainable Development—adopted by world leaders in September 2015
Sustainability	Meeting the needs of the present without compromising the ability of future generations to meet their own needs while also considering the needs of the other life systems on the planet

1

THE PERSONAL, SOCIAL, EMOTIONAL AND CITIZENSHIP DIMENSIONS OF SUSTAINABILITY EDUCATION

SARAH LEONARD

LINKS TO CCF

1.5, 7.3, 7.4

SUSTAINABLE DEVELOPMENT GOALS

GOAL 13: Climate Action

KEY WORDS

Ethos; personal development; social and emotional learning; eco-anxiety; citizenship

> **CHAPTER OBJECTIVES**
>
> This chapter will:
>
> - Consider children's emotional responses to the environment and how children might be affected by changes to the climate.
> - Explore how the classroom environment can support children to share their feelings about, and understanding of, environmental change and sustainability.
> - Review how a focus on personal development can support children to become active citizens with the skills to participate in a more sustainable world.

Introduction

I've come to a frightening conclusion that I am the decisive element in the classroom. It's my personal approach that creates the climate. It's my daily mood that makes the weather... In all situations, it is my response that decides whether a crisis will be escalated or deescalated and a child humanized or dehumanized.

(Ginott, 1972, p15)

This chapter explores two elements of how education can support children and young people to navigate the complex issue of the environment and sustainability by effectively supporting children's personal development. The first part focusses on developing our awareness of children's potentially complex thoughts and emotions about the environment and sustainability and why we need to be sensitive to these. The second considers how particular strands of the curriculum (particularly personal, social, health, economic – PSHE – and citizenship education) can help create classrooms where children's perspectives and concerns are explored. We shall suggest ways they can learn how to be active, responsible citizens, empowered to do something about the challenging and important social issue of sustainability. As Froebel (cited in Lilley, 1967, p41) noted, 'I want to educate people to be free, to think, to take action for themselves'.

> **REFLECTIVE QUESTION**
>
> Return to the quotation at the beginning of this chapter. How can you set the emotional climate in the classroom?
>
> How might the emotional climate help children talk about the meteorological climate?

The environment and sustainability: Managing sensitive and challenging topics in the classroom

In 1992, the United Nations Framework Convention on Climate Change (UNFCCC) recognised education as essential for responding to climate change. It is a message echoed in many subsequent publications both global (UNICEF, 2021) and local (DfE, 2022). The fact that learning is a complex process is undisputed (Wray, 2018), but there is an inevitable additional layer of complexity when learning includes sensitive or challenging topics which might provoke personal or emotional reactions.

Climate change is such a topic, and terms such as climate anxiety and eco-anxiety are starting to be part of everyday language (Clayton and Karazsia, 2020; Hickman, 2020). Anxiety is often regarded in negative terms, but an experience of unease or worry, and even fear, is part of human experience; it can help us to find out more information or compel us to look for solutions, something that may be particularly useful when thinking about sustainability and environmental protection (Hickman et al., 2021). Equally, it is important to recognise that some level of climate anxiety is in no way irrational – data and evidence about the impact of the changing climate is incontrovertible. The 2023 IPCC report (2023, n.p.) identified that 'human-caused climate change is already affecting many weather and climate extremes in every region across the globe. This has led to widespread adverse impacts and related losses and damages to nature and people'.

Given that climate anxiety may be a potentially useful and understandable response, is there a need to be concerned about children's worries about this topic? Research suggests that there is, for two reasons: firstly, for children, climate anxiety may be compounded by having relatively little power in taking action; secondly, climate change can be associated with a range of other emotions such as guilt, anger or fear, which have the potential to cause the anxiety to become overwhelming (Diffey et al., 2022; Hickman, 2020; Hickman et al., 2021). Children have also not fully developed the ability to regulate their emotions or to balance them with information about the technologies or progress which may help address climate change.

How might children feel about the environment?

The psychological impact of climate change on children and young people is relatively under-researched (Hickman, 2020; Wu et al., 2020), but this is starting to change. In 2022, for example, the Children's Society's 'Good Childhood Report' explored the views of 2,000 UK children to establish views on wider social issues. The environment was top of participants' concerns (even above a new pandemic, crime and online safety), with 4 in 10 children reporting that they felt 'very' or 'quite' worried about it. Hickman et al. (2021) surveyed 10,000 children and young people aged 16–24 from ten countries including the UK and USA, Finland, India and the Philippines. Just over two-thirds of the participants felt 'afraid' or 'sad' about climate change, with figures higher for those from countries where the impact of the crisis is felt more directly. Approximately three-quarters of those young people asked agreed that 'the future is frightening' and 55% responded 'yes' to the statement 'humanity is doomed' (Hickman et al., 2021, p868). These responses are mirrored in a smaller scale, qualitative study by Diffey et al. (2022) in which interviews were undertaken with children and young people of a similar age range and from a mixture of high (UK, UEA), upper middle (Jamaica, South Africa) and lower middle (India, Philippines) income countries. In spite of their diverse geography, the interviewees shared significant concern about climate crisis and experienced feelings of fear and hopelessness, feelings which persisted over time but increased at times when the impact of climate change was immediate to them or was being reported globally. As in Hickman et al.'s (2021) research, these emotions were exacerbated by immediate risk to self, family or community.

> ## REFLECTIVE QUESTION
>
> Do the responses of young people to climate change surprise you?
>
> When teaching potentially challenging or sensitive topics, it is important to recognise and respond to children's different emotions and personal experiences.
>
> - Is there a way of gathering information about children's understanding and feelings *before* a lesson? Perhaps you could create a 'worry box' or a 'question bank' for children to post their concerns anonymously.
> - Think about your class. Some children may have been directly and negatively affected by climate change (see next section) and some may come from homes where the topic is never discussed or is actively dismissed. How will you plan for this *range of experience*?
> - How do *you* feel about the topic? This should also be factored in because you will be managing the way it is handled and need to do this sensitively and with self-awareness. It is important that information shared is factual and accurate and that you neither disregard children's questions or worries nor cause or add to add to their anxiety.

Acknowledging children's direct and indirect experience of climate change

The impact of climate change is now part of most children's experience. UNICEF's (2021, p11) report identifies that 'almost every child on earth (>99 per cent) is exposed to at least 1 of these major [droughts, floods, severe weather] climate and environmental hazards, shocks and stresses' and, as is the case globally, there is also inequality in experience locally that teachers will be aware of. Whilst children most significantly affected by climate change reside predominantly in lower- or middle-income countries, either as a result of their geography or because there is less infrastructure to mitigate the effects (ND-Gain, 2023), even in higher income countries there is still a greater impact on some than others – there is a social justice component of climate change (Preston et al., 2014). The extreme temperatures in the UK in the summer of 2022 will have affected most primary-aged children, but some of those living in major conurbations – particularly those from lower socio-economic circumstances – were likely to experience these effects more adversely, as temperatures in cities rose higher than those in more rural areas and there was potentially less access to green spaces (Willshire, 2022). Some coastal areas are more likely to experience extreme flooding, and populations at risk of these experiences are also amongst the most deprived in the country (Climate Just, 2022). There is much discussion about the pollution of the sea and rivers; children and their schools are part of the communities affected by these issues.

Schools also work with increasingly diverse pupil populations, some of whom will have first-, second- or third-generation links with family and communities in locations which have experienced the direct impact of serious climate related events. Whilst those pupils living in other countries are physically safe, the potential emotional impact of seeing these events exists and should be acknowledged and responded to in classrooms where children's feelings and questions can be explored. There is clear evidence that the most effective approach to well-being and mental health is to secure opportunities to be positive and action focussed, but in doing this, children's voices should not be silenced (Hickman, 2020).

Hickman (2020) and Diffey et al. (2022) also report that children can face contradictory messages. Their feelings and questions might not be addressed by parents and other professionals (often because adults are not sure how to manage such complex questions and concerns) and they do not feel listened to. On the other hand, hopes for the future and for addressing these issues also lie with them; they are portrayed as the potential solution for all things climate related. To address this, Hickman (2020) argues for a position where adults support children through 'internal activism' – listening carefully to and understanding how children feel – accompanied by 'external activism' where they are supported to take action in the world:

> *Both feeling sad and recycling, feeling angry and lobbying politicians, feeling guilty and planting bee friendly plants, feeling grief and supporting school climate strikers. We can both take action in the outer world and also give attention to inner relational landscapes, our inner emotional climate crisis.*
>
> (Hickman, 2020, p422)

Personal development: Developing children's voice and empowering action on sustainability

So far, we have acknowledged that learning about the environment and climate change might be challenging, but children are clear that they seek knowledge and opportunities to be heard in relation to these topics. There is a role for knowledge acquisition through the full range of curriculum subjects but central to this is pupils' social and emotional learning and their personal development.

Personal development can be seen as a collection of approaches, some related to a school's ethos, vision and values and the implementation of its key policies such as anti-bullying, inclusion, behaviour amongst others. Other aspects are related to specific areas of the curriculum including spiritual, moral, social and cultural development (SMSC) which encompass fundamental British values (DfE, 2014), careers education in secondary schools and citizenship education. Personal development should also be provided through the now statutory relationships, sex and health education (RSHE) and non-statutory PSHE (DfE, 2021b).

REFLECTIVE QUESTION

Looking at the varied opportunities for personal development above, how might you use these to support sustainability education. Do these opportunities reflect Hickman's (2020) concept of 'internal and external activism'?

Personal, social and emotional development

Children's social and emotional skills, and their holistic personal development, is known to have a positive impact in a host of ways. Social aptitude supports academic learning, and when children develop personally, they become resilient, respectful of the views of others and able to communicate in appropriate ways (EEF, 2019). The centrality of personal development is evident in the Early Years Foundation Stage (EYFS) where personal, social and emotional development is recognised as a prime area of learning through which young children can be supported to 'manage their emotions, develop a positive sense of self, …to persist' (DfE, 2021a, p23). This strand of learning reflects the importance attached to the development of executive functions (attentional and cognitive flexibility, working memory and inhibitory control, or the 'go/no-go' decision) which allow an individual to plan and organise, to manage and regulate emotions and behaviours, and to problem solve (Whitebread et al., 2019). If we want children to explore and engage with (and ultimately take action) about challenging or sensitive topics, strengthening this range of personal attributes is paramount.

PSHE, sometimes referred to as the 'curriculum for life' (PSHE Association, 2017, p19), covers core content such as health, well-being, online safety and relationships, whilst concurrently developing other important personal and social skills including communication and resilience, critical thinking and empathy. It is in these ways, Baggaley (2019) argues that PSHE complements the facts and knowledge acquired through the rest of the curriculum and secures pupils' emotional literacy, the ability to make confident decisions, to form effective community connections, to protect their own well-being and to take action even in difficult times. Thus, PSHE responds directly to Hickman's (2020, p422) call for adults to support children's 'internal and external activism'; it can support children's understanding of how to take action whilst at the same time building personal and interpersonal skills and attributes.

Citizenship education

Citizenship education – non-statutory in key stages one and two but identified by the DfE (2015, p1) as supporting schools to plan a 'full curriculum' – is 'centrally important in instilling in children a sense of hope for the future and a sense of empowerment as active agents of change' (Nohilly, 2022, p226). It should allow children to recognise both their individual development and their role within the local and global community, knowing that their actions can influence 'local, global and national issues and political and social institutions' (DfE, 2015, p3). It is here that learning about the environment and sustainability is explicitly included. Importantly, this includes learning about some of the issues discussed in the previous section of this chapter – the direct and indirect impact of climate change and sustainability and awareness of issues of social justice: 'that resources can be allocated in different ways and that these economic choices affect individuals, communities and the sustainability of the environment'; (DfE, 2015, p4). The citizenship education guidance does not shy away from tackling challenging and complex issues with children and does not underestimate what children can engage with – but as acknowledged in the first part of this chapter, the classroom climate must support this.

In the classroom

Supporting personal development

The DfE's (2022) sustainability and climate change strategy proposes curriculum adaptations and changes in a range of subjects, specifically in personal development and PSHE. The guidance acknowledges that 'teachers are best placed to understand the needs of their pupils' (DfE, 2021b, n.p.), and these opportunities can serve as a powerful vehicle for or implementing the proposed changes when carefully planned.

Any teaching of personal development – including through PSHE or citizenship education – should be structured so that there is continuity and progression in the curriculum. This will ensure that children build skills in executive functioning and interpersonal interactions and can become more adept at articulating their thoughts on complex issues. The expectations set out in the citizenship guidance by the DfE (2015) and the PSHE association's (2023) planning guidance on the 'community and responsibility' strand of the curriculum are helpful documents to support this. The EYFS guidance is also extremely useful for all teachers; continuing to think about personal social emotional development (PSED) as a *prime area* of learning beyond the EYFS (DfE, 2021a) can help ensure that the subject is not only taught as a stand-alone area of learning and given due time within the curriculum but also that it is integrated into other curriculum areas, for example through carefully planned, developmentally appropriate group work, opportunities for problem solving and the explicit teaching of how to overcome challenges when learning. This will occur in all learning and teaching thus developing children's skills and attributes for when they learn directly about climate, diversity and the environment in any curriculum area. It can also support environment-focussed events or projects used to bring sustainability to the forefront of learning and teaching in school.

Hold a school Conference of the Parties (COP) to choose some sustainability actions the school community can achieve together. Every child can be involved with age-appropriate contributions linked either to a single action or to different actions taken in different phases or year groups. Children in KS2 should be involved in the organisation and presentation of ideas for discussion (potentially supported by members of the community or other experts), but all children can be involved in making decisions and taking action.

The table below takes biodiversity as a theme, but other ideas such as sustainable school travel, reducing food waste or reusing rather than recycling could be organised similarly (Table 1.1).

Table 1.1 *Developing sustainable themes across primary age phases*

EYFS	KS1	KS2
Create a natural sensory area with children, allowing them to choose what to plant that will provide an array of colour, textures, sound and scent. Grow some plants from seed so that children appreciate the wonder of the life cycle. Use natural materials to enhance the sensory nature of the space - shells, bark, mulched leaves, cones and petals.	Choose an area of the school grounds to 'rewild'. Plant native species to start the process. Plan for monitoring the growth of plants (and the arrival of new ones) and the presence of birds and insects over time so that the impact can be evaluated.	Undertake a biodiversity survey of the school environment and decide how this can be increased. Encourage dialogue and interaction with the local community so that change might be affected in the local environment, beyond the school boundaries; this potentially opens up discussion about providing biodiverse spaces in nearby private gardens or land used for other purposes such as farming, or thinking about how pollution might be reduced on local roads.

The EEF (2019) guidance on supporting social and emotional aspects of learning is a further useful tool for securing effective practice with suggestions on teaching strategies (recommendations one and two) providing a wealth of ideas to support effective classroom practice. When thinking about this dimension of learning, it is also important to be aware of your own thoughts and emotional responses to sensitive or challenging topics so that you manage an environment in which children are given accurate and balanced information. Using school policies and working with experienced colleagues to understand how to manage challenging questions and discussions, alongside protecting your own well-being, will help create a classroom in which sustainability – its challenges and its promise – are fully embedded in all aspects of learning.

CHAPTER SUMMARY

This chapter has considered the range of complex personal and emotional responses children may have when considering environmental change and sustainability. It has identified that effective learning and teaching opportunities must recognise these responses, balancing the need to acknowledge them without amplifying anxiety. Embedding well-structured and sensitively constructed PSHE and citizenship education can do this in two ways: by supporting children articulate and understand their emotional responses and by developing them as citizens who understand their own power to act. Sustainability requires knowledge of the environment and how our ecosystems work and an emotional engagement with the complex challenges of its protection – an affective as well as an intellectual response. Personal, social, emotional and citizenship dimensions of learning are uniquely positioned to secure both for children.

Further reading and resources

https://www.footprintnetwork.org/resources/educational-resources/
There is a host of useful resources for helping children to think about attainable sustainable action (and develop a fuller understanding of all the SDGs) available through Global Footprint network. The materials are available in multiple languages and there is access to further research for teachers.

References

Baggaley, J. (2019) *What Should We Tell the Children? Climate Change and the School Curriculum.* Available at: https://pshe-association.org.uk/evidence-and-research/a-curriculum-for-life-case-statutory-pshe-education (Accessed: 23 April 2023).

Clayton, S. and Karazsia, B. T. (2020) Development and validation of a measure of climate change anxiety. *Journal of Environmental Psychology*, 69: 101–434. https://doi.org/10.1016/j.jenvp.2020.101434

Climate Just (2022) *Which places are disadvantaged?* Available at: https://www.climatejust.org.uk/which-places-are-disadvantaged (Accessed: 23 April 2023).

Department for Education (2014) *Promoting Fundamental British Values through SMSC.* Available at: https://www.gov.uk/government/publications/promoting-fundamental-british-values-through-smsc (Accessed: 23 April 2023).

Department for Education (2015) *Citizenship Programmes of Study: Key Stages 1 and 2*. Available at: https://www.gov.uk/government/publications/citizenship-programmes-of-study-for-key-stages-1-and-2 (Accessed: 23 April 2023).

Department for Education (2021a) *Development Matters. Non-statutory Curriculum Guidance for the Early Years*. Available at: https://www.gov.uk/government/publications/development-matters--2 (Accessed: 23 April 2023).

Department for Education (2021b) *Personal, Social, Health and Economic Education*. Available at: https://www.gov.uk/government/publications/personal-social-health-and-economic-education-pshe/personal-social-health-and-economic-pshe-education (Accessed: 12 March 2023).

Department for Education (2022) *Sustainability and Climate Change: A Strategy for Education and Children's Services Systems*. Available at: https://www.gov.uk/government/publications/sustainability-and-climate-change-strategy/sustainability-and-climate-change-a-strategy-for-the-education-and-childrens-services-systems (Accessed: 21 April 2023).

Diffey, J., Wright, S., Uchendu, J. O., Masithi, S., Olude, A., Juma, D. O., Anya, L. H., Salami, T., Mogathala, P. R., Agarwal, H. and Roh, H. (2022) "Not about us without us" – the feelings and hopes of climate-concerned young people around the world. *International Review of Psychiatry*, 34(5): 499–509. https://doi.org/10.1080/09540261.2022.2126297

EEF (2019) *Improving Social and Emotional Learning in Primary Schools*. Available at: https://educationendowmentfoundation.org.uk/education-evidence/guidance-reports/primary-sel (Accessed: 23 April 2023).

Ginott, H. G. (1972) *Teacher and Child: A Book for Parents and Teachers*. Scribner Paper Fiction.

Hickman, C. (2020) We need to (find a way to) talk about … Eco-anxiety. *Journal of Social Work Practice*, 34(4): 411–424. https://doi.org/10.1080/02650533.2020.1844166

Hickman, C., Marks, E., Pihkala, P., Clayton, S., Lewandowski, R. E., Mayall, E. E., Wray, B., Mellor, C. and van Susteren, L. (2021) Climate anxiety in children and young people and their beliefs about government responses to climate change: a global survey. *The Lancet Planetary Health*, 5(12): 863–873. https://doi.org/10.1016/S2542-5196(21)00278-3

Intergovernmental Panel on Climate Change (2023) *AR6 Synthesis Report: Climate Change 2023*. Available at: https://www.ipcc.ch/report/sixth-assessment-report-cycle/ (Accessed: 17 March 2023).

Lilley, I. (1967) *Friedrich Froebel: A Selection from His Writings*. Cambridge: Cambridge University Press.

Nohilly, M. (2022) *Teaching Climate Change in Primary Schools: An Interdisciplinary Approach*. Edited by A. M. Dolan. Oxon: Routledge.

Notre Dame Global Adaptation Initiative (2023) *ND-Gain Country Index*. Available at: https://gain.nd.edu/our-work/country-index/rankings/ (Accessed: 23 April 2023).

Preston, I., Banks, N., Hargreaves, K., Kazmierczak, A., Lucas, K., Mayne, R., Downing, C. and Street, R. (2014). *Climate Change and Social Justice: An Evidence Review*. Joseph Rowntree Foundation. Available at: https://www.jrf.org.uk/report/climate-change-and-social-justice-evidence-review (Accessed: 23 April 2023).

PSHE Association (2017). *A Curriculum for Life. The Case for Statutory Personal, Social, Health and Economic (PSHE) Education*. Available at: https://pshe-association.org.uk/evidence-and-research/a-curriculum-for-life-case-statutory-pshe-education (Accessed: 23 April 2023).

PSHE Association (2023) *Community and Responsibility*. Available at: https://www.citethemright-online.com/sourcetype?docid=b-9781350927964&tocid=b-9781350927964-34 (Accessed: 23 March 2023).

The Children's Society (2022) *The Good Childhood Report 2022*. Available at: https://www.childrenssociety.org.uk/information/professionals/resources/good-childhood-report-2022 (Accessed: 22 April 2023).

United Nations (1992) *United Nations Framework Convention on Climate Change*. Available at: https://unfccc.int/resource/docs/convkp/conveng.pdf (Accessed: 21 April 2023).

UNICEF (2021) *The Climate Crisis Is a Child Rights Crisis: Introducing the Children's Climate Risk Index*. New York: United Nations Children's Fund (UNICEF). Available at: https://www.unicef.org/reports/climate-crisis-child-rights-crisis (Accessed: 29 December 2023).

Willshire, M. (2022) Climate change made UK heatwave more intense and at least 10 times more likely. Available at: https://www.imperial.ac.uk/news/238772/climate-change-made-uk-heatwave-more/ (Accessed: 23 April 2023).

Whitebread, D., Grau, V., Kumpulainen, K., McClelland, M., Perry, N. and Pino-Pasternak, D. (2019) *The Sage Handbook of Developmental Psychology and Early Childhood Education*. Sage. https://doi.org/10.4135/9781526470393

Wray, D. (2018) Looking at learning. In T. Cremin and C. Burnett (eds.), *Learning to Teach in the Primary School*, 4th edition. Oxon: Routledge, pp66–76.

Wu, J., Snell, G. and Samji, H. (2020) Climate anxiety in young people: a call to action. *The Lancet Planetary Health*, 4(10): 435–436. https://doi.org/10.1016/S2542-5196(20)30223-0

2
CREATING HARMONY THROUGH CURRICULUM DESIGN

RICHARD DUNNE AND EMILIE MARTIN

LINKS TO CORE CONTENT FRAMEWORK

1.1, 3.1, 4.6, 4.7

SUSTAINABLE DEVELOPMENT GOALS

GOAL 4: Quality Education
GOAL 7: Affordable and Clean Energy
GOAL 13: Climate Action

KEY WORDS

Harmony principles; agency; interconnectedness; sustainability actions; sustainability themes; learning enquiries; nature connection

CHAPTER OBJECTIVES

This chapter will:

- Explore ways to provide opportunities for children to engage meaningfully with issues of sustainability and climate change.
- Draw on recent research and policy to highlight how issues of sustainability are currently represented in the primary school curriculum.
- Outline a 'Harmony' framework for teaching and learning which supports children in developing a deep connection with the natural world.
- Provide practical suggestions of ways in which the curriculum can be reworked and reimagined to promote a new way of learning inspired by principles of Harmony in Nature.

Introduction

We have lived our lives by the assumption that what was good for us would be good for the world. We have been wrong. We must change our lives, so that it will be possible to live by the contrary assumption, that what is good for the world will be good for us.

(Wendell Berry, 1969)

At this point in time, faced with the increasingly urgent challenges of climate change and biodiversity loss, the above quote from the novelist, environmentalist and farmer Wendell Berry summarises so well the shift in outlook that we need to embrace, and which is so overdue. It is time that we learn to see ourselves as part of the natural world rather than separate from it. It is time that we acknowledge that our well-being is inextricably linked to the well-being of our wider world. It is time that we adjust our outlook, our lifestyles and our actions accordingly in order to adjust our course from the one that currently lies ahead of us.

An interconnected worldview, which places humankind within the natural world, has been in existence for many years amongst Indigenous cultures and certain religions. This way of seeing our world teaches us that if we damage or degrade the natural world, there is a direct impact on us. The crisis of perception that has led to so much destruction now has to change. We *are* nature and we need to live in harmony with natural systems and learn how the principles or features of these systems can be our guide, as we look to live in more sustainable ways. The official invitation to the coronation of King Charles III, a champion of the natural world, put nature centre stage, with references to nature including wildflowers, butterflies and bees adorning the design. This is the direction of travel we must now take, one in which we develop practices that work in harmony with nature and ensure our own well-being in the process.

Education has a key role in shifting perspectives and priorities, as well as equipping young people with the skills, knowledge and attributes they need to address the issues, including climate change and biodiversity loss, which threaten our collective well-being now and in the future.

What does the curriculum guidance suggest?

As it currently stands, the primary National Curriculum makes few explicit references to learning about climate change and other wider issues of sustainability, although it should be noted that this varies across the UK.

Year 4 children in England will learn in Science, for example, about the threats posed by changing environments to living things and the positive and negative impacts of human activity on natural environments (DfE, 2013). However, there are few explicit references to issues of environmental sustainability beyond this. However, as we will consider in the next section, recently implemented initiatives at the policy level, most notably the Department for Education's policy paper 'Sustainability and Climate Change: A Strategy for the Education and Children's Services Systems' (2022), are promoting action on environmental issues alongside the curriculum taught in schools. In time, we would hope there are opportunities to make deeper links between the two.

With reference to the curriculum taught in schools in Northern Ireland, the Council for the Curriculum, Examinations & Assessment states that teachers should be given 'considerable flexibility to make decisions about how best to interpret and combine the requirements so as to prepare young people for a rapidly changing world' (2007, p2). This level of autonomy for environmentally minded educators to bring into the classroom issues of sustainability, which constitute some of the most urgent challenges young people need to respond to in our rapidly changing world, is also echoed in Wales. Schools here can use the framework set out in the Curriculum for Wales (2022) to develop their own curricula, provided these address the 'four purposes' of the curriculum; these include the requirement that schools support learners in becoming 'ethical, informed citizens who… show their commitment to the sustainability of the planet' (Curriculum for Wales, 2022, n.p.).

Meanwhile, in Scotland, environmental sustainability is a key strand in the Curriculum for Excellence (2019). Of the four capacities at the heart of the curriculum, one stresses the importance of enabling young people to become responsible citizens who are able to evaluate environmental issues effectively. The curriculum itself includes outcomes relating to biodiversity and interdependence, energy sources and sustainability and the processes of the planet.

REFLECTIVE QUESTIONS

Where and how do you teach children about learning to live with nature?

Do you find this easy or challenging to plan for in your school curriculum?

How is sustainability represented in children's educational experience?

One of the clearest indications that many young people believe that the current curriculum content does not adequately address environmental issues, including climate change, is evidenced by the presentation in Parliament earlier this year of the Climate Education Bill (2023) – awaiting its second reading at the time of writing. Written by students, if passed into law the Bill would make it mandatory for issues relating to climate change and sustainability to be integrated into the primary and secondary school curriculum.

However, there is clear evidence that the education sector across the UK is waking up to the need to put the sustainability and climate change agenda increasingly at the heart of learning. To give just two examples of this: The Curriculum for Wales is underpinned by the Well-being of Future Generations Act (2015) and gives schools much greater freedoms to design their own curriculum with reference to their local context and communities, and a much more nature-connected way of learning. The Department for Education in England has a sustainability and climate change strategy that, whilst not statutory, is gaining prominence alongside the existing curriculum with opportunities to bring the learning to life through sustainability-based and nature-based activities. These include the Nature Park to increase biodiversity on school grounds and the Climate Action Award to recognise action to address the climate crisis (Natural History Museum, 2022).

While there is still a long way to go before schools are truly walking the talk on this agenda, the signs are at last more encouraging that it is being given the attention it deserves. There are still very real questions about teachers' capacity to deliver on sustainability and climate change. These questions pertain to their knowledge and understanding of the issues, as well as the pressure they face due to the timetable constraints. The Teach the Future's 'Teach the Teacher' campaign (SOS-UK and Teach the Future, 2021) is highlighting and providing support in this regard. Learning about sustainability and climate change is an essential component of a good education and we need to make sure the process is engaging and enjoyable, as much as it is a serious matter, and to make space for it in an already crowded primary school curriculum. The Harmony Project's cross-curricular approach based on projects of learning helps with the latter, as we will see later in this chapter.

How can we give young people opportunities to become the climate leaders of tomorrow?

In addition to giving young people opportunities to acquire knowledge and understanding about issues relating to climate change and wider sustainability issues, there is also the question to address in the education of how we support them in developing the skills and agency they need to act on these issues. Andreas Schleicher, Director, OECD (Organization for Economic Co-operation and Development) Directorate for Education and Skills, defines student agency as 'the capacity to set goals, reflect and act responsibly to effect change. The concept of agency is rooted in the belief that students need to develop the ability and the will to positively influence their own lives and the world around them' (OECD, 2021, para. 7).

The results of the 2018 Programme for International Student Assessment (PISA) assessment, the first of these international OECD studies to include a focus on student agency relating to sustainability, revealed that while four in five (89%) 15-year-olds in participating countries said they knew 'something' about the issues of climate change and global warming, only three in five (59%) said they felt empowered to act to improve things. The actions they were most likely to take as a result of their sense of empowerment were largely simple individual actions such as reducing energy consumption – a great first step but not really comparable with the 'bigger picture' actions we would want our climate leaders of the future to be equipped to make. Commenting on the results, Schleicher noted:

Schools need to do better in helping students develop a sense of self-efficacy, agency and responsibility. Only in this way can young people unleash their knowledge and energy to build sustainable cities, start sustainable businesses, push the innovation frontier for green technologies, rethink individual lifestyles, back ecologically responsible policy making, and, most importantly, strike the right balance between meeting the needs of the present and safeguarding the ability of future generations to meet their own needs.

(OECD, 2021, para. 18)

Of course, it is not only schools but also our wider education systems, encompassing policymakers and teachers, national curricula and the curricula of individual education settings, which share responsibility for supporting students in developing the sense of their own self-efficacy, agency and responsibility for leading on solutions to the environmental challenges we face.

If schools and education settings are going to be successful in giving students more agency and responsibility to lead on ways to solve these environmental challenges, a number of key changes need to take place.

Firstly, we need to put the sustainability and climate change agenda firmly at the heart of learning so that teachers see it as a core component of what they teach, rather than an add-on or something done outside of the curriculum. This means looking at opportunities to address issues of sustainability and climate change within the learning process so that students develop a really good understanding of the issues and learn what they can do about them in age-appropriate ways.

Alongside this, it is time to shift to a more 'joined-up', interdisciplinary model of learning that allows young people to draw on skills, knowledge and understanding gained in different areas of the curriculum. This reflects the highly interconnected nature of the world we are part of, and the challenges we face.

We also need to give students opportunities to apply their subject skills, knowledge and understanding to the issues that so concern many of them. This approach gives learning greater relevance and, if done well, is likely to motivate students to take the learning into their own lives. In order to foster a sense of agency in young people, we need to ensure they have opportunities to act. In the subsequent sections of this chapter, we shall look at developing a Harmony approach to teaching and learning in more detail, and how to help students to develop a sense of their own agency through the practical application of 'sustainability actions'.

A new framework for teaching and learning

Inspired by the vision of King Charles III, explored in his book *Harmony: A New Way of Looking at Our World* (2010), a Harmony approach to education re-frames learning around natural laws and principles that ensure the resilience and balance of systems in Nature. When applied to teaching and learning, they help to show the world as an interconnected whole and provide a coherent and meaningful framework through which National Curriculum objectives can be delivered. When we apply them to our own lives, they help us to adopt healthier, more sustainable ways of living. This is the path we believe education needs to take.

In this section, we shall explore concepts around learning through the Harmony approach through a series of reflective questions. We shall consider how a new framework for teaching and learning can help children understand how to live in more harmonious and sustainable ways, now and in the future.

> **REFLECTIVE QUESTIONS**
>
> Our sense of separation from nature is deeply at odds with the simple truth that, as living things, we are entirely interconnected with other living things in the natural world, and this **is** why it is important that children and young people have opportunities to form a deep sense of connection with the natural world.
>
> - With reference to a class or a group of children you have worked with, or drawing on your curriculum knowledge, what role does the natural world play in the education of children in early years settings and primary schools?
> - What is the relationship between a sense of connection and a sense of responsibility? How are these two concepts interrelated?
> - Think of a time when you have felt connected to nature. How did this experience affect your outlook, feelings or actions more widely?

The benefits of exposure to natural settings for the individual are well-documented, with research identifying a range of positive outcomes including improved cognitive function, brain activity, blood pressure, mental health and sleep (Jimenez et al., 2021), and, for young people's learning specifically, attainment, progress and attendance (Natural England, 2016).

These outcomes are, of course, highly desirable. However, if we move beyond an anthropomorphic view of the benefits of connection with nature, we might consider how it can motivate us to adopt more sustainable behaviours to protect and restore the well-being of the natural world. In other words, when considering why a deep sense of connection with the natural world is important, we might ask not just what nature can do for us, but what we can do for nature.

Ives et al. (2018) identify several key forms of nature connection, from material connections (what we take from the natural world) to experiential connections, including recreational activities in natural settings, cognitive connections (encompassing knowledge, beliefs and attitudes), emotional attachments and philosophical connections (consideration of our relationship with the natural world). Of these, they argue that the cognitive, emotional, and philosophical connections are the ones most likely to result in transformative change when it comes to embracing more sustainable ways of living and being. To facilitate the development of a deep sense of connection with nature, they suggest that: 'Structural change may often be necessary to enable interventions for connecting people with nature to be implemented or benefits realised. For example, educational policy may need revising to allow school students' greater interaction with nature as part of curricula' (Ives et al., 2018, n.p.).

The Harmony approach restructures the content of the primary curriculum so that children have the opportunity to learn *about* nature, as stipulated in the National Curriculum science programmes of study, *in* nature in order to bring learning to life and give a practical dimension to what is learnt, but importantly also *from* nature and what nature teaches us through what we call its principles of

Harmony. Through this approach, children can forge experiential, cognitive, emotional and philosophical connections with the natural world.

As an example of what this kind of learning might 'look like', in a Harmony curriculum framework, children in Year 2 focus for one half-term on the enquiry question: 'Why are bees so brilliant?'. They learn how bees in a hive work together and about the symbiotic relationship between bees and flowering plants (learning *about* nature). They observe bees in their natural habitat and, if resources allow work with a beekeeper to care for bees (learning *in* nature), then consider what we can learn about interdependence from bees that we could apply to our own lives (learning *from* nature).

REFLECTIVE QUESTIONS

As we consider what best practices in education about sustainability and climate change might look like, skills and knowledge are important but so too are factors such as motivation and confidence.

- Why is helping children to develop a sense of their own agency an important part of education about sustainability and climate change? How can this be facilitated?
- Think of someone you have had experience working with whom you consider to be an effective leader or a leader of change. What qualities did they possess that make you think of them in this way?
- Think of a time in your own life when you have had to implement change. What was it that made you believe you could achieve this? If you lacked belief, what helped you to overcome this?

In addition to putting nature at the heart of teaching and learning, the Harmony approach also emphasises the importance of action for sustainability. The Harmony curriculum framework is structured around half-termly 'enquiries of learning', each with its own associated 'sustainability action'. These are practical, child-led projects, challenges or campaigns arising from the learning which give children experience of leading change. Examples of sustainability actions linked to enquiries of learning in the early years, KS1 and KS2 are shown in Table 2.1.

Table 2.1 Enquiry questions and positive actions

Year group	Enquiry question	Sustainability action
Year 1	What will we find at the seaside?	Beach (or local area) clean-up
Year 2	What do I need to be healthy?	Cooking with local, seasonal ingredients
Year 3	Where in the world does our food come from?	Growing food organically
Year 4	What are the cycles of our solar system?	Leading 'Earth Hour' for the school community
Year 5	What journey does a river take?	Finding ways to save water
Year 6	How are we connected to Antarctica?	Monitoring and reducing energy use

Giving children consistent opportunities in their learning from a young age to lead change, to work with others to achieve common goals and to see first-hand the impact that their actions can bring about, helps them to see themselves as sustainability and climate leaders.

What do teachers developing a Harmony approach to education in their settings tell us about its impact? What do children who are engaging with this way of learning have to say?

The Harmony Project works with a range of primary education settings to help them put sustainability and nature at the heart of teaching and learning. The reflections of headteachers and teachers in schools developing a Harmony approach highlight three key benefits. Firstly, they recognise that the Harmony approach helps children to look outwards and understand that they are part of something much larger than themselves. Secondly, it helps them to develop a sense of environmental stewardship – that we are collectively responsible for ensuring the health and well-being of the planet and that they have a part to play in this. Thirdly, they begin to recognise themselves as 'agents of change' and to understand that they have the power to affect positive change.

Consider the following comments made by participating school communities on the impact that the Harmony Project approach to education has achieved in their settings:

> *Reviewing our curriculum through the Harmony Project 'lens' pulls together with the school's vision and values to prepare our children (and their families) to become 'agents of change' for a more sustainable future.*
> Roy Sewell, Headteacher at St Mary's CE First School & Nursery, Ferndown, Dorset

> *Children develop a really good understanding of their place in the world and the impact of people's choices.*
>
> *They are able to speak confidently and passionately about global issues – they have a voice.*
>
> *Children are developing and embedding a sense of moral purpose with regards to guardianship of their world.*
> Comments from staff at South Farnborough Infants, Farnborough, Hampshire

> *Pupils benefit from rich and meaningful learning experiences across all national curriculum subjects. These are drawn together through the harmony' principles which enable pupils to understand how their learning experiences interconnect.*
> Ofsted report for St John's CE Primary School, Dorking, Surrey

In the classroom

In this section, we shall look at some more starting points for schools and educators interested in developing a Harmony curriculum in their settings. When we consider the role that a Harmony approach to education can have in bringing about a transition to more environmentally sustainable ways of living and being, we have a clear sense of where we are going. But how do we get started? The first steps towards developing a Harmony approach to education in a school or another education setting will be as diverse as the settings themselves – there is no 'one size fits all' approach.

REFLECTIVE QUESTIONS

Based on your knowledge of a school or class you have worked with, what might some 'ways in' to developing a Harmony approach be?

Great learning starts with the learner, their prior knowledge, skills and interests. This principle can also be applied to introducing or implementing change.

- How do school values resonate with the principles of Harmony that underpin a Harmony approach?
- Think about the context of the school (this could be its local community or the physical features of its setting). How might this inform the 'first steps' you take to develop a Harmony approach?
- Think about a particular class and the interests of the children and staff in it. What would appeal to them as a first project or focus for learning that is linked to a principle of Harmony in Nature?

For some schools, the first step might be to start to draw teaching and learning in each year group together each half-term under the 'umbrella' of an overarching enquiry question or theme (some examples of possible enquiry questions are provided in Tables 2.1 and 2.2). Doing so offers important opportunities to organise the content of learning in a more cross-curricular way that allows children to make connections between subject-specific content. This more 'joined-up' curriculum structure helps learning make sense for children and reflects the true highly interconnected nature of the world they are part of.

The planning overview shows how content from subjects across the curriculum can be brought together within the framework of a learning enquiry. A link to the planning overview can be found in the Further Reading and Resources section of this chapter.

Other settings might take a single sustainability theme as a whole-school focus and embed this in learning in all-year groups. Some examples of how this might be achieved for a biodiversity sustainability focus are given in Table 2.2.

Table 2.2 Single lines of enquiry with a focus on biodiversity

Sustainability theme: Biodiversity	
Year group	**Enquiry question**
Year 1	Which is my favourite wildflower and why?
Year 2	Why are bees so brilliant?
Year 3	Why should we preserve the biodiversity of the rainforest?
Year 4	How are animals adapted to survive in the Sahara?
Year 5	How can we ensure our oceans stay amazing?
Year 6	Where do Arctic animals migrate to?

Another approach still would be to focus on the principles of Harmony in Nature that are at the heart of the Harmony approach to education. These are principles we see at work in nature – and which ensure the well-being of natural systems – from which we can learn to live in more sustainable, more harmonious, ways. These include the principle of the Cycle and the principles of interdependence, Diversity and Adaptation.

A school or other education setting might begin working with these principles by aligning them with its values. For example, through the lens of the principle of Diversity, values such as appreciation, fairness and respect might be explored, with the principle of interdependence aligning well with the values of co-operation, responsibility, and trust. Alternatively, an education setting might prioritise aligning principles of Harmony in Nature to learning. A Year 1 learning enquiry which asks children 'What will we find at the seaside?' and a Year 6 enquiry which asks 'How are we connected to Antarctica?' can both be linked to an exploration of the principle of interdependence, by looking at the dynamic balance found in coastal ecosystems such as rockpools (Year 1) and the wider environmental consequences of our lifestyles and actions on one of our planet's polar regions (Year 6).

What might a new framework for teaching and learning that puts sustainability and nature at the heart of the curriculum look like?

The overview of planning for a Year 6 learning enquiry, 'How are we connected to Antarctica?' can be accessed on the Harmony Project website (details can be found in Further Reading and Resources for this chapter). This shows how National Curriculum objectives in different subjects can be drawn together in a way that allows children to make links between their learning in different areas of the curriculum. Each row of the overview shows the content covered in each subject over a six-week period, while the learning each week (the content of each column) is themed around a weekly question.

To drill a little deeper into some of the subject-specific content, the maths investigation that features in week 1 of this enquiry sees children working with real-life surface temperature data collected at a monitoring station in Antarctica to determine how this has changed over time and reflect on what the link with climate change is. This covers the following National Curriculum objectives:

- Use negative numbers in context and calculate intervals across zero.
- Calculate and interpret the mean as an average.

Meanwhile, the English unit in week 2 focusses on planning and creating diary entries (recounts) written by a modern-day Antarctic explorer and covers the following National Curriculum objectives:

- Plan by noting and developing initial ideas, drawing on reading and research where necessary.
- Draft and write by selecting appropriate grammar and vocabulary.
- Evaluate and edit by assessing the effectiveness of own writing and others' writing.
- Draft and write narratives, describing settings and atmosphere.

This helps children to connect with the sights and sounds of Antarctica and to consider what it might feel like to experience being there.

> **CHAPTER SUMMARY**
>
> In this chapter, we have explored how a new, cross-curricular framework for delivering National Curriculum objectives can help teachers and their students explore issues relating to climate change and environmental sustainability. We have explained how principles that ensure the health, resilience and dynamic balance of systems in nature can shape this framework and support children in developing a deep sense of connection with nature and helped you to consider how to implement principles of Harmony in your school curriculum.

Further reading and resources

www.theharmonyproject.org.uk/teaching-resources/medium-term-planning/protect-antarctica
The planning overview on the Harmony Project website shows how content from subjects across the curriculum can be brought together within the framework of a learning enquiry.

https://www.theharmonyproject.org.uk/practice
For more information about the principles of Harmony in Nature discussed in this chapter as well as others, visit The Harmony Project website.

Dunne, R. (2020) Harmony: A new way of looking at and learning about our world – A teacher's guide.
The Guide provides inspiration and practical information for educators seeking to apply the principles of Harmony in Nature to their practice.

Charles, C. et al. (2018) Home to us all: How connecting with nature helps us care for ourselves and the earth, children & nature network.
This report presents the growing body of evidence that people's relationship with nature profoundly influences their behaviours toward the Earth. Available at: https://www.iucn.org/resources/grey-literature/home-us-all-how-connecting-nature-helps-us-care-ourselves-and-earth

Department for Education (2022) Sustainability and climate change: a strategy for the education and children's services systems.
This document recognises the role that education plays in engaging with the climate crisis and in equipping young people with the skills they need to work towards a healthier future for our world. It discusses how the creation of more environmentally sustainable school grounds and settings can help facilitate change and how the knowledge and understanding young people have about sustainability issues can be developed. Available at: https://www.gov.uk/government/publications/sustainability-and-climate-change-strategy

Richardson, M. and Butler, C. W. (2022), The nature connection handbook: a guide for increasing people's connection with nature.
This guide recognises that a sense of connection to nature improves our ability to take action on climate change and other pressing environmental issues. It summarises research on nature's connection and sets out pathways to help improve our connection with nature. Includes case studies and examples of activities that can promote a sense of connection to the natural world. Available at: https://finding-natureblog.files.wordpress.com/2022/04/the-nature-connection-handbook.pdf

References

Berry, W. (1969) *The Long-Legged House*. Barclay, CA: Counterpoint Press.

Council for the Curriculum, Examinations and Assessment (2007) *The Northern Ireland Curriculum Primary*. Available at: https://uk.ccea.org.uk/learning-resources/northern-ireland-curriculum-primary

Climate Education Bill (2023) *Private Members' Bill*. Available at: https://bills.parliament.uk/bills/3405

Department for Education (2013) *National Curriculum for Science Key Stage 1 and 2*. Available at: https://assets.publishing.service.gov.uk/government/uploads/system/uploads/attachment_data/file/425618/PRIMARY_national_curriculum_-_Science.pdf

Department for Education (2022) *Sustainability and Climate Change: A Strategy for the Education and Children's Services Systems*. Available at: https://www.gov.uk/government/publications/sustainability-and-climate-change-strategy/sustainability-and-climate-change-a-strategy-for-the-education-and-childrens-services-systems

Education Scotland (2019) *Curriculum for Excellence*. Available at: https://scotlandscurriculum.scot

HRH Prince of Wales, Charles, Juniper, T. and Skelly, I. (2010) *Harmony: A New Way of Looking at Our World*. London: Harper Collins.

Ives, C. D., Abson, D. J. and von Wehrden, H. et al. (2018) Reconnecting with nature for sustainability. *Sustainability Science*, 13: 1389–1397. https://doi.org/10.1007/s11625-018-0542-9

Jimenez, M. P. et al. (2021) Associations between nature exposure and health: a review of the evidence. *International Journal of Environmental Research and Public Health*, 18(9): 4790. Available at: www.mdpi.com/1660-4601/18/9/4790

Natural History Museum (2022) *National Education Nature Park and Climate Action Awards*. Available at: https://www.nhm.ac.uk/about-us/national-impact/national-education-nature-park-and-climate-action-awards-scheme.html

Natural England (2016) *Links between Natural Environments and Learning: Evidence Briefing*. Available at: https://publications.naturalengland.org.uk/publication/5253709953499136

OECD (2021) *Education at a Glance 2021: OECD Indicators*. Available at: https://www.oecd-ilibrary.org/education/education-at-a-glance-2021_b35a14e5-en

Schleicher, A. (2021) *Green at Fifteen – What Schools Can Due to Support the Climate, Commentary on Results of PISA 2018*. Available at: https://oecdedutoday.com/green-at-fifteen-schools-support-climate/ (Accessed: 26 May 2023).

SOS-UK and Teach the Future (2021) *Teach the Teacher*. Available at: https://www.teachtheteacher.uk/

Welsh Government (2022) *Designing Your Curriculum, Curriculum for Wales*. Available at: https://hwb.gov.wales/curriculum-for-wales/designing-your-curriculum/

3
LEARNING TO CARE ABOUT OUR WORLD IN THE EARLY YEARS

SARAH SPRAKE AND EMILY ROTCHELL

LINKS TO CORE CURRICULUM FRAMEWORK

2.2, 3.1, 4.7

SUSTAINABLE DEVELOPMENT GOALS

GOAL 3: Good Health and Well-being
GOAL 4: Quality Education

KEY WORDS

Sustainability; play; early years; environment; ecology; social; cultural; economic agency; inclusivity; choice; empathy

CHAPTER OBJECTIVES

This chapter will:

- Consider education for sustainability from an early childhood perspective, using examples from international curriculum development, research and policy.
- Describe key themes of agency, inclusivity, choice, empathy and hopeful pedagogy emerge and resonate with early child development and practice.
- Consider the affinity between teaching and learning about sustainability and the holistic curriculum of early years, focussing on how the foundations and principles for this learning can be woven through provision.

Introduction

The roots of sustainable thinking and doing begin in children's earliest encounters with the world around them. Children begin to develop their understanding of nature and their reciprocal relationship with it from the moment they start to explore the world. The United Nations (UN) Educational, Scientific and Cultural Organization (UNESCO, 2012) report emphasises that Education for Sustainable Development (ESD) should be integrated at all education levels, starting from early childhood and that children from a young age can be introduced to, and become aware of, aspects related to the three key pillars of sustainable development: environmental and ecological concerns, social and cultural implications, and economic aspects (Brundtland, 1987). So how do we approach sustainability in the early years? Do we explain to very young children what sustainability is? Where is a good starting point for our youngest children to learn about 'meeting the needs of the present without compromising the ability of future generations to meet their own needs (Brundtland, 1987, p16)?' This can be quite a daunting task for early years practitioners. Davis (2009) showed that research into sustainability education in the early years was a limited area, but more recently there has been an increase in research into this area of education specifically focussing on the youngest learners.

This chapter explores education for sustainability from an early childhood perspective using examples from international curriculum development, research and policy. Key themes of agency, inclusivity, choice, empathy and hopeful pedagogy emerge and resonate with early child development and practice. The affinity between teaching and learning about sustainability and the holistic curriculum of early years, focussing on how the foundations and principles for this learning can be woven through provision is also considered.

Early Childhood Education for Sustainable Development

To consider sustainable thinking and doing in the early years, it is useful to review research and approaches to sustainability and environmental education from an early years' perspective. Pramling, Samuelsson and Kaga (2010) in Bamber (2020) propose seven notions that are embedded in a sustainable environment for social life and economy: respect, reduce, reflect, reuse, repair, recycle and responsibility. These '7Rs' underline the basic principles children need in order to foster love and respect towards nature. In this way ideas, attitudes, beliefs and behaviours are obtained that assure thinking and living in a sustainable way. Kim and Dreamson (2020) state that Early Childhood Education for Sustainability (ECEfS) is becoming internationally recognised as an important means for young children to develop their attitudes and behaviour towards sustainability. Korkmaz and Yildiz (2017) note that different views give rise to the many different approaches to pedagogy and curriculum used in ESD internationally, which are holistic, experiential, critically reflective, collaborative, problem-based, systemic and/or participatory, as outlined in Table 3.1.

Table 3.1 Approaches to pedagogy and curriculum for ESD

Approach to ESD	Brief description of the approach	EYFS possible example (we have only mentioned a few here, of course, there are many more)
1. Holistic	The curriculum has sustainability woven throughout.	All areas of the EYFS have links to sustainability. This could involve all The UN SDGs.
2. Experiential	The curriculum is flexible, allowing new ideas to be tried out.	Can we reduce the amount of water we use? Let's try out some ideas and see which are the most effective e.g. always turning taps off after washing our hands, collecting rainwater to water our plants. *
3. Critically reflective	The curriculum involves reflecting on the curriculum and making changes in relation to this.	Responsibility: Consider how we are already responsible for our environment and how we might take this further. For example, a setting may already recycle paper, now they will consider how they can reuse more of it. **
4. Collaborative	Staff and pupils work together to think of ways to become more sustainable.	Staff and pupils decide together that they want to grow and use some of their own herbs/fruit/vegetables and compost any waste. They create ideas boards together on how they will do this.
5. Problem-based (or an alternative may be solution-based)	The enquiry leads to questions being posed and potential solutions created.	A potential problem arises, which is then woven into curriculum planning, and potential solutions are found. For example, How can we keep our classroom warmer in winter?
6. Systemic	Considering environmental, economical and social aspects of sustainability together.	How can we improve our outdoor area? • For ourselves, other people who use it and for visitors. • How can we use the resources we have or can get to do this most effectively? • How can we best work as a team to achieve a good outcome?
7. Participatory	Involving everyone in the setting (and wider environment) in the decision-making process.	Considering how we can bring together the school community and the wider community in a collaborative allotment project.

*Check if your local water company provides ideas, resources and/or grants for reducing water usage.
**Check if you can access any paper recycling workshops for your pupils, or perhaps make your own.
Source: Adapted from Korkmaz and Yildiz (2017).

Warwick et al. (2017, p28) assert that 'Early years practitioners have a vital and exciting role to play in helping to nurture in young citizens ways of being that enable them to participate in the creation of more sustainable futures in their everyday lives', and argue that the vital role of early years practitioners is to playfully engage children with a sense of appreciation and value of the natural and social world by encouraging a sense of compassionate connection, convivial relationship and civic capacity. Rather than having a problem-based approach (see Table 3.1), Warwick et al. (2017) suggest that in the early years, a more suitable starting point should be formulated. They suggest instead a more playful engagement with a sense of appreciation and value of the natural and social world. 'A nurturing ground for children to develop a sense of wonder and innate curiosity about their life-worlds' (Warwick et al., 2017, p30). This approach is aimed at innovating towards *pedagogies of hope*. This illustrates that the approaches in Table 3.1 are not mutually exclusive, but here is a different approach: 'hope' can potentially incorporate parts of some other key ingredients of good early years practice. For example, the *pedagogy of hope* also aims to nurture children's collaborative creativity (Warwick et al., 2017).

In addition to developmentally appropriate pedagogy, the situated context of an early year's setting within its wider community will provide authentic and personal opportunities for curriculum design. Owens et al. (2022) argue that 'A school vision can drive a purposeful curriculum in relation to the climate crisis, and that there are opportunities for schools to identify what they will prioritise and this will be reflected through their selection of content'. For example, this can be achieved by selecting elements of Table 3.1, and beyond that, what schools want to incorporate into their own curriculum in relation to their setting, As well as using statutory documentation such as the Early Years Foundation Stage (EYFS) statutory framework (Department for Education, 2014), Owens (2022) suggests personalising it to suit the need and chosen focus in regards to sustainability education and that, teaching in current times to ensure a sustainable outcome for all requires more than core knowledge, so the vision should consider a curriculum that incorporates learning about, through and for the times we are living in. This means selecting content with opportunities for pupils to gain factual knowledge, recognise and share emotive aspects of learning and think about values, develop empathy and have opportunities for agency. Ideally a melding of curriculum, ethos, action and lifestyle.

REFLECTIVE QUESTIONS

Which of the 7Rs resonate with your own practice?

Are there any of the approaches that you would particularly like to develop in your own practice? Why is that and how might you action this?

Sustainability, early years and international practice (Scotland, Eco-Schools, Boyd)

Schools will often draw on curriculum guidance, or programmes to develop curriculum, and often these may be whole school approaches, which require adapting for early years provision. In this section, we explore three examples of curriculum guidance and examine the themes which emerge from each of these.

Eco-Schools

The Eco-Schools programme is a seven-step framework that empowers young people to make a difference in their school, local community and beyond. The programme is currently implemented in 73 countries worldwide (including The United Kingdom and Ireland). Korkmaz and Yildiz (2017) state that the goal of the Eco-Schools programme is innate to sustainable development, and the programme includes all three pillars of sustainability:

1. An environmental dimension, which aims to raise environmentally conscious individuals (Cincera et al., 2015)

2. A sociocultural dimension because its activities require continuous communication with parents and other community members

3. An economic dimension of sustainability since the programme emphasises conscious consumption and conservation by focussing on themes such as energy, water and recycling (Kadji-Beltran, 2002)

Learning for sustainability is an entitlement for all learners within Scotland's curriculum (see Further Reading). It aims to weave together global citizenship, sustainable development education and outdoor learning to enable learners, educators, schools and their wider communities to build a socially just, sustainable and equitable society. It supports the development of knowledge, skills and values at the heart of the curriculum's four capacities, helping to nurture learners as responsible citizens and effective contributors.

Boyd et al. (2021) assert that 'a key aspect of education for sustainability in the early years is creativity... about thinking divergently, "outside the box" and being solution-focussed. Being solution focussed would correlate well with pedagogies for hope – what positive impacts can practitioners and settings have in terms of sustainability?' (2021, p9). In this document, they aim to support early years practitioners and parents to engage with the sustainable development goals (SDGs), learning more about our responsibilities to each other and the world in which we live. Their work has an emphasis on education for sustainability through the 17 SDGs and Science Technology Engineering and Mathematics (STEM).

Whilst there is a focus on STEM in Boyd et al.'s work (2021), they also prioritise the characteristics of effective teaching and learning from the EYFS. These are:

- Playing and exploring – children investigate and experience things, and 'have a go'.

- Active learning – children concentrate and keep on trying if they encounter difficulties and enjoy achievements.

- Creating and thinking critically – children have and develop their own ideas, make links between ideas and develop strategies for doing things.

(EYFS, DfE, 2021, p16)

Boyd et al.'s (2021) document also draws on specific areas of the EYFS such as *Understanding the World* and the prime area of *Communication and Language*.

From this review of research, programmes and approaches, common themes emerge. In each, sustainability is inextricably linked with nurturing attitudes and community, with a view of the child as connected to the world around them and having agency in their learning. Authentic, concrete experiences are foregrounded in pedagogical approaches with the role of the practitioner central to children's developing knowledge and understanding.

In the following section, we shall now explore implications for practice in early years settings and where children may naturally encounter opportunities for playful, hopeful opportunities for sustainable thinking and doing.

In the classroom

During the early years, children are developing their understanding of self, emotions, and feelings and how they relate to the wider world. Young children's perception of the world starts with themselves, and this gradually expands during their first five years of life. This view of development resonates with the themes which emerge from the review of research and practice in this chapter so far, which has identified some common themes, such as agency, nurturing practice and implementing hopeful approaches to pedagogy. These approaches to pedagogy and provision in the early years nurture children's developing ideas about themselves, the world and their role within it; in this way, children's sense of environmental responsibility develops from a breadth and variety of experiences. It is important to remember that early years education plays a key role in embedding beliefs and dispositions, that children will carry with them as they grow and develop, as Chawla (1998) reminds us:

> *This complexity may make the challenge of environmental education more difficult, but it also makes it more hopeful. Just as ecosystems are more resilient when they contain an abundance of species that can form diverse adaptations to change, so is the future more hopeful if diverse paths lead people into environmental commitments.*
>
> (Chawla, 1998, p381)

Children's holistic development happens when they are actively engaged in an environment that interests and motivates them. Active, hands-on experiences are vital to children's early encounters with sustainability, through their interactions with the world and its resources.

Community and play

Sustainable thinking and doing develops from the individual child's starting points. In the early years, children are developing their sense of self and their confidence to explore, whilst developing agency and voice, learning to care for themselves and others: the building blocks of knowing about community and connections. In early years educational settings, children are at the heart of a shared community and the interactions between home, school and the wider community can foster a sense of belonging. Welcoming families into settings, during daily routines or learning events, enables this sense of community to thrive; children gain a sense of how places and people are connected.

As their experience of the world develops, children may seek to engage with changing play experiences. Children's play develops in tandem with their evolving perspectives of the world around them. It progresses from solitary play to playing alongside others, developing simple interactions and enabling them to engage in collaborative play. In practice, children are unique, play is diverse and development is individual; so, practitioners can support play by observing and enabling play experiences with children retaining agency. As children begin to attend early education settings, they may experience more interactive play with their peers, and through these early experiences, they may experience using shared resources for the first time. As children develop their play and become more confident to be part of small groups, they might learn that they can achieve a goal by working with others. These are likely to be children's first experiences of community and communality.

The early years classroom can reflect the expanding world of the children who play and learn within it. The role play area can reflect the identities of the children who play there, so they see their wider world included in this space. Using authentic resources will enable children to feel secure and build on their understanding through play. Children may use this area to practise and revisit routines of their homes play out their personal experiences and will learn about the lives of peers too. Children are learning to look after resources while finding out that resources can be used up and run out. A set of shared resources between the educational setting and home can be created too, such as sharing libraries for books or toys, sharing recipes or recycling facilities.

Things to consider:

- Fostering relationships and connections between a setting and community will support children's developing understanding of their wider world.

- Children's identities can be reflected in the classroom setting, consider role play and small world areas – do these relate to the children's experiences and extend their perceptions?

- Giving children independence and agency to look after classroom spaces and resources will nurture awareness of responsibilities.

- Are there opportunities to create shared resources between home and the educational setting such as recipes, story bags, libraries of books or toys?

Environment

Through early interactions with the natural world, children experience the relationship between humans and nature; they begin to understand the impact they have on the environment and the impact the environment has on them. For example, selecting clothing for going outside: investigating the impact of stamping in a puddle; a footprint in the sand; of feet treading a well-worn path through the grass,. The foundational learning of these small interactions with the world begins to develop an understanding of more complex concepts, such as that once plucked from its stem a leaf stops growing and begins to decay.

Outdoors, in natural landscapes, there are abundant opportunities to enhance critical thinking skills to overcome real challenges. Children's curiosity and motivations are nurtured through playful learning opportunities in an environment where natural processes are lived experiences. Children learn to respect and value nature, and understanding and developing an attachment to a natural environment make children more likely to want to protect nature in later life.

The resources and spaces available to early years educational settings are varied, but meaningful interactions with nature can be large or small scale. The image in Figure 3.1 depicts a child engaging with water. By observing this child's play, it was possible to see the learning emerging from the sequence of play. The children learned they were able to redirect the flow and affect the movement of the water just by altering the position of their hands. These small interactions may create the foundation for later conceptual learning (see Figure 3.2).

Figure 3.1   A child engaging in water lay in an outdoor setting

What is water like? Where does it come from? Where does it go? What does it do? Where can we find it? How can we use it? What do we call these water features? What is the difference between a canal and a river? What is my nearest river called? Where are the biggest rivers and lakes in the UK? What are they like? How does the water cycle work? Where are the world's biggest freshwater sources? Why are rivers important for trade and development?

Figure 3.2   Example of children's developing geographical understanding from EYFS to KS2, Owens et al. (2022)

This demonstrates the significance of playful interactions with nature, regardless of whether these are large or small scale, whether in a purpose-built outdoor space or part of a daily opportunity. For example, from contributing to the development of a school farm or allotment beds to growing herbs on a windowsill, a child encounters growth and nature. Produce, even in tiny quantities, can be shared at home so that children can see the rewards of their endeavours. Small containers of soil can be just as endlessly fascinating as larger areas, and a trickle of water or a puddle can present as many opportunities for play as larger sources. Inclusive open-ended activity without a fixed outcome such as digging or watering supports children's understanding of their relationship with the earth without the pressure of producing a predetermined result.

Things to consider:

- Do you use outdoor play to support children's developing understanding of their relationship with nature?
- Do you ensure play, indoors and outdoors, is inclusive for all learners and is adapted to meet the needs of children's stages of development?
- What natural processes are children gaining experiences of in your setting or during the learning experiences that you provide?
- How do you make sure that great value is placed on small opportunities for interactions with nature?
- How do you provide time for open-ended activity and value that as crucial for children's exploratory play and inclusivity for all learners?

Supportive practice, routines and pedagogy

The effectiveness of play-based, nature-rich approaches to pedagogy has been established by research (Ardoin and Bowers, 2020). Embedding playful pedagogy for sustainability requires careful consideration. Bilton (2007) discusses the implications of an adult directing play in the context of a den-building opportunity, where the activity is only authentic if the child retains the agency in designing their space. Pressoir (2008) also emphasises the value of playful pedagogies in the context of environmental education stating that 'children are capable of understanding complex ideas about the environment particularly when suitable play-based pedagogies are used' (Pressoir (2008), in Edwards et al., 2012, p17). There will also be many opportunities to incorporate sustainable thinking and doing into daily routines which become embedded in practice and naturally become part of children's developing actions towards the world. For example, communal mealtimes, the way resources are displayed and treated, caring for living things, and children's agency in constructing and maintaining their learning spaces, all provide valuable opportunities to open dialogue around sustainability and resourcefulness.

Supportive adults who are fully engaged with quality interactions to scaffold curiosity and provide opportunities for interests to be followed will enable children's developing ideas about the world to thrive. Skilled practitioners will know when to intervene, when to prompt children's thinking through open-ended questions and importantly to know when children need space and time to think to develop their ideas through uninterrupted play. Children learn from observing those around them, so the approaches and care about others and the world shown by the practitioners in early education settings will have an impact on the child's developing views. Adults can model caring behaviours by providing a learning environment in which children have agency and voice, which will support developing ideas about community and sustainability. Practitioners can make subtle changes to the provision to reflect children's interests while maintaining familiar consistent provision that will enable children to revisit and recreate their ideas in new ways.

REFLECTIVE QUESTIONS

- How is learning about sustainability embedded into routines in your setting?
- How do children have agency in developing provision?
- How do interactions with practitioners' scaffold thinking and doing for sustainable futures?

CHAPTER SUMMARY

Sustainability in the early years is inextricably linked with nurturing attitudes and community, with a view of the child as connected to the world around them and having agency in their learning. Authentic, concrete experiences are foregrounded in pedagogical approaches with the role of the practitioner central to children's developing knowledge and understanding. This chapter is just a starting point in exploring sustainability in the early years Curriculum. Consider further exploring international curriculum development and policy when working towards a potentially empathetic, solution-focussed, inclusive and hopeful pedagogy for sustainable development in the early years.

Further reading and resources

https://www.amightygirl.com/mighty-girl-picks/top-children-s-books-on-the-environment
A selection of Children's Books on the environment, curated by amightygirl.com

https://www.ecoschools.global/
Eco-schools Global encourages young people to engage in their environment by allowing them the opportunity to actively protect it. It starts in the classroom; it expands to the school and eventually fosters change in the community at large.

https://hwb.gov.wales/repository/publishers/ad23d962-3658-49b9-bc66-808c19c1378a
Eco-schools Wales resources hub

https://education.gov.scot/education-scotland/scottish-education-system/policy-for-scottish-education/policy-drivers/learning-for-sustainability/
Education Scotland: Learning for Sustainability

https://feeacademy.global/

The Foundation for Environmental Education Academy is one of the world's largest environmental education organisations, prioritising climate action across to address the urgent threats of climate change, biodiversity loss and environmental pollution. Their educational programmes, Eco-Schools, Learning About Forests and Young Reporters for the Environment, empower young people to create an environmentally conscious world through a solutions-based approach.

https://hundred.org/en

HundrED aims to help every child flourish by giving them access to quality education. They believe that with education innovations school systems can be transformed, and students can be equipped with the skills to thrive as global citizens.

https://www.eecera.org/sig/sustainability-in-early-childhood-education/

The hub of EECERA (European Early Childhood Education Research Association)'s Sustainability in Early Childhood Education Special Interest Group.

https://www.wildlifetrusts.org/

The Wildlife Trusts are a grassroots movement of people who believe that we need nature and that nature needs us. There are 46 individual Wildlife Trusts, each of which is a place-based independent charity with its own legal identity, formed by groups of people getting together and working with others to make a positive difference to wildlife and future generations, starting where they live and work.

UNESCO (2012) Education for Sustainable Development: Good Practices in Early Childhood Education for Sustainable Development in Action. Good Practices N°4 – 2012. United Nations Educational, Scientific and Cultural Organization. Paris.

References

Ardoin, N. and Bowers, A. (2020) Early childhood environmental education: a systematic review of the research literature. *Education Research Review*. https://doi.org/10.1016/j.edurev.2020.100353

Bamber, P. (ed.) (2020) *Teacher Education for Sustainable Development and Global Citizenship: Critical Perspectives on Values, Curriculum and Assessment* (Critical global citizenship education). New York: Routledge. https://doi.org/10.4324/9780429427053

Bilton, H. (6 September 2007) 'All about dens' in Nursery World magazine. Available at: https://www.nurseryworld.co.uk/features/article/all-about-dens

Boyd, D., King, J., Mann, S., Neame, J., Scollan, A. and McLeod, N. (2021) *An Early Childhood Education for Sustainability Resource That Embeds the Sustainable Development Goals and STEM into Pedagogical Practice*. NCFE: Liverpool John Moores University. Available at: https://www.ncfe.org.uk/media/xbcbjrfj/early-years-sustainability-resource.pdf

Brundtland, G. H. (1987) *Our Common Future Report of the World Commission on Environment and Development*. Geneva: UN-Document A/42/427.

Chawla, L. (1998) Significant life experiences revisited: a review of research on sources of environmental sensitivity. *Environmental Education Research*, 4: 4 369–382. https://doi.org/10.1080/1350462980040402

Cincera, J., Kroufek, R., Simonova, P., Broukalova, L., Broukal, V. and Skalík, J. (2015) Eco-school in kindergartens: the effects, interpretation, and implementation of a pilot program. *Environmental Education Research*, 3: 1–18. https://doi.org/10.1080/13504622.2015.1076768

Davis, J. (2009) Revealing the research 'hole' of early childhood education for sustainability: a preliminary survey of the literature. *Environmental Education Research*, 15(2): 227–241. https://doi.org/10.1080/13504620802710607

Department for Education (2021) *Development Matters*. Available at: https://www.gov.uk/government/publications/development-matters--2

Department for Education (2014) *Statutory Framework for the Early Years Foundation Stage*. Available at: https://www.gov.uk/government/publications/early-years-foundation-stage-framework--2

Edwards, S., Moore, D. and Cutter-Mackenzie, A. (2012) Beyond 'killing, screaming and being scared of insects' learning and teaching about biodiversity in early childhood education. *Early Childhood Folio*, 16(2): 12–19.

Kadji-Beltran, C. (2002) *Evaluation of Environmental Education Programmes as a Means for Policy Making and Implementation Support: The Case of Cyprus Primary Education* (PhD diss.). Warwick University.

Korkmaz, A. and Yildiz, T. G. (2017) Assessing preschools using the Eco-Schools program in terms of educating for sustainable development in early childhood education. *European Early Childhood Education Research Journal*, 25(4): 595–611. https://doi.org/10.1080/1350293X.2017.1331074

Kim, S. and Dreamson, N. (2020) Culturally inclusive early childhood education for sustainability: a comparative document analysis between Australian and Korean curricula. *European Early Childhood Education Research Journal*, 28(5): 712–730. https://doi.org/10.1080/1350293X.2020.1817242

Owens, P. (2022) *Teaching in a Climate Crisis: Some Provocations and Thoughts*. Primary Geography Number 108 Summer 2022.

Owens, P., Rotchell, E., Sprake, S. and Witt, S. (2022) *Geography in the Early Years: Guidance for Doing Wonderful and Effective Geography with Young Pupils*. Sheffield: The Geographical Association.

Pressoir, E. (2008) Preconditions for young children's learning and practice for sustainable development. In I. Pramling Samuelsson and Y. Kaga (eds.), *The Contribution of Early Childhood Education to a Sustainable Society*, pp57–66. Paris: UNESCO. Available at: https://unesdoc.unesco.org/ark:/48223/pf0000159355

UNESCO (2012) *Shaping the Education of Tomorrow: 2012 Report on the UN Decade of Education for Sustainable Development*. Available at: http://unesdoc.unesco.org/images/0021/002166/216606e.pdf Accessed: 19 April 2016.

Warwick, P., Warwick, A. and Nashm, K. (2017) Towards a pedagogy of hope. In V. Huggins and D. Evans (eds.), *Early Childhood Education and Care for Sustainability: International Perspectives*, 1st edition. Routledge. https://doi.org/10.4324/9781315295855

4
BECOMING CONSERVATION CHAMPIONS THROUGH SCIENCE LEARNING

DEBORAH POPE

LINKS TO CORE CURRICULUM FRAMEWORK

3.3, 3.6, 4.2

SUSTAINABLE DEVELOPMENT GOALS

GOAL 15: Life on Land

KEY WORDS

Natural world; biodiversity; conservation; big ideas; scientific enquiry; science capital; citizen science

> ### CHAPTER OBJECTIVES
>
> This chapter will:
>
> - Examine the role of science learning in developing children's understanding of the natural world.
> - Explore how the principles and 'big ideas' of science help teachers to identify age-appropriate opportunities to develop children's ecological awareness within the national curriculum.
> - Evaluate the importance of science literacy in preparing learners for future active citizenship.
> - Exemplify practical approaches to teaching this area in the primary classroom.

Introduction

Bringing nature into the classroom can kindle a fascination and passion for the diversity of life on earth and can motivate a sense of responsibility to safeguard it.

(David Attenborough, 2011)

Why should we aspire for children to become conservation champions? To conserve something indicates an action to protect it from being wasted, lost, changed or destroyed. Our survival is dependent on the earth's natural resources, including air, water, soil, minerals, fuel, plants and animals. Conservation practices are central to caring for these resources for the future benefit of all living things. The children we teach now will inherit the problematic legacy of climate change and loss of biodiversity. It is our responsibility to ensure that they are prepared and empowered with the knowledge, understanding, skills and attitudes to meet the challenges that lie ahead. In its sustainability and climate change strategy for education policy paper (Department for Education 2022), the government has identified science education as a natural home for much of this activity. A new science model curriculum focussed on nature is promised by 2023. To align, the same focus is adopted in this chapter. It will examine what science has to offer children's developing ecological knowledge and how we might best encourage children through science learning to become environmentally responsible, active citizens in the future. We shall look at some of the research and theory in this area and consider related approaches in the context of the primary science curriculum. Following a discussion of the evidence, we shall explore how we might apply some of these ideas in practice.

Why science?

> ### REFLECTIVE QUESTIONS
>
> Why do you think that the government has chosen science as the focus subject for much of the sustainability and climate change strategy for education? To what extent do you agree?

Policy background

For decades, there have been calls for environmental education to be given greater priority in education policy. More recently, the issue of climate change has been brought to the forefront due to an urgent need to tackle global challenges (IPCC, 2021; UNESCO, 2017). In 2022, the government published its sustainability and climate change strategy for the education and children's services systems in England (DfE, 2022) in response to the global crisis. The strategy includes plans for a science model curriculum with teaching resources, focussing on the recognition of native species, along with science professional development for teachers. A further, and perhaps more innovative, initiative includes the creation of a virtual National Education Nature Park. Working in partnership with a range of organisations, the education sector will be supported to map all the land across the education estate with a view to enhancing the biodiversity of one large, virtual nature park.

While there is much to be welcomed in the Department for Education (DfE) strategy, it raises some questions, too. Evidence suggests that there is already insufficient science teaching in primary schools. The Wellcome Trust's (2017) 'State of the Nation' report on UK primary science education found that, across year groups, on average 58% of classes were not receiving at least two hours of science per week and 12% of schools were not teaching weekly science to any year groups. The research also found that many teachers reported low confidence in teaching science. These research findings suggest that it might not be straightforward for teachers to integrate the additional curriculum materials. Given that no change is anticipated to the statutory curriculum for primary science, it becomes important to evaluate the content that exists and identify opportunities to make meaningful connections to climate change and sustainability.

The nature of science

Science is concerned with investigating the world around us, to provide explanations of how and why things happen. The body of knowledge established by the scientific community represents those ideas that are currently considered to be most plausible. New evidence emerges regularly through scientific research that advances current thinking. Such evidence has demonstrated that intensive farming and fishing, urbanisation and climate change are impacting global biodiversity. In the UK, wildlife populations have decreased by 58% since 1970 (State of Nature Report, 2019). In the same time period, more than half of British farmland birds have declined or been lost, for instance, the lapwing, the cuckoo and the turtle dove. There are many more examples in the report, and the newest version, State of Nature Report, 2023, shows an even more alarming picture (see further reading).

Primary science education is focussed upon well-established theories: national curriculum programmes of study act as signposts to foundational concepts and processes that build progressively to help children to make sense of the world around them. These key ideas form the basis for children's science literacy, so they cannot be neglected. They also provide the framework within which to develop children's ecological awareness. We can illustrate to children the relevance of science and its dynamic nature, by integrating current evidence about biodiversity and the conservation practices that offer hope in preserving natural ecosystems, without shifting focus from the fundamentals.

Scientific knowledge and understanding

> **REFLECTIVE QUESTION**
>
> What role do you think scientific knowledge plays in developing children's environmental attitudes and behaviours?

To develop expertise in science, children need to build both their substantive knowledge (science content) and disciplinary knowledge (working scientifically), as reiterated in Ofsted's recent research review for science (2021).

Substantive knowledge

Substantive knowledge represents conceptual knowledge of scientific ideas. Scientific concepts need to be taught explicitly. Children's understanding can be enhanced by the teacher selecting the most pertinent analogies, illustrations, examples and demonstrations to increase the effectiveness of their explanations. The importance of building on children's prior knowledge has long been acknowledged in primary science practice; teachers use a range of techniques to elicit children's existing ideas, such as drawing, concept mapping or discussion of 'concept cartoons'.

One of the trickier aspects of teaching younger children about climate change and sustainability is the fact that many of the underpinning ideas are scientifically complex, requiring a level of conceptual understanding that is, frequently, beyond the expectations for the children's stage in learning. For example, recognising gas as a state of matter makes its first appearance in the Year 4 programme of study (aged 8–9), so understanding the impact of greenhouse gases is potentially problematic. In a science learning context, our aim is always for secure conceptual understanding. If there are weaknesses in prior knowledge, children are more likely to develop misconceptions. For that reason, if we wish to embed the teaching of ideas connected to biodiversity and conservation within existing school science curricula, we must ensure that children's conceptual learning does not sit in 'silo' topics. Building conceptual connections within and between topics is a central principle if our aim is for children to develop deeper scientific understanding.

> ### PAUSE FOR THOUGHT
>
> #### Big ideas of science education
>
> *The goal of science education is not knowledge of a body of facts and theories but a progression towards key ideas which enable understanding of events and phenomena of relevance to students' lives.*
>
> (Harlen, 2010, p2)
>
> In 2009, with the aim of articulating a common purpose for science education, an international group of scientists, engineers and science educators distilled science learning into ten 'big ideas' *of* science and four 'big ideas' *about* science that were relevant to all learners through their years of compulsory schooling. The framework of 'big ideas' supports teachers to ensure the science curriculum has a purpose in building and connecting smaller ideas towards these bigger organising ideas that can explain the world.

Example of building towards a 'big idea' in the topic of plants

In Figure 4.1, the key ideas are drawn from the national curriculum programmes of study for the plants topic across Years 1–3. It shows how the key ideas are built in the curriculum but also how the sequence might simply end with the role of the flower in the life cycle. By placing some more emphasis on the role of insect pollinators, we can build further, from the unifying idea of reproduction to the interdependence between the plants and the insect pollinators (e.g. bees, wasps, moths, butterflies and flies), in which the plant relies on the insect and the insect needs the plant for food (pollen and nectar). As shown in the diagram, taking this approach naturally leads to the eighth 'big idea' (Harlen, 2010); it gives a purpose to the learning sequence and helps children to see the significance of what they are learning, not as isolated facts, but as an overarching idea that can be applied in many specific contexts.

The curriculum sequence is fundamental to understand this topic. Whilst retaining these key ideas at the heart of children's learning experiences in the topic, it is possible to create meaningful opportunities to enrich their understanding of biodiversity and conservation, such as growing vegetables in a school garden and identifying the plant parts we eat, surveying plant diversity in the school grounds and designing planters to encourage pollinators. Rather than taking anything away from core science activities, these additional elements can offer a greater sense of purpose to the children's science learning.

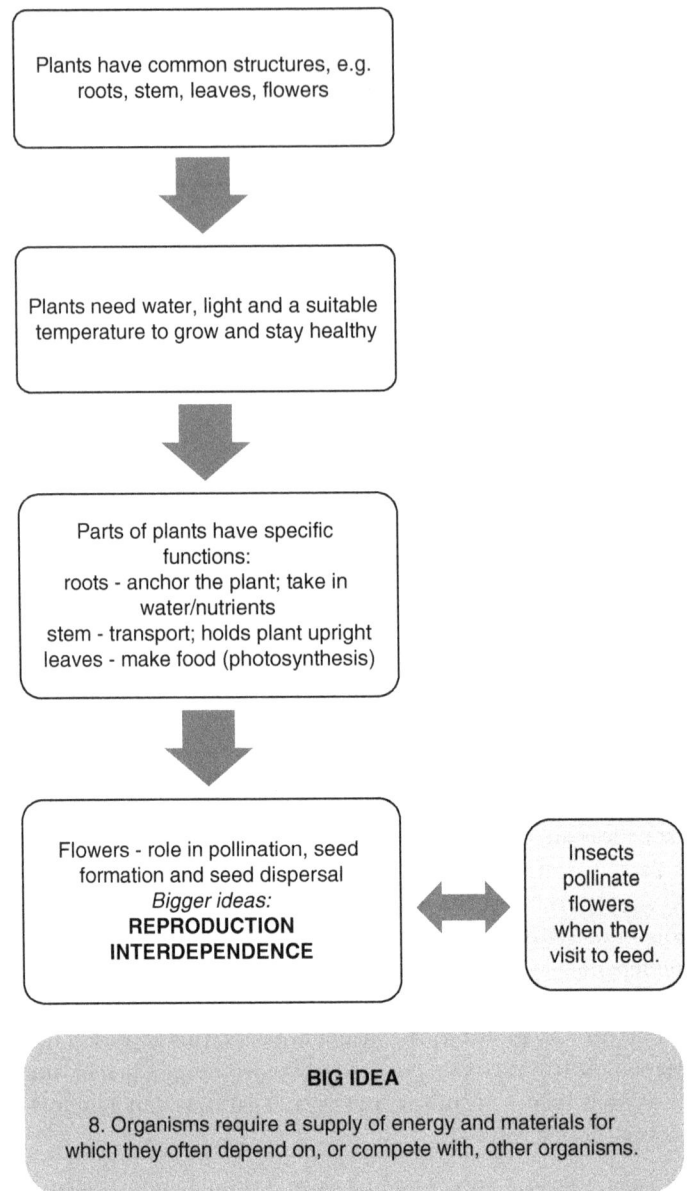

Figure 4.1 Building towards a 'big idea' in the plants topic

Disciplinary knowledge

Disciplinary knowledge encompasses understanding about the nature of science and the working practices of scientists used to build knowledge, along with skills used to collect and analyse evidence across a range of types of enquiry. This does not equate simply to doing practical work and collecting data (Ofsted, 2021). For scientific enquiries to be purposeful, the work must support and apply the teaching of specific concepts. Skamp (2007) coined the term 'heads, hearts and hands-on science' to capture the necessary interplay between the cognitive, affective and experiential elements of effective science learning. The interconnectedness between disciplinary knowledge and substantive knowledge brings meaning to science, as illustrated in the example in Figure 4.2.

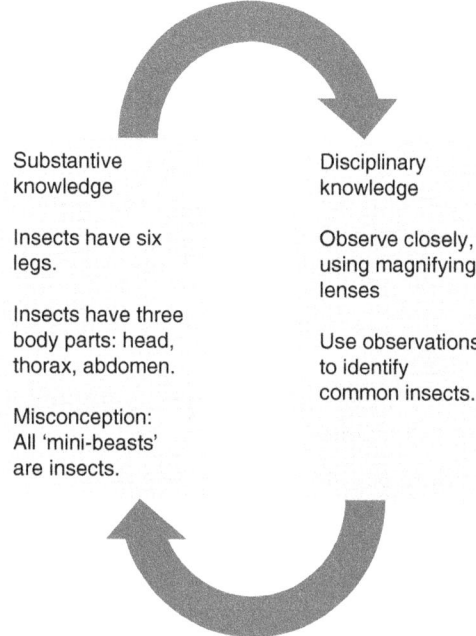

Figure 4.2 Example of the interplay between substantive and disciplinary knowledge

There are six types of enquiry that children should have the opportunity to engage with over time. Some scientific ideas lend themselves well to being investigated via a particular type of enquiry. A focus on the natural world can offer rich opportunities to work beyond the familiar fair testing scenario, as shown by the examples in Table 4.1.

Table 4.1 Examples of questions to be answered through different enquiry types

Type of enquiry	Investigation
Comparative/fair testing	How does light affect plant growth?
Research using secondary sources	Which plants are good for attracting pollinators?
Observation over time	How does the hazel tree in the playground change over the year?
Pattern seeking	Where do we find the most woodlice?
Identifying, grouping and classifying	Which of these invertebrates are insects and which are not?
Problem-solving	Design a bird feeding station for the school grounds.

Investigative work in science provides an opportunity for children to be taught, and to practise, associated skills of scientific enquiry relating to planning and carrying out investigations, collecting, presenting and interpreting data, and drawing conclusions. Enquiry skills are embedded progressively within the working scientific programmes of study in the national curriculum. Once again, it is important that you teach children these skills explicitly, with appropriate scaffolding for their stage of learning.

Children as agents of change

A line of reasoning frequently encountered in policies is that if children become more knowledgeable about the environment, they will become more connected to nature and can be engaged as agents of change for the environment in their homes and communities (Bourn, 2021). It requires children to transfer environmental concerns raised in school into their everyday lives with a view to them influencing environmental attitudes and behaviours of people around them. Although this is a neat argument, there is more for us to consider.

> ### PAUSE FOR THOUGHT
>
> In their classic paper, Hungerford and Volk (1990, p18) asserted that ecological knowledge was not a good predictor of environmental behaviour:
>
> > If environmental issues are to become an integral part of instruction designed to change behaviour, instruction must go beyond 'awareness' or 'knowledge' of issues. Students must be given the opportunity to develop the sense of 'ownership' and 'empowerment' so that they are fully invested in an environmental sense and prompted to become responsible, active citizens.
>
> More recently, the findings of a study by Carmi et al. (2015), reinforced the major role of emotions. Although they found ecological knowledge to be important, whether that knowledge has a significant effect on behaviour was determined by emotions.

These studies, and others like them, reveal to us that scientific knowledge is only one part of the solution. In the illustrative 'bicycle' model on climate change by Cantell et al. (2019), knowledge is represented by just one wheel. Knowledge must be applied and evaluated critically, so the other bicycle wheel represents thinking skills, and both wheels are connected by the chain ('action'). The model incorporates other key elements, including emotions, identity, values and participation. The different components work together as a dynamic system, just like the parts of a moving bicycle. The model resonates with the idea of scientific literacy; science education should develop relevant transferable knowledge, skills and attitudes for life. To have a look at Cantell's bicycle activity, see the Further Reading and Resources for this chapter.

According to Skamp (2011, p4), scientifically literate citizens understand the world around them and can engage critically in debates about science-related issues. They make informed choices about matters that impact their lives and the environment, with respect for evidence. To enable this through primary science education, the challenge is two-fold: the need not only to connect children to nature but also to increase their connectedness to science in a way that is empowering.

> ### PAUSE FOR THOUGHT
>
> **The ASPIRES project**
>
> Through a five-year study, Archer et al. (2013) sought to explore and understand what influences the likelihood of a young person aspiring to a science-related career. They found that family 'science capital' was key. Drawing upon the ideas of the French sociologist, Pierre Bourdieu, in relation to 'capital', the concept of 'science capital' was developed to encapsulate 'all the science-related knowledge, attitudes, experiences and social contacts that an individual may have' (p6). The research highlighted the need to build science capital from the primary phase of education for more young people to identify science as being 'for them'.

Primary Science Capital Teaching Approach

The Primary Science Capital Teaching Approach (PSCTA) (Nag Chowdhuri et al., 2021) is a reflective model devised as a way to put into practice the ASPIRES project research findings about science capital. It uses the metaphor of your science capital 'bag' holding all your 'science-related interests, knowledge, relations and behaviours' (p12). The approach has much to offer to the teaching of biodiversity and conservation due to its inclusive foundation of starting with learners' needs and interests. It supports student voice and agency through personalising and localising learning with real-life examples that are relevant to the child. We need children to see science as 'for them' irrespective of whether they go on to have science-related careers. The aim of the approach is to use scientific knowledge, processes and skills to act on issues that matter to children and their lives, building science identity and agency. Rather than studying the natural world as something external to them, children develop their voices through participation.

> ### REFLECTIVE QUESTIONS
>
> Consider your own science capital.
>
> How might this influence your teaching of science?

Connecting children to nature

The benefits of learning science outside the classroom are well-documented (e.g. Harlen and Qualter, 2018) in relation to helping children to make abstract concepts real, developing their aptitude in different environments and motivating young people to become active caretakers of the environment. When visiting locations off-site, there are multiple opportunities for children and teachers to benefit from the expertise of specialist staff at museums, zoos and wildlife centres, or places of work such as farms, supermarkets and garden centres. Natural locations, such as parks, woods and seashores, frequently offer access to rangers for school visits. Interacting with experts builds children's science capital, which, in turn, increases the relevance of the learning to children's future lives.

To care for the environment, you must experience it on a regular basis over time, so working within the school grounds is often the most accessible way to do this. We must recognise that teachers are sometimes apprehensive about undertaking surveys of plant and animal diversity on the school grounds, due to concerns about the limitations of their own natural history knowledge. This is where resources produced by organisations, such as The Woodland Trust, can offer support with activities involving the identification of wildlife.

Citizen science

Another way that teachers can be supported through expert communities is through involvement in citizen science projects which use collaborative volunteer research to collect, or explore, data (Bonney et al., 2009). Submitting observation data to collaborative projects shows children the value of their contributions, empowering them to participate in collective action. A familiar example is the Royal Society for the Protection of Birds (RSPB) Big Schools' Birdwatch which is a simplified survey of birds in the school grounds that feeds into the Big Garden Birdwatch – the UK's largest citizen science wildlife survey (540,000 participants in 2023). Citizen science forms an integral part of the DfE strategy introduced at the start of this chapter, in relation to the creation of a virtual National Education Park. It is anticipated that children will have opportunities to engage in community science projects, wildlife monitoring and data analysis, with a view to enriching their skills and future career opportunities. This offers much potential for children's opportunities to interact with a range of experts from partnership organisations for the duration of their school years. There is significant potential to connect children with nature in their local contexts, so promoting a sense of ownership, whilst building their science capital through their active participation in conservation-orientated communities.

In the classroom

In this section, we shall look at some examples of how you can provide opportunities to develop children's understanding of biodiversity and conservation through their science learning. The school grounds are a natural extension of the classroom, but we know that effective learning beyond the classroom boundaries is best supported by meaningful preparation and follow-up.

Using the school grounds

Increasingly, primary schools have some well-developed areas on the grounds to support children's interactions with the natural world. If there are areas still to be developed, involve the children in

4 Becoming conservation champions through science learning

their design, creation and upkeep. Additionally, draw upon the expertise of parents and carers too. You will be surprised at what can come into being through collaboration. If your school is located in an intensely urban area with little access to nature, even within the school grounds, you may need to use community facilities, such as visiting allotments or community gardens. The main advantage of having ready access to nature, even in small areas, is how regularly the spaces can be used by all year groups, enabling integration within the school curriculum. Useful elements to develop include:

- A gardening area
- Trees/shrubs (see The Woodland Trust free trees for schools scheme)
- Log piles/bug hotels
- A bird-friendly area with feeders, bird table, bird bath and nesting boxes
- A patch of unmown grass at the edge of the school field or a grassed area
- A pond (can be as simple as a pond in a pot)

Resources

Gardening

Most educational suppliers offer bulk kits of age-appropriate tools:

- Gloves
- Kneeling pads
- Hand trowels and forks
- Hand rakes
- Watering cans
- Garden brush
- Recycled plant pots/containers
- Shovel
- Spade
- Dutch hoe
- Fork
- Leaf rake
- Soil rake

Nature study

- Magnifiers
- Collecting pots
- Pooters
- White trays
- White sheet (for a tree shake)
- Plastic spoons/soft paintbrushes (to transfer invertebrates with care)
- Sweep net/pond dipping net
- Digital cameras
- Easi-speak microphones
- Binoculars
- Clipboards
- Pencils/paper
- Identification keys for plants and invertebrates (see The Woodland Trust website for good online examples)

The RSPB website has instructions for making some of these resources from recycled materials. See the Further Reading and Resources section of this chapter for a link.

Ideas to try with your class

YEAR 1

Topic: Plants and seasonal changes

Activity: Adopt a tree

Choose an accessible deciduous tree in the school grounds (or nearby) as the focus for a year-long observational investigation. Visit the tree throughout each season for children to record their observations about the leaves, bark, buds, blossom and fruit. Consider what might be growing at the base of the tree and on the bark. Do they notice any animal activity in, on, or by the tree? Record what the weather is like at the time of each observation. However, you choose to approach the recording of children's work, remember to add each season sequentially for ready comparison, for instance, on a long-term wall display or in a large class project book. This helps children to know that it is the same living tree that takes on a different appearance through the seasons.

YEAR 2

Topic: Habitats

Activity: Shake a tree

When studying habitats, this is a good way to survey which invertebrates are living in a tree (or shrub). Choose a tree with some lower-hanging branches. Spread out a white sheet on the ground beneath it before giving the tree branch, or shrub, a gentle shake, or tapping the branch with a stick. The children can hold the sheet up at the edges if it helps. Collection jars can be placed gently over the invertebrates so the children can observe them more closely using magnifiers. They could also use pooters to collect specimens, or transfer them carefully using a soft paintbrush to a container. This is a perfect opportunity to teach children how to respect wildlife and how to always return living things to the place you found them, unharmed. Use simple identification keys to sort and identify some of the invertebrates collected. Compare with the invertebrates found elsewhere, for instance under a log pile.

YEAR 3

Topic: Plants – The role of the flower in plant reproduction

Activity: Flower dissections

Often when children are introduced to the names and functions of the structures within a flower in the context of sexual reproduction, it is through the medium of stylised diagrams. This is an important stage for clarifying that the male stamen comprises the anther (containing pollen) and the filament, while the female carpel comprises the ovary (containing the ovules), style and stigma. For increased relevance though, the children need to connect with the magnificent diversity of these flower structures in different plant species. Through careful dissection of specimens, children can peel away the petals of each flower to reveal the structure. Creating a display of the dissection encourages a slow and steady pace. Children can arrange the petals, stamens, and cross-sectioned carpel onto background paper to exhibit their findings. The arrangement can either be photographed or stuck down to the paper. Comparisons can be made between flowers of different plant species in relation to the number/colour/length of stamens and the shape/colour/length of carpels, for example. Shop-bought cut flowers tend to be more suitable, in preference to removing flowers from the school grounds.

YEAR 4

Topic: Habitats

Activity: How are living things harmed, or helped, by changes to the environment?

Undertake a Bioblitz activity to survey a grassed area. Place a quadrat (or hula hoop) in the area to be sampled, and the children identify as many living things as possible within the defined space in a set time. The aim is for children to recognise how many living things co-exist and how they depend on each

(Continued)

other. For example, in a neatly mowed lawn you will find invertebrates (e.g. worms, woodlice, beetles, grasshoppers and spiders), that make the lawn an important foraging site for insectivorous birds such as blackbirds, robins and pied wagtails. The children might also identify other plants growing amongst the grass, such as moss (good nesting material) and dandelions (seeds eaten by goldfinches and house sparrows; flowers pollinated by bees, hoverflies and butterflies).

Introduce the scenario of changing the lawn area, with a couple of possible options: (1) replace it with artificial grass or (2) leave it unmown for longer. The children can investigate what the effects of each change would be on the biodiversity of the micro-habitat, using research through secondary sources. Findings can be presented in a range of formats, for instance, a slideshow presentation, an information leaflet, or a debate. Argumentation is a key aspect of scientific literacy and this activity presents an excellent opportunity to motivate children to take a position on the issue and to act as an advocate for it. Relate their findings to current issues, like the No Mow May Movement and campaigns against artificial grass to illustrate how individual actions can make a difference. A visit to a wildlife meadow is a powerful stimulus to engage children's emotions.

YEAR 5

Topic: Life cycles

Activity: Gardening for butterfly conservation

Make learning about the butterfly life cycle more purposeful by considering how that knowledge can help us to conserve butterfly populations. Children will already know about the importance of butterflies as pollinators. Butterflies will visit gardens if they can feed on suitable nectar plants; the nectar provides energy for butterflies to fly and find a mate. This helps butterflies in different ways depending on the time of year. In spring, butterflies are emerging from winter hibernation or returning to Britain from warmer climes (e.g. southern Europe) and need to refuel. In autumn, butterflies need to build their energy reserves to survive winter hibernation or a return migration journey. Set a problem-solving investigation for the children to create a planting plan for the school grounds that will provide flowers to attract butterflies for the whole season. The project could include elements of surveying the school grounds for butterfly activity, and research from secondary sources to explore which plant species are most attractive.* Interviewing an expert is also a good idea, whether visiting a garden centre/nature reserve or inviting a guest speaker into the classroom.

Additional challenges can be introduced by considering how to encourage butterflies to breed in the garden. For this, butterflies need the right foodplants* for egg laying and for the growing caterpillars to feed upon. Realising the class plan will promote ownership, and can be as simple as setting up some planters in suitable locations. Ongoing population monitoring and engagement with a relevant citizen science project will create empowerment through their active participation in making a difference.

---

*Good plants to attract butterflies are lavender, wallflower, primrose, bluebell, verbena bonariensis and bird's-foot trefoil. Caterpillar foodplants include holly, nasturtium, bird's-foot trefoil, sorrel, thistles and nettles.

YEAR 6

Topic: Evolution and inheritance

Activity: Bird feeders and evolution

In this Year 6 Evolution topic, the key idea is that variation exists in all natural populations, whether it is the differences in eye colour in humans or the height of sunflowers. Those individual plants or animals that have advantageous characteristics in relation to survival and reproduction are more likely to produce new offspring, which are like them. This means that those characteristics, or adaptations, become more prevalent in the population. Through this mechanism of natural selection, variation leads to evolution over long periods of time (deep time).

This activity builds on the knowledge children gain from learning about Darwin's historical study of finches. You will introduce the work of contemporary evolutionary biologists and consider some current research findings published in 2017. International teams collaborated to study the common garden bird, the great tit, *Parus major* (Yes, they will giggle!). The biologists analysed historical beak length data and screened over 3,000 birds across three natural sites: one in the UK and two in the Netherlands. They found that more of the birds in the UK had longer beaks, and those in the Netherlands had shorter beaks, even though they were the same species. What was surprising to the researchers was that this evolutionary change had happened in a relatively short time, with beak length increasing since the 1970s. What do they think was driving this change? Birds' beaks are usually adapted to the food they eat. British people love to feed birds and we spend twice as much on bird feeders than people in mainland Europe. The researchers tagged the birds from the UK site to see how much time they spent visiting bird feeders. Those with longer beaks spent more time at the feeders than those with shorter beaks. So, their theory is that the bird feeders are driving evolutionary change, emphasising how human behaviour impacts the natural world.

You can present the details of the study in lots of different ways but some direct instruction will be important to make sure that children have fully understood the tricky ideas involved and to build on prior learning. Children could try out the theory by doing a comparative test to see if longer tweezers are better than shorter ones for reaching seeds inside a bird feeder and holding on to them.

CHAPTER SUMMARY

In this chapter, the importance of the fundamental elements of science education has been foregrounded, but also the need for us to go further to inspire children's respect for the beauty of the natural world, engaging their emotions and sense of ownership. If we build children's science capital and connect them to nature in purposeful ways, we open the doorway for future active citizenship as ecologically responsible adults. For some, you will light the spark for their future careers.

Further reading and resources

www.wwf.org.uk/sites/default/files/202005/Climate_Change_Education_Bicycle_Model.pdf
Cantell's bicycle activity (WWF)

https://www.rspb.org.uk/fun-and-learning/for-teachers/lesson-plans-and-supporting-resources/detective-equipment/
The RSPB website has instructions for making some of these resources from recycled materials.

State of Nature report, 2023 https://www.nationaltrust.org.uk/our-cause/nature-climate/state-of-nature-report-2023

Citizen science

Big Schools' Birdwatch (www.rspb.org.uk)

Big Butterfly Count (www.butterfly-conservation.org)

BeeWalk/Pollinator Monitoring Scheme/iRecord (https://www.bumblebeeconservation.org)

Nature's Calendar (www.woodlandtrust.org.uk)

Royal Entomological Society's Annual Insect Week (www.royensoc.co.uk)

UK Ladybird Survey (www.coleoptera.org.uk)

Weather Observations Website (https://wow.metoffice.gov.uk)

Zooniverse (www.zooniverse.org)

References

Archer, L., DeWitt, J., Osborne, J., Dillon, J., Wong, B. and Willis, B. (2013) *ASPIRES Report: Young People's Science and Career Aspirations, Age 10–14*. London: King's College London.

Attenborough, D. (2011) The Natural Curriculum: inspiring children to learn with nature. In *ASE Annual Conference*. University of Reading, Reading, UK.

Bourn, D. (2021) *Education for Social Change: Perspectives on Global Learning*. London: Bloomsbury.

Bonney, R. et al. (2009) Citizen science: a developing tool for expanding science knowledge and scientific literacy. *BioScience, 59*(11): 977–984.

Cantell, H., Tolppanen, S., Aarnio-Linnanvuori, E. and Lehtonen, A. (2019) Bicycle model on climate change education: presenting and evaluating a model. *Environmental Education Research, 25*(5): 717–731.

Carmi, N., Arnon, S. and Orion, N. (2015) Transforming environmental knowledge into behavior: the mediating role of environmental emotions. *The Journal of Environmental Education, 46*(3): 183–201.

Department for Education (2022) *Sustainability & Climate Change: A Strategy for the Education & Children's Services Systems*. Available at: https://www.gov.uk/government/publications/sustainability-and-climate-change-strategy/sustainability-and-climate-change-a-strategy-for-the-education-and-childrens-services-systems

Harlen, W. and Qualter, A. (2018) *The Teaching of Science in Primary Schools*, 7th edition. London: David Fulton.

Harlen, W. (ed.) (2010) *Principles and Big Ideas of Science Education*. Available at: www.ase.org.uk

Hungerford, H. R. and Volk, T. L. (1990) Changing learner behavior through environmental education. *The Journal of Environmental Education*, 21(3): 8–21.

IPCC (2021) *Climate Change 2021: The Physical Science Basis Summary for Policymakers*. Geneva: IPCC.

Nag Chowdhuri, M., King, H. and Archer, L. (2021) *The Primary Science Capital Teaching Approach: Teacher Handbook*. London: University College London.

Ofsted (2021) *Research Review Series: Science*. Available at: www.gov.uk

Skamp, K. (2007) Conceptual learning in the primary and middle years: the interplay of heads, hearts and hands-on science. *Teaching Science*, 53(3): 18–22.

Skamp, K. (2011) *Teaching Science Constructively*. Auckland: Cengage Learning.

State of Nature Partnership (2019) *State of Nature Report 2019*. British Trust for Ornithology. Available at: https://www.bto.org/sites/default/files/publications/state-of-nature-2019-report-uk.pdf

UNESCO (2017) *Education for Sustainable Development Goals: Learning Objectives*. Paris: UNESCO.

Wellcome Trust (2017) *'State of the Nation' Report of UK Primary Science Education*. London. Wellcome Trust.

5
TEACHING FOR SUSTAINABILITY WITHIN DESIGN AND COMPUTING EDUCATION

SUSAN OGIER AND LYNDA CHINAKA

LINKS TO CORE CURRICULUM FRAMEWORK

1.6, 2.1, 3.1, 3.2

SUSTAINABLE DEVELOPMENT GOALS

GOAL 14: Life Below Water
GOAL 15: Life on Land

KEY WORDS

Creativity; design; innovation; man-made; digital; technologies; Design Thinking; consumerism, circular economies

5 Teaching for sustainability within design and computing education

CHAPTER OBJECTIVES

This chapter will:

- Consider the role of sustainability within design education and computing.
- Contextualise and understand sustainability in man-made and digital environments.
- Explore the role of digital literacy in developing an awareness of conservation and sustainability through computing.
- Explore how learning in Design and computing can equip children for the future.
- Link to current research theory and appropriate pedagogies.
- Explore ways that sustainability may be taught through Design and computing by suggesting practical approaches to teaching this area in the primary classroom.

Introduction

Whether we like it or not, we are all avid consumers of goods and technologies. We have grown accustomed to engaging and interacting with many different types of technologies as a matter of course, whether these are mechanical or digital. Our lives are suffused by these, so much so that we often do not realise the extent to which we rely upon them. We have come to expect that in our daily lives, we have access to a whole range of materials, products, resources, etc. and we might begin to feel it is within our rights to have these things at our disposal. Goods and new products are touted by advertisers as the next best things, and we all clamour to buy the latest gadget or 'must-have' item – but for how long is this a sustainable attitude? Maybe it is true that we have become used to a high-maintenance lifestyle, but this has been at great expense to the earth's natural resources, as the cost of materials – and the current cost of living crisis – has forced us all to look more carefully at where we spend our hard-earned cash. Perhaps this is a good time to re-evaluate what we spend our money on and allow ourselves to become more thoughtful about ethical consumerism, as well as how we promote this way of thinking to the next generation. A number of high-profile individuals around the world such as Mia Mottley, Prime Minister of Barbados, Congresswoman Alexandria Ocasio Cortez, USA and Jacinda Ardern, former Premier of New Zealand, all make the case for urgency in addressing the changes that need to be made in relation to the sustainability of our world.

Enter the role of the designer! In this chapter, we shall explore how ecologically sound design can be placed at the centre of learning when teaching design and computing in primary schools. We all use terms such as *sustainability* and *conservation*, as part of our everyday conversations, but do children know what these words mean in relation to their everyday lives, and do they understand how they can have the power to change things for the better?

Sustainability and the man-made world

The term 'sustainability' can be brought to life in the classroom by raising topics that are concrete to children – for instance, saving the planet for their future, conserving, or making the most of natural resources that are no longer in plentiful supply around the world (not just in the UK): water, gas and electricity. They need to understand the importance of being sustainable or operating in a sustainable way because of the dangers that the planet faces. Children need to be taught what sustainability means in the man-made world today and the challenges that affect our planet. Some of these challenges are already being experienced locally by folks here in the UK: shortage of energy supplies, extreme weather patterns that have resulted in flooding, landslides and the unusual appearance of Thor the Walrus, who appeared in Southampton and Scarborough in December of 2022 (Osbourne, 2022). The massive marine mammal would ordinarily have been expected to journey to much colder climes, but due to the loss of sea ice habitats animals are now affected by climate change (Mckie, 2023). Children need to learn that many of the events and catastrophes that take place around the world and in this country are a result of an approach to living our lives that up until now has sustained us. However, this approach is unlikely to do so in the future due to what is an increasingly rapid change in our climate.

Classroom learning through the use of various digital tools and technologies can centre on the effects of climate change, wildlife conservation and protecting endangered species that have been affected by huge-scale climate events. We are often imperilled by the choices we make and the way that we live our lives with the added effect of destroying our surroundings. A recent newspaper article stated that 'The lives of walruses, like those of polar bears and seals, are changing. All are living at the frontier of climate change, and all are suffering as a result' (Attenborough, 2023 cited in Mckie, 2023).

Diversity aids understanding

Children can use their interest and love of technology to develop their digital skills and use this to gain substantial learning about sustainability through creative design and computing projects. Children can be taught about sustainability and climate change through activities that relate to creating man-made products that have zero or little impact on the environment, and which can be achieved in a fun and interactive way. This is vital to ensure that children feel empowered to be agents of change and to develop a sense of hope for the future. Such is the diversity of our classrooms today, that it is likely that some pupils will have direct links to places around the world where planetary crises are already taking place, and this can be a great starting point for a design project. The diversity of children and their backgrounds is a good stimulus for teaching topics such as climate change and food security – something that children are now experiencing first-hand, for example having groceries like tomatoes and eggs being rationed or unavailable. Projects that are relevant to primary-aged children could 'draw on learners cultural knowledge and experiences' to inform the curriculum and therefore provide likely classroom topics. (Raspberry Pi Working Group, 2021, p6). Culturally relevant pedagogies in computing would see pupils, including those from diverse backgrounds, learn how these planetary crises are affecting local communities. This would be a topic of interest because some children would be motivated by their own family histories and connections.

> **REFLECTIVE QUESTION**
>
> Consider the cultural histories of children in your class. Make a list of potential topics that you could use to plan a design project that draws on their cultural heritage. What considerations would you need to make or mitigate against?
>
> Children might have family or friends who are personally impacted by the effects of the climate emergency, for example, wildfires in Europe, or drought in the Horn of Africa. By planning relevant and real-world projects for children, we can show children that there are many solutions to the world's problems and encourage and motivate them to develop imaginative responses of their own.

Design and computing in the curriculum

Computing in the national curriculum has an inspiring 'purpose of study', stating that 'a high-quality computing education equips pupils to use computational thinking and creativity to understand and change the world' (DfE, 2013b, p1). This is true enough, especially now that we are so heavily dependent on digital literacies in relation to global citizenship and safe practices using social media and the internet. The fundamental role of digital practices in industry will be vital for today's children as they grow up into a future world. The National Curriculum Programme of Study for computing is ambitious in its acknowledgement of future learning needs amidst fast-moving changes in a global environment. 'Computing also ensures that pupils become digitally literate – able to use and express themselves and develop their ideas – at a level suitable for the future workplace and as active participants in a digital world' (DfE, 2013c). The role of computing education is to embed an understanding of the way that real-life technologies may be used to produce sustainable efficiencies in everyday life. Teaching children greater digital awareness enables them to fully participate as digital citizens with a growing awareness of sustainability in the world around them. As critically conscious individuals, they can participate by making and creating technologies towards outcomes that have long-term benefits for the world around them. For sustainable futures, children can use digital tools to investigate and analyse environmental issues around parts of the world, or they can use online calculators to calculate their carbon footprint. By learning about how systems work and about the technologies that we use daily, they understand the efficient use of those technologies to encourage sustainable practice. For example, the use of eco-friendly search engines like Ecosia, which plants trees for every search made, or Ocean Hero, which collects plastic bottles from the seas.

There are two national curriculum areas that cover 'Design': Design and Technology and Art Design. The English national curriculum for Design and Technology at KS1 and two acknowledges that this area of learning draws on skills and knowledge from across the curriculum – in sciences, arts and computing. The purpose of the study asks teachers to consider how they can enable children to use creativity and imagination to 'design and make products that solve real and relevant problems within a variety of contexts', and to 'develop a critical understanding of its impact on daily life and the wider world' (DfE, 2013a, p1). These aims are important to consider in relation to our focus on learning about sustainability and mitigating against the climate emergency within design. However, once we look at the subject content requirements, much of the critical values-based rationale indicated in the purpose of the study disappears in favour of functionality and skills.

Art (craft) and design as a subject area in the national curriculum allows primary teachers to specifically think about design in a different way, as here it is naturally attached to a more fluid conception of the process of design, than the functional qualities forefronted in the national curriculum for Design and Technology. This same concept is highlighted by the National Society for Education on Art and Design (NSEAD): 'Design does not remain a static concept, but is typically concerned with improving our quality of life through the creation of objects of beauty, functional products or products that are both functional and have style or an aesthetic' (NSEAD, n.d.). NSEAD also states that finding a definition for what 'design' actually means is not quite as simple as it might first seem, and quotes The British Design Council (2009), who muddy the water even further by telling us that 'design is everywhere – and that's why looking for a definition may not help you grasp what it is'. Whilst this is not particularly helpful to us as primary teachers, the Design and Technology Association (DATA) gives us some clear guidance on how we can plan to teach children about design: It must be about being 'something for someone with some purpose' (Ryan, n.d.). A sense of purpose is perhaps one of the key aspects that has given us all a fresh focus. The climate emergency is forcing us all to change how we interact with the man-made world. Of course, design IS everywhere – but our job is to critically evaluate existing design now, and to make changes in the way we live and how we design for the future. This starts in the classroom by encouraging the next generation of designers to engage with the need to reduce human impact on the environment.

Understanding ourselves as consumers

If we accept, as the British Design Council suggests above, that we – especially in the Western world – are bound by design in how we interact with the man-made world and its objects, there must come a point when we recognise our responsibility for the form that any future design will take. Up until recent history we have celebrated 'throwaway' culture as a sign of advancement and progress in human development (MacArthur, 2018). Whether it is the clothes on our backs or the food on our table, as a society we have grown accustomed to having what we want, when we want it, and consecutive governments and large corporations have encouraged this whilst reaping financial rewards for the seemingly endless desire of the population to consume the latest and newest items on the market. Since the 1950s and the mass marketing of plastic, we have been able to buy items so cheaply that we feel no attachment to them and consequently think nothing of discarding objects that we have grown tired of, with very little regard for where they will go or what might happen to them. We now know that these objects are not only filling landmass, but have spilled into our oceans, being consumed there by sea life, and suffocating and strangling sea creatures too. Microplastics are now in our own food chain, the potential negative consequences are subject to much current research (Blackburn and Green, 2021). Rapid developments in technological design, whilst often making our lives easier, have also negatively impacted upon the environment through 'planned obsolescence' (Zhang, 2022), exacerbated by global pressures for societies to constantly be in a state of economic growth. But the backlash has begun. The way we have used materials, food stuffs and objects in the past is no longer sustainable for our future. There is a growing understanding of our place within nature, and that we are simply part of nature – it is not just there for us to help ourselves to and to conquer, so systems, practices and mindsets will need to change in the model that we provide for the children we teach.

> **REFLECTIVE QUESTIONS**
>
> How conscious are you of how you use and create resources in/for your classroom?
>
> What impact does this have on how children in your class use objects and materials?

Design for positive change

As citizens and as teachers, and therefore influencers, we hold a great deal of power. An Eco-Awakening (2021) is a report by The Economist Intelligence Unit (EIU), commissioned by the World Wildlife Fund for Nature (WWF), disseminating research that measured awareness, engagement and action for nature on a global scale. This research shows that consumers are changing their behaviour in response to an awakening understanding of the serious decline of species on our planet that will affect us all. For example, they found that online searches for sustainable goods have increased globally by 71% since 2016, and this is forcing corporations and businesses to take notice and change their practices, particularly in the cosmetics, pharmaceutical, fashion and food sectors (EIU, 2021). Other design industries, such as architecture, are at the forefront of innovation and developing cleaner, greener practices that are revolutionising the built environment. An ecologically supportive 'circular economy', for example, is promoted through three principles, with *design* as the core driver: (1) eliminating waste and pollution, (2) circulating products and materials (at their highest value) and (3) regenerating nature (Ellen MacArthur Foundation, n.d.). Children's experiences in learning about design in school should reflect the nature of design in the real world, and to facilitate this we might start by looking at how we currently teach design principles and question whether these are fit for purpose, if we are to move to the concept of designing for a circular economy, and placing caring for our planet before desire and greed for more 'stuff'. It is worth remembering here that the guidance available to support design learning in the current national curriculum is at least ten years old, and this should make us wonder whether that is good enough too, as the world has already changed beyond recognition since this was published in 2013.

Creativity and design thinking

It is well known that creativity is a key skill necessary for the future (Forbes, 2018) and that today's children will need the whole range of attributes that is afforded by being able to think imaginatively and to solve – or maybe just to cope with – problems that we are currently storing up as a global society (Kupers et al., 2019; Robinson, 1999). Many theories have emerged over the past few decades around what makes an individual 'creative', or what might lead someone to believe they are not creative! Runco and Sakamoto (1999) remind us that creativity is as much a social and developmental construct, as it is to do with personal and educational experiences, and as such the concept is highly complex. Amabile (1997) purports that everyone has the potential to be creative, and this occurs when an individual's expertise in their chosen field coincides with task motivation and critical thinking, which can also be affected by social environments and emotions. Craft, too, explains that we all have the potential to be creative in different contexts, in what she describes and Little c and Big C: Big C being genius level and Little c being the small acts of everyday creativity – the ability to acknowledge 'possibility thinking' and to live with, and even embrace, ambiguity (Craft, 2000, 2001). This is a useful definition for us in the context of the creative capacity that all children will need in order to face their futures. It is essential that children are equipped with tools that will enable them to be the game changers we need and to be able to function in a world that we cannot easily predict.

Design Thinking is a concept that relates closely to the idea that everyone has the capacity for creativity and innovation. According to Razzouk and Shute (2012), Design Thinking encompasses the skills acquired through creative practices, such as the ability to experiment, problem solve and analyse, as well as taking risks and resilience. These skills do not just apply to arts subjects but are common in science research and engineering too (Razzouk and Shute, 2012). So not just soft skills after all, as these are the skills our young people are going to need by the shed load. Promoting flexible and creative thought is at the centre of how we encourage children to develop their creative capacities, and this is explained clearly in the Royal Academy of Engineering Report, *Thinking like an Engineer: Implications for the Education System* (Lucas et al., 2014). The report stresses that particular 'habits of mind', such as curiosity, openness, resilience, resourcefulness, collaboration, reflection and ethical consideration, are essential in a child's education, in order to encourage their natural drive to design and develop ideas, and build creations of their own.

PAUSE FOR THOUGHT

Our responsibility is to inform, educate and prepare children not just for today but for tomorrow's world. The role of design for a sustainable future, whether it is through digital technologies or physically making and creating is a vitally important area for children's education. We have no time to waste now in rethinking what we do with primary-aged children to prepare them for their futures.

In the classroom

In this section, we shall look at a few examples of how you can plan for computing and Design projects that will focus on building knowledge and understanding about sustainability and ethical practice. These ideas will help you to ensure children develop their creative capacities whilst promoting minimum impact on the environment.

5 Teaching for sustainability within design and computing education

Modelling sustainable practice in the classroom

This Table 5.1 will help you to change commonly used resources to environmentally friendly alternatives.

Table 5.1 Eco-friendly alternatives to replace everyday resources

Traditional practice	Eco-friendly alternative	Benefits
PVA glue	Cellulose paste Or make your own! http://ecochildsplay.com/2009/02/26/homemade-glue-for-kids-crafts/	Plastic-free
Sellotape	Paper tape https://small99.co.uk/materials/packaging/alternatives-to-plastic-tape-sellotape/	Non-plastic
Recycled materials: yoghurt pots and plastic bottles	Fibre pots Or make your own pots from newspaper https://www.gardenersworld.com/how-to/diy/how-to-make-paper-pots/ If you do use plastic, ensure it is recycled correctly and that the children are involved in that.	Plastic-free
Glue sticks	These are made from recycled plastic, so will still need to be disposed of properly https://www.greatart.co.uk/bic-ecolution-glue-sticks.html	Solvent-free Recycled casing
Paper	Use recycled paper: sugar paper, cartridge paper, card, etc. https://www.recycledpapercompany.co.uk/	Cuts down fewer trees
Pencils and colouring pencils	https://www.dryadeducation.co.uk/spectrum-watercolour-pencils-eco-boxes?acc=d8dca8c4afd498484c77e93cb81ae46c	packaging: recycled pulp. unlaminated and recyclable = less wastage in production.

Projects to try with your class

NURSERY AND RECEPTION

Computing and design

Project: Is this a computer?

Concept: Our homes and lives are filled with computers; many more than any young learner can count – but do they recognise a computer when they see it?

Activity: Show children a collection of objects from home and from school.

(Continued)

Arrange them in any order and then ask the children to sort them into those that are computers and those that are not. Objects could include camera, phone, scales, pen, book, teddy, other toys, cash register, paintbrush, calculator, plant, keyboard or anything else you can think of.

This works well as a specific guided teacher's activity. Children could be asked to predict which of the items that might be computers in the future.

YEAR 1

Computing and design

Project: Make your own device: What are the parts of a computer or mobile phone?

Concept: The design of computers and hand-held devices is changing and developing all time. Very often this leads us to desiring the next model and discarding older versions. Shulte (2008, p111) argues that familiarity with everyday devices encourages a willingness to interact with such digital artefacts for social reasons in the long term; therefore, if children understand how computers are made, they will become conscious of how to recycle and repurpose in ethical ways. Ongoing research in Germany sees young people taught how to repair or restore defective everyday devices that ordinarily would simply be thrown away. Find out more here in this article by Childs (2022): https://www.raspberrypi.org/blog/repair-cafes-computing-education-hello-world-19/

Activity: Use cardboard and paper to cut out shapes to symbolise different parts of a computer. Children can deconstruct old computers or discarded mobile phones to find out more about the components and understand what they are for. Look at the main components of a computer and name them (e.g. control unit, monitor; mouse, screen, monitor, keyboard etc.).

Children use pre-cut shapes to make their own design of a computer (Luikas, 2017, p56). What new features will they want or need? They can cut their own new shapes and assemble the parts together.

Make an interactive display with the designs and parts of the redundant computers or devices. Ask the children to write labels for the components: Can they match the name of the component to the part?

Involve the children in recycling the components once the work is finished and the display comes down! https://www.recycleyourelectricals.org.uk

Resource: https://www.bbc.co.uk/bitesize/topics/zymykqt/articles/z9myvcw

YEAR 2

Computing and art and design

Project: Rewilding: Create a digital leaflet, a photo story about caring for nature and the environment.

Concept: Urban and suburban gardens are increasingly important spaces for wildlife in our nature depleted country (Wildlife Trust, No date). Children will gain a sense of purpose by being able to communicate their understanding of how we need to support insects and wildlife in our gardens and outdoor spaces. They will use processes such as photography and drawing to create illustrations that will encourage their readers to allow nature to thrive in

Activity: Talk to the children about the importance of insects in the ecosystem and introduce the concept of 'rewilding'. Take the children on a walk in the local environment. Ask children to make notes of where they see common flowers, such as dandelions and daisies: these might be in unusual places, such as between paving stones. Try to visit a park or place where you can find a biodiverse range of fauna, such as a park. Ask them to look carefully to see if they can spot any insects. The children can use sketchbooks to draw and make nature notes on the outing. Compare how many insects are found in another area where there are no flowers or fauna.

Back in class, ask them to design and create a photo story with text. Try to discourage the reader from having over manicured gardens and outdoor spaces. Ask children to save their edited images and upload them to a desired location on the school's computer system and then once their design is complete onto the school's intranet, school's social media platform or website.

Resource: https://www.adobe.com/express/create/leaflet

YEAR 3

Computing and art and design

Project: Recycled Digital Artefact

Concept: The project reinforces the importance of recycling and its impact on sustainability. It encourages children to think creatively and consider environmental issues that are important to them. Developing a sense of consumerism and preservation are helpful values that can be instilled in the classroom. This activity demonstrates the way that a digital artefact may be created and produced using existing materials. Nothing has gone to waste!

Activity: Select a theme that focusses on ethical issues, e.g. Children collect recycled materials from the kitchen cupboard: cardboard boxes, plastic containers, bottles and newspaper. They explore the materials and surfaces and cut up into random shapes. They use a digital art programme like Paint 3D to create a digital artefact. Children upload photos of the materials that they have designed and assembled onto the computer. In Microsoft Paint 3D they use one or two tools to manipulate and transform their design.

Children can learn and discuss the way local amenities are used to support sustainability in their local area. The rise in the use of charity shops and upcycling places can be discussed in a way that helps promote responsible and environmentally conscious behaviour. Children can be encouraged to reduce waste by using repurposed goods or purchasing second-hand clothes. Which charity shops do they know? and use? The class teacher can provide their own examples of items of clothing or objects in the home that have been purchased in some of these places.

YEAR 4

Computing

Project: Create algorithms in a coding project

Concept: Create an animation using block-based code about Vanessa Nakate a leader in Climate Justice and UNICEF Goodwill Ambassador.

Visit the United Nations website https://www.un.org/en/climatechange/vanessa-nakate-climate-change-is-about-people and find out about a young Uganda woman who brought the climate crisis that is happening in Africa to the world's attention. Remind children that many of the issues of sustainability affect countries that have done little to cause or contribute to the problems that our planet faces. Children can benefit from the understanding of climate change and its effects are about people.

Activity: Children create simple algorithms using block-based code to depict a story about Vanessa Nakate. Children can use child-friendly search engines to conduct their own independent research to find out images and facts about Vanessa Nakate. Class teachers can prompt thinking about why she isn't very well known here in the UK. Model the use of the art editor in Scratch as a starting point. Show the children how to draw their own version of Vanessa's image using the tools in the palette to create a character (Sprite). Next, the character is now ready to be coded. Children can also be taught how to import images into Scratch. Simple algorithms using simple sequences of blocks of code can then be created in a variety of ways, e.g. Vanessa in conversation with another character.

For those that are new to coding, ideas can be further developed with the support from this guide: https://scratch.mit.edu/ideas

Once the children are familiar with using their newly chosen or independently designed characters, do reintroduce the correct terminology for the characters – Sprites.

YEAR 5

Art and design and computing

Project: Textile design using Hapa Zome

Concept: Children will question the use of fast fashion and understand the challenges of the fashion industry as a major polluter. They will learn about current efforts by designers to provide alternative materials that have little or no impact on the planet and develop practical knowledge to create their own fabric designs.

Activity: Introduce children to the new generation of fashion designers who are forefronting an ethical, environment-friendly approach to the fashion and textile industry.

Look at designers, such as Tolu Coker: https://www.wallpaper.com/fashion/tolu-coker-the-artist-creating-clothing-for-equity-and-social-change or look at sustainability statements on brands such as G-Star Raw https://www.g-star.com/en_ca/raw-responsibility-sustainability

Ask children to research and find facts about why the fast fashion industry is bad for the planet. https://www.bbc.co.uk/bitesize/articles/zdrw47h

Tell the children they are going to create a textile design using natural and sustainable materials. Cut cotton or hemp squares: two per child. Children place material on a flat, tough surface, such as a wooden block. They arrange cut flowers on one sheet and cover with the second. They then bash with a hammer until the colour is released from the flowers and printed onto the fabric. They can then use needles and coloured threads to embellish their designs.

Find out how to Hapa Zome here: https://caitlynirwin.com/blog/what-is-hapa-zome-printing

Scan the designs into the computer and use editing software to develop the design to be used for wrapping paper or wallpaper, curtain fabric or cushion covers.

A development of this might be to create a range of block-based coding software for example children can create simple algorithms in Scratch about sustainable clothing. Children can write code for eco-friendly clothing and consider the use of sustainable materials like recycled paper or renewed plastic.

YEAR 6

Computing

Project: Data Visualisation – Thor's Journey

Children learn how to gather data and present information about the way climate events affect animal well-being. Children can design a timeline that charts the key events in Thor's journey, from his arrival on the shores of England including previous and subsequent sightings. Demonstrate the way that sightings can be analysed. The children can be taught how to analyse the data to identify patterns and trends. They create charts or graphs to show the frequency of Thor's sightings over time and in different locations. The children's work can culminate in an infographic. They create an infographic to summarise all the facts and information they have found about Thor's journey. They include illustrations, images, digital art, charts and graphs to make the data presented interesting and easy to understand. An online presentation can also be devised as an alternative with a variety of media to add interest. This can be designed for a younger audience – another year group in the school.

The news story of Thor the Walrus could be used as a starting point: https://www.rspb.org.uk/our-work/rspb-news/rspb-news-stories/thor-the-wandering-walrus/.

Suggested online tools include Canva, Digimaps, Google Sheets or Piktochart. Search tasks can be conducted using child-friendly search engines such as Swiggle, Kiddle or any of Google search tools with suitable preferences enabled beforehand.

CHAPTER SUMMARY

In an already overcrowded curriculum, it can be hard to think about how to plan for teaching climate change and sustainable living. As teachers, however, we need to be convinced of the merit of this for ourselves, and we hope this chapter has helped you consider your own feelings and fears in how we use and view the man-made world. Through practical, fun, real-world projects, children will find their voice as designers of the future: Digital literacy is a strand in computing that can be used for teaching many of these projects because these are the skills children growing up into tomorrow's adults will need. Because children use the internet regularly and are participants in a global world, they can learn about the responsible use of materials, technology, tools and devices – and to be the agents of change that are no longer optional for our future survival.

Further reading and resources

Eco-friendly Search Engines.

https://www.ecosia.org/
Ecosia, which plants trees for every search made.

https://oceanhero.today/
Ocean Hero, collects plastic bottles from the seas.

https://www.youtube.com/watch?v=OcO1O99UoUs
This video explains the 'Cradle to Cradle' concept.
Lots of lovely ideas and recourses for sustainable design and computing projects on these websites:

https://www.stem.org.uk/primary

https://www.greenlivingtips.com/

References

Amabile, T. M. (1997) Motivating creativity in organisation: on doing what you love and loving what you do. *California Management Review*, 40(1): 39–58.

Blackburn, K. and Green, D. (2021) The potential effects of microplastics on human health: what is known and what is unknown. *Ambio*. 2022 March. 51(3): 518–530. https://doi.org/10.1007/s13280-021-01589-9

Childs, K. (2022) Repair cafes in computing education. Hello world, Issue 19, June 2022. Available at: https://www.raspberrypi.org/blog/repair-cafes-computing-education-hello-world-19/

Craft, A. (2000) *Creativity across the Primary Curriculum*. London: Routledge.

Craft, A. (2001) Little c creativity. In A. Craft, B. Jeffrey and M. Leibling (eds.), *Creativity in Education*. London: Continuum.

DfE (2013a) *National Curriculum, Art and Design, Key Stages 1 and 2*. Available at: https://assets.publishing.service.gov.uk/government/uploads/system/uploads/attachment_data/file/239018/PRIMARY_national_curriculum_-_Art_and_design.pdf

DfE (2013b) *National Curriculum, Computing, Key Stages 1 and 2*. Available at: https://assets.publishing.service.gov.uk/government/uploads/system/uploads/attachment_data/file/239033/PRIMARY_national_curriculum_-_Computing.pdf

DfE (2013c) *National Curriculum, Design and Technology, Key Stages 1 and 2*. Available at: https://assets.publishing.service.gov.uk/government/uploads/system/uploads/attachment_data/file/239041/PRIMARY_national_curriculum_-_Design_and_technology.pdf

Economist Intelligence Unit (2021) *An Eco Awakening: Measuring Global Awareness, Engagement and Action for Nature*. WWF and EIU. Available at: https://f.hubspotusercontent20.net/hubfs/4783129/An%20EcoWakening_Measuring%20awareness,%20engagement%20and%20action%20for%20nature_FINAL_MAY%202021%20(1).pdf?utm_referrer=https%3A%2F%2Fexplore.panda.org%2Feco-wakening

Ellen MacArthur Foundation (n.d.) Available at: https://ellenmacarthurfoundation.org/

Kupers, E., Lehmann-Wermser, A., McPherson, G. and van Geert, P. (2019). Children's creativity: a theoretical framework and systematic review. *Review of Educational Research*, 89(1): 93–124. https://doi.org/10.3102/0034654318815707

Lucas, B., Hanson, J. and Claxton, G. (2014) *Thinking Like an Engineer: Implications for the Education System*. Available at: www.raeng.org.uk/thinkinglikeanengineer

Luikas, L. (2017). *Hello Ruby, Journey inside the Computer, Feiwal and Friends Book*. New York: Macmillan Publishing group.

MacArthur, E. (2018) Why Our Throwaway Culture Has to End. National Geographic. Available at: https://www.nationalgeographic.co.uk/environment-and-conservation/2018/06/why-our-throwaway-culture-has-to-end

Mckie, R. (2023) Thor the disoriented walrus enthralled Brits, but cut no ice with climate sceptics. *The Guardian*. Sunday 8 January. Available at: https://www.theguardian.com/commentisfree/2023/jan/08/thor-the-disoriented-walrus-enthralled-brits-but-cut-no-ice-with-climate-sceptic

Osbourne, M. (2022) The unusual European journey of Thor the Walrus. *Smithsonian Magazine*. Smart News, March 2023. Available at: https://www.smithsonianmag.com/smart-news/the-unusual-european-journey-of-thor-the-walrus-180981734/

Powers, A. (2018) Creativity is the skill of the future. *Forbes*. Available at: https://www.forbes.com/sites/annapowers/2018/04/30/creativity-is-the-skill-of-the-future/?sh=1432e8d04fd4

Raspberry Pi Working Group (2021) *Culturally Relevant and Responsive Computing in the Classroom: A Guide for Curriculum Design and Teaching*. Raspberry Pi report. Available at: https://static.raspberrypi.org/files/research/Guide+to+culturally+relevant+and+responsive+computing+in+the+classroom.pdf

Razzouk, R. and Shute, V. (2012) What is design thinking and why is it important? *Review of Educational Research*. Available at: https://doi.org/10.3102/0034654312457429

Robinson, K. (1999) *All Our Futures, National Advisory Committee on Creative and Cultural Education*. Available at: https://www.sirkenrobinson.com/read/all-our-futures/

Runco, M. R. and Sakamoto, S. O. (1999) Experimental studies of creativity. In Sternberg, R. J. (ed.), *Handbook of Creativity*. Cambridge: Cambridge University Press, pp35–61.

Ryan, T. (n.d.) *Are You Really Teaching Design and Technology?* Available at: https://www.designtechnology.org.uk/media/3226/are-you-really-teaching-dtv2_x264.mp4

Schulte, C. (2008) *Duality Reconstruction – Teaching Digital Artifacts from a Socio-technical Perspective.* ISSEP 2008, LNCS, 5090, pp110–121. Available at: https://link.springer.com/content/pdf/10.1007/978-3-540-69924-8_10.pdf

Zhang, T. (2022) *You Are Throwing Away Your Future: The Effects of a Throwaway Society.* The Science Survey. Available at: https://thesciencesurvey.com/editorial/2022/04/23/you-are-throwing-away-your-future-the-effects-of-a-throwaway-society/

6
EXPLORING THE CLIMATE IN CONTEXT THROUGH GEOGRAPHY

ANTHONY BARLOW

LINKS TO CORE CURRICULUM FRAMEWORK

1.6, 2.1, 3.1, 3.2

SUSTAINABLE DEVELOPMENT GOALS

GOAL 11: Sustainable Cities and Communities
GOAL 13: Climate Action
GOAL 15: Life on Land

KEY WORDS

Geography; phenomena; concepts; scheme; composite; component; climate; weather; local; locality; people; environments

CHAPTER OBJECTIVES

This chapter will:

- Describe the role of curriculum-making in relation to teaching key concepts in geography.
- Consider the role of climate change and teaching the weather within geographical concepts.
- Contextualise and locate climate teaching in schools' localities.
- Link to current research theory and appropriate pedagogies.
- Explore ways that weather and climate may be taught through geography by suggesting practical approaches to teaching this area in the primary classroom.

Introduction

As pupils progress, their growing knowledge about the world should help them to deepen their understanding of the interaction between physical and human processes…Geographical knowledge, understanding and skills provide the frameworks and approaches that explain how the Earth's features at different scales are shaped, interconnected and change over time.

(DfE, 2013)

Scale and perspective present challenging aspects to focus upon within the geography curriculum. We are constantly moving between local, regional, national and global. Where do we put the emphasis when we are trying to teach about big processes relating to the environment? Understanding the interactions and connections, the 'big picture' view of geography, can sometimes be lost when teachers plan. This chapter will argue that through a focus on conceptual understanding in a local context, teachers can have more success in this area, and we can help our children know more and understand more about geography and about environmental issues. Through relevant, age-appropriate, local and UK perspectives rather than just through distant, 'big-geography' perspectives we can build a 'sense of scale' and connection to what these perspectives look like in the everyday.

Concepts and climate

A focus on conceptual understanding will help build up a child's ability to transfer the knowledge they are learning into new and novel situations and support their wider understanding (Ofsted, 2019). Think about an issue like serious flooding. We can see the effect of extreme rainfall on locations on the news, we could try to put ourselves in people's shoes, but this is still very much removed from our lived experience. It is often a story about somewhere beyond, somewhere unknowable. For example, this account about floods in Europe was written in 2021: EU.

On 14 and 15 July 2021, a flood event affected parts of Belgium, Germany and surrounding countries, causing more than 200 fatalities and resulting in large socioeconomic impacts.

(Copernicus, online)

Large socioeconomic impacts – what might these be? It is the connections created by this singular physical event that interest geographers. The event is one thing, but the human geography story is quite another. My perspective is that when we teach about events like this, we should focus at the same time on what's happening to us nearby. Could this happen in our local water courses, would the amount of land covered in tarmac in our local high streets and to our denuded local hills cause similar problems? All teachers of geography should be aware of these local perspectives when we consider continental or global problems, and to work towards supporting children's explanations of geographical phenomena at this range of scales.

By building local knowledge and perspectives into our conceptual understanding we will build a stronger *composite* understanding (Ofsted, 2019), a stronger schema, than if we just focus on a singular case study perspective or de-contextualised thinking.

The grammar of geography

The curriculum neglects to foreground the **grammar** of geography, as Lambert suggests (2017). He describes this as 'the acquisition and development of systematic conceptual knowledge that informs geography's "relational" understanding' (2018, p12). There is a challenge here in connecting concepts – the local and continental, the observable and knowable – and it is one of the key challenges for any geography teacher. For people like myself, educating pre-service teachers, we know that with limited initial education in England in geography (Catling, 2014b), and with limited continuing professional development alongside planning or release time for teachers, means that ways to do this are often misunderstood. This is crucial when we have big global challenges such as migration, globalisation and our theme here of climate change. How do the small pieces fit together into a coherent whole at each stage?

REFLECTIVE QUESTIONS

Read these two extracts from Mackintosh's thinking.

> *Research has shown that the perceptions children have of physical features and processes are closely related to their experiences, but the affective dimension of children's encounters with the physical environment has been neglected. Geography should... take into account the children's prior ideas in their choice of concepts to be taught, the order of their teaching and particularly their choice of learning experiences, with clear purposes for each activity... we must 'start where the children are at'...*
>
> (Mackintosh, 2010, p71)

> *Evidence suggests that there has been little, if any, progress in children's knowledge and understanding in physical geography since Piaget, despite access to television images, travel and the national curriculum.*
>
> (Mackintosh, 1999, p70)

- Do you agree with this?
- What role do you think the affective domain might play in geography learning?

Curriculum planning problems?

One of the problems in common with other foundation subjects is that primary geography is taught sporadically, through units of learning which sometimes do not connect together very well.

While ideas of what to teach abound the composite, conceptual ideas remain less well understood. Ofsted's Research Review (2021) highlights concepts which should be included:

- Place
- Space
- Scale
- Interdependence
- Physical and human processes
- Environmental impact
- Sustainable development
- Cultural awareness
- Cultural diversity

(Ofsted, 2021a)

REFLECTIVE QUESTIONS

- How many of these terms could you define?
- How many of these could you explicitly link to a unit of study that you teach, and how are they listed on your curriculum mapping documents?
- Importantly for this chapter, which of these link to a study of the environment, the climate or teaching weather?

Climate and curriculum-making in geography – Critical challenges

Teaching about the challenges of the world today and the issues we face in relation to the environment is one area where teachers can often be swayed by current affairs. For example, acid rain in the 1980s, the depleting ozone layer in the 1990s, fairtrade and farming, plastic waste, the oceans and now climate change. All these issues have one interesting component: they are all human-induced problems.

Since the 1960s, future-oriented geography has been a feature of geographical study and it has focussed on different aspects as worries have waxed and waned in the popular imagination from population growth to 'rising unemployment, mounting injustice and a deteriorating environment' from the 1970s and beyond (Huckle, 1983, p59). Most recently the focus has arguably been on single-issue themes such as waste and, particularly, ones such as single-use plastic waste and the oceans. While undoubtedly these stories of how we live now through the lens of the mountains of waste we produce (Barlow, 2017 Catling et al.), they all have at their heart the issue of finite space, resources or capacity for us to continue as we are. When considering curriculum-making, we should focus on both human geography as well as the wider picture of systemic failure.

Ofsted suggests a systems approach: 'Research shows how important it is to ensure that pupils understand how human and physical processes interact to influence and change landscapes, environments and the climate, as well as how human activity relies on the effective functioning of natural systems' (Ofsted, 2021a).

The bigger systems in our world can get lost. The four most commonly cited that we should consider teaching are as follows in Table 6.1:

Table 6.1 Four most common 'big' systems

Atmosphere (weather and climate)	Hydrosphere (rivers, river basins, seas and oceans)
Lithosphere (landforms)	Biosphere (animals, plants and soils)

Standish has consistently challenged what he sees as political interference in school geography and the tendency to replace a core body of knowledge and understanding with a relativist focus on 'values'. Fairtrade, in particular, comes in for criticism from Standish who says 'the issue has been removed from its wider social and political context, making it solely a matter of individual consciousness' (2009, p45). A school curriculum risks being politicised. Standish suggests that the geography curriculum has become a site for political concerns rather than teaching pupils difficult and abstract theories like climate science, we have opted to engage pupils' interest in other 'trendy topics' (Standish, 2007, 2009).

When we teach about local areas, we need to have data to show that our partial and limited views can be supported by longer-view evidence. These partial views might be called generalisations. The Ofsted Research Review (2021) suggests that considerable thought needs to be given to challenging pupils' generalisations. Children might have already developed views on climate change, formed by these generalisations, and it is important that we approach the issue without contributing to eco-anxiety.

The Department for Education supports this:

> *The challenge of climate change is formidable. For children and young people to meet it with determination, and not with despair, we must offer them not just truth, but also hope. Learners need to know the truth about climate change – through knowledge-rich education. They must also be given the hope that they can be agents of change…*
>
> (DfE, 2022)

For anyone teaching geography, with the curriculum's myriad bits of knowledge, the question is, how does this fit into an overall 'schema' of what geography actually is? The challenge that Ofsted, in England, has set us is to get better at building a sense of sequence, a progressive set of conceptual ideas and coherence within this sometimes sprawling subject. This challenge can be even the case with centrally planned or bought-in schemes of work when exposed to the realities of your children and your context. It is this local context I want to focus on in this chapter.

Planning for climate concepts: The ultimate sprawling idea!

If we think of those European 2021 floods, we can teach this as a singular event, a problem in itself. It is when we ask *why* that good geography occurs: Why there? Why then? Why was it so bad?

Any big conceptual or composite ideas are made up of many component parts, this is similar to what Lambert describes as the area's grammar. Understanding weather, as a component of the English national curriculum, is essential in order to explore the effects of climate change. Below is a partial set of components relating to an understanding of global atmospheric circulation, all of which can contribute to extreme weather events (see Figure 6.1).

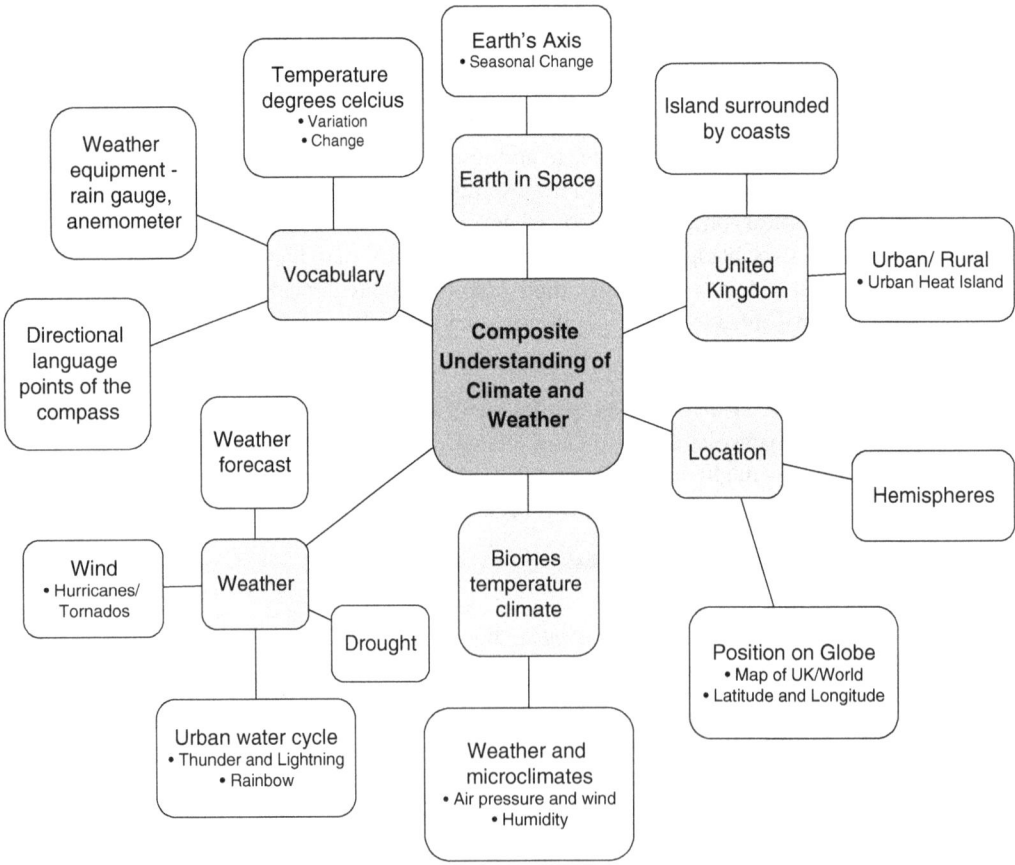

Figure 6.1 Component parts in the geography curriculum — leading to an understanding of weather and climate

Research shows how important it is to ensure that pupils understand how human and physical processes interact to influence and change landscapes, environments and the climate, as well as how human activity relies on the effective functioning of natural systems. Indeed, several authors are critical of the false divide that can be presented between physical and human environments. Successful curriculum plans ensure that pupils gain the knowledge needed to explain the relationship between processes and their impact in different locations and at different times (Ofsted, 2021b).

The challenge, again, for teachers is how to consider what these component parts are that build up to this bigger picture understanding. My argument is that this is even more important when teaching about climate change to avoid a sense of impossibility in the task.

> **REFLECTIVE QUESTIONS**
>
> What have you taught about this big concept?
>
> Have you taught it with any sense of possibility thinking (Hicks, 2010) or have you taught it with a sense of catastrophe?

In the classroom

The 'In the classroom' section is designed to help you to think through six teaching weather and climate activities. It will consider 'hyperlocal' perspectives and day-to-day perspectives. It will also help you to explain these phenomena. It then links to the UK's weather and considers the urban water cycle and the ways this can be seen and explained in different localities. Finally, we will consider perspectives on the regional and our UK climate's future.

Hyperlocal perspectives: The wind

Look outside of your window. Has the weather changed, what do you notice Has it changed in the past hour since you have been reading this chapter?

The wind might be seen as a straightforward and basic concept. Look at this description from Kirsty McCabe from the Royal Meteorological Society.

> In simple terms, wind is the movement of air…caused by pressure differences, which in turn were caused by temperature differences…it all starts with the sun. As the sun warms the earth's surface, the atmosphere warms too. But thanks to our hills and oceans, the heating is uneven, not to mention that the poles receive less solar energy than the equator.

This suggests a reasonably simple explanation of wind power but reading the rest of Kirsty's article 'What is wind?' will demonstrate how complex this system actually is.

You will find a link to this article as well as some practical resources to help teach about the wind from the Geographical Association in the Further Reading and Resources section of this chapter.

Pupils can then combine the wind direction information with recordings of the predominant weather type on that day using wind rose (see the Further Reading and Resources of this chapter for more information). Wind direction is named after the direction it comes from, not the direction it is blowing towards. Compare the wind roses with a world map and explore how the direction of the wind can bring different weather conditions because of where it comes from.

Day-to-day perspectives: How should we teach about weather?

Weather is the day-to-day experience of our world, what we get and not what we expect to get through different months or seasons. So, climate is the general weather over a long period which can be seen to change. As the Met Office suggests, 'the major difference between weather and climate is the timescale. Weather occurs over hours or days. Climate, however, refers to the average of all weather that takes place over a much longer period, usually years or decades' (Met Office, online).

REFLECTIVE QUESTIONS

Listen to a weather forecast and focus on the language used:

- What is the general story that the meteorologist/presenter is trying to get across?
- How successful is this?
- Giving children a weather forecast to create is actually a complex task so how would break down this task into small steps?

Explaining day-to-day perspectives: How might we explain the UK's weather?

The weather an air mass brings is determined by the region it has come from and the type of surface it has moved over. As our weather is determined by the dominance of one mass at that time, there is no mixing. This is one of the reasons why our weather can be so different from one day to the next. This is demonstrated in the chart below (see Figure 6.2).

6 Exploring the climate in context through geography

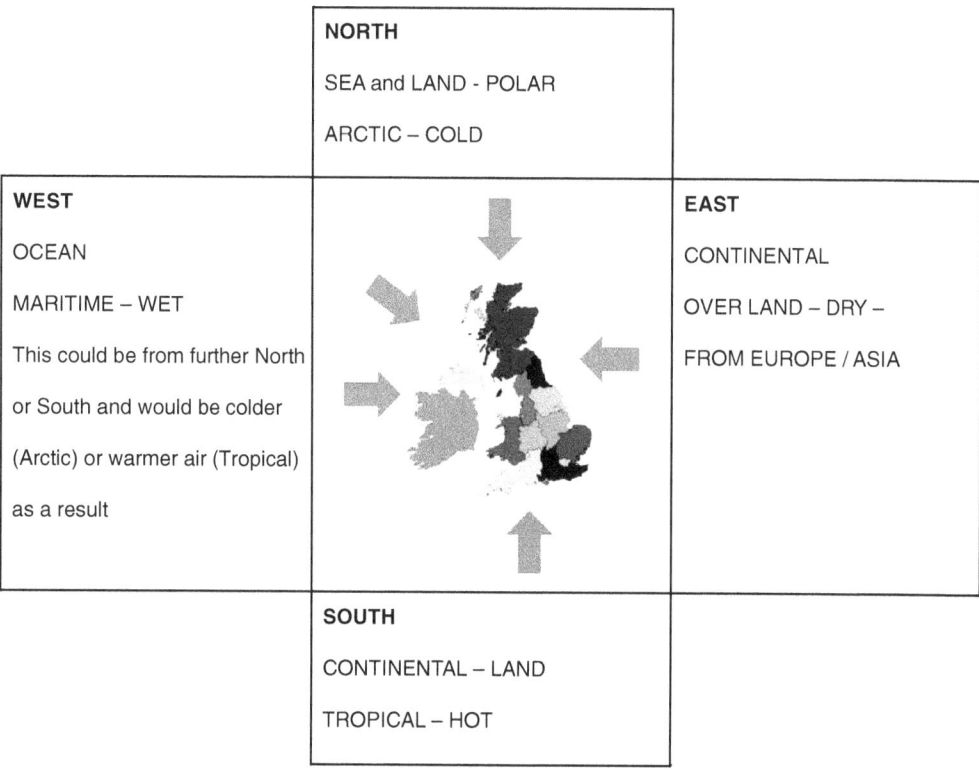

Figure 6.2 UK weather Diagram by author; Clipart source: Openclipart.

The best way to explain this to children is to show them the effect of air masses moving. Use a large space like a field and ask them to run around in groups, taking the role of the different air masses. Then bring out one group as the Jet Stream and see how everything will change. For an example of this watch the BBC clip, The Battle of the Weather Fronts, linked in the Further Reading and Resources section of this chapter.

Help the children to understand how global systems of air pressure are being affected by man-made actions.

For example, the heating of the oceans and deforestation changes the conditions that are needed to regulate air flow across the planet.

Explaining rainfall perspectives: Teaching the urban water cycle

All weather is localised. You might know of times when you have been driving and driven through the rain or heard of people near you who have experienced very different weather despite their proximity. Our experiences can be very varied depending on whether you are by the coast, inland, surrounded by high-rise buildings or by the countryside. Use the Thames water link in the Further Reading and Resources to help you to consider the whole range of aspects in teaching the water cycle.

Consider the implications of poor water management and the subsequent effects of drought – see Chapter 7. Exploring the history of humans and their environment.

ACTIVITY: THE URBAN WATER CYCLE AND SUSTAINABLE URBAN DRAINAGE SYSTEMS

Go for a water walk around your school site.

- Look for areas where grass has been worn away – who caused this? Was it humans or small-scale erosion?
- Look for shortcuts that have been created – sometimes called desire lines or elephant paths, again something that can be exacerbated by the action of water.
- Look for full or dry puddles or dips in the land – where does water collect?
- Look for potholes in the ground or road – how have these holes been created? How are they getting worse?
- Look for rotting wood or peeling paint where the action of the water has caused damage to the building – Look for streaking caused by water.
- Look for badly drained and marshy ground – why is it so muddy? What do the dips in the land and the slopes do to manage the water locally? Where does it pool or collect?
- Look for pipes and gutters that manage the water that falls on the roof – see where the water goes into the drains and think about where these drains lead to.
- Look for moss and green mould and for plants growing between paving stones – micro cracks where life starts to flourish, nourished by regular watering from the rain.

Survey your school grounds for the impact of water and take some pictures. Consider taking them when there is a downpour. What evidence can you find for the effect of rainfall?

Create an information pack with a series of images showing the effect of water on the environment. Use this as a discussion point with the children. Research strategies that are being developed within urban design to manage water. The city of Sheffield, for example, has created areas to capture water and to manage rainfall (see the Grey to Green website linked in the Further Reading and Resources section for more information).

Could we create areas like this in our school? Who is responsible for the upkeep of our school grounds?

Extreme weather events

REFLECTIVE QUESTIONS

As this chapter was being planned, we had an extremely hot summer in the UK. My memory is of multiple days of over 30-degree heat and many days approaching 40 degrees. We had wildfires in

> local Surrey Hills, as though the weather was more like that in Southern Spain. It was, to me, an outlier year. Was I right in thinking this?
>
> What are your weather memories? Can you remember particular outlier years? Do you think they have become more frequent? Does this indicate something of a change to the climate story over time?

The Met Office indeed reported that 2022 was indeed a year of records: 'All four seasons in 2022 were in the top 10 warmest on record for the UK. Winter was the eighth warmest, spring the fifth warmest, summer the fourth warmest and autumn the third warmest 2022 has been dominated by higher-than-average temperatures' (Dr Mark McCarthy, Met Office, Press Office, 2022).

What we need to do is look at the longer view. I recommend that you consider looking at the way the data is presented from the Weather Spark website for your geographical region. We might also turn to an assessment from the Met Office to get a more longitudinal view. See the Further Reading and Resources section for more information. You might also look at the Climate Stripes activity in Chapter 11. Understanding our world challenges through Mathematics. Understanding our world challenges through Mathematics.

Conclusion

The subject of geography is often seen as 'dry' and based on substantive knowledge, a 'pub-quiz' geography approach (Barlow and Whitehouse, 2019). What this means is that learning is atomised and disconnected, and we don't achieve a 'golden thread' (Spielman, 2022), a sequence which leads to sustained progress across teaching in the primary years. This is compounded by the lack of understanding of the nature of geography and the disciplinary approach that a thorough understanding of its concepts can lead to. Geography is essentially the study of our planet, our home. The changes that the Anthropocene has brought to our planet must be included in the study of geography.

As we conclude, therefore, we should perhaps consider the peril that faces us in relation to climate change. This is the sobering truth, again with reference to the Met Office's perspective:

> *Sea levels around the UK will keep rising [...] Parts of the UK will be in danger of flooding, with low lying and coastal cities at particular risk. Farming in the UK will be affected by climate change, [...] with more droughts expected, water may not be as easy to access, making it harder for farmers to plan the growing season. Some crops we grow today may also be unsuited to higher temperatures. Floods, storms, and extreme heat can cause damage to buildings, disrupt transport, and affect health.*
>
> (Met Office, n.d.)

Monbiot suggests that we should recognise that this is a point in time for united, concerted action, rather than piecemeal, or superficial responses: 'All this time, environmentalists have been telling people we face an unprecedented, existential crisis, while simultaneously asking them to recycle their bottle tops and change their drinking straws' (2022). This chapter aimed to show how some small geography can help point towards the big story of climate change. Geography 'seeks to make sense of the world and its people, places and environments through explanatory relationships' (Ofsted, 2021a).

These relationships have a time and space perspective, they are about how we live now, how we have come to be and how we might live in the future. Future-oriented geography has a long history in the study of geography since the 1960s and it has focussed on different aspects as worries have waxed and waned in the popular imagination (Huckle, 1983). Most recently the focus has arguably been on single-issue themes such as waste and, particularly, ones such as single-use plastic waste and the oceans. While undoubtedly these stories of how we live now through the lens of the mountains of waste we produce (Barlow, 2017 in Catling et al.), they all have at their heart the issue of finite space, resources or capacity for us to continue as we are. Whilst single-issue themes are undoubtedly important, this chapter has sought to demonstrate the significant linkage between local and global climate concerns.

CHAPTER SUMMARY

This chapter has focussed on using local conditions linked to global trends to support the teaching of climate change. We have investigated local weather phenomena to help us understand how these are connected to global systems. Activities in the classroom focus on developing an understanding of geographical processes, linking to the concepts of scale and perspectives (local - to national - to global).

What this chapter seeks to do is to look at the big picture climactic story and to try to see some local and UK perspectives on how this can be taught to primary-aged children. Without climate education being rooted in a sense of local environments that children live in we miss the positive story of small-scale stories and increasing mitigations that can improve a sense of place in the locality to provide positive changes. All geography is local or at least needs to start out that way for our youngest learners.

Further reading and resources

https://weatherspark.com/
The WeatherSpark website provides climate reports with the weather by month, day, and hour. Here you can compare temperature over a number of years.

https://www.metoffice.gov.uk/weather/learn-about/met-office-for-schools
The Met Office provides a number of resources specifically designed to teach weather and climate in schools.

https://www.greytogreen.org.uk/innovation
Read about Sheffield's innovative drainage system and the impact it has had on Sheffield's Biodiversity and Green Spaces.

https://www.thameswater.co.uk/about-us/responsibility/education/the-water-cycle
Read about the urban water cycle to help you to consider the whole range of aspects in the teaching the water cycle.

https://www.bbc.co.uk/programmes/p00j4xjr
The Battle of The Weather Fronts – Chris Hollins explains how weather fronts help to create our weather in Britain.

https://geography.org.uk/wp-content/uploads/s/01/OTR-Wind-rose-2023.pdf
See an example of a Wind Rose here.

https://www.rmets.org/metmatters/what-wind
What is wind? Kirsty McCabe demonstrates how complex the wind system actually is.

https://geography.org.uk/wp-content/uploads/2023/01/OTR-Weather-vane-2023.pdf
Practical support in teaching about the wind is available on the Geographical Association website.

https://www.rmets.org/resources/all
The Royal Meteorological Society provide a number of useful resources to aid in your teaching.

References

Barlow, A. (2017) in Catling, S. (Ed.) (2017). *Reflections on Primary Geography*. Sheffield: The Register of Research in Primary Geography.

Barlow, A. and Whitehouse, S. (2019) *Mastering Primary Geography*. London: Bloomsbury.

Catling, S. (2014a) Giving younger children voice in primary geography: Empowering pedagogy - A personal perspective. *International Research in Geographical and Environmental Education*, 23(4): 350–372.

Catling, S. (2014b) Pre-service primary teachers' knowledge and understanding of geography and its teaching: A review. *Review of International Geographical Education Online*, 4(3). Available at: https://rigeo.org/wp-content/uploads/2021/05/Pre-Service-PrimaryRIGEO-V4-N3-3.pdf

Catling, S. (2017) Reflections on Primary Geography: Preceedings prepared for the 20th Charney Primary Geography Conference 2017; Conference participants' prospectives on primary education Sheffield: Register of Research in Primary Geography.

Copernicus Online ESOTC 2021 | EUROPE | THEMATIC Flooding in Europe. Available at: https://climate.copernicus.eu/esotc/2021/flooding-july (Accessed: 25 June 2023).

Department for Education (2013) *National Curriculum for Georgraphy, Key Stages 1 and 2*. Available at: https://assets.publishing.service.gov.uk/government/uploads/system/uploads/attachment_data/file/239044/PRIMARY_national_curriculum_-_Geography.pdf

Department for Education (2022) *Policy Paper Sustainability and Climate Change: A Strategy for the Education and Children's Services Systems*. Available at: https://www.gov.uk/government/publications/sustainability-and-climate-change-strategy/sustainability-and-climate-change-a-strategy-for-the-education-and-childrens-services-systems

Geographical Association. *Curriculum Making*. Available at: https://geography.org.uk/curriculum-making/

Hicks, D. (2010) The long transition: Educating for optimism and hope in troubled times. *3rd Annual Conference of the UK Teacher Education Network for Education for Sustainable Development/Global Citizenship.* Available at: https://www.researchgate.net/publication/285232652_The_Long_Transition_Education_for_optimism_and_hope_in_troubled_times (Accessed: 25 June 2023).

Huckle, J. (1983) Values education through geography; a radical critique. *Journal of Geography, 82*(1983): 59–63. Available at: https://huckleorguk.files.wordpress.com/2020/10/huckle1983b.pdf

Lambert, D. (2017) Thinking geographically. In M Jones (ed.), *The Handbook of Secondary Geography.* Geographical Association, pp20–29.

Lambert, D. (2018) *Geography, Capabilities and the Educated Person.* Available at: https://discovery.ucl.ac.uk/id/eprint/10058011/1/chapter3_lambert%20F.pdf

Mackintosh, M. (2010) *Children's Understanding of Rivers.* Available at: https://www.tandfonline.com/doi/abs/10.1080/10382040508668365

Mackintosh, M. (1999) Children's views in physical geography, *International Research in Geographical & Environmental Education*, 8(1): 69–72. https://doi.org/10.1080/10382049908667592

Met Office (n.d.) Effects of climate change. Met office. Available at: https://www.metoffice.gov.uk/weather/climate-change/effects-of-climate-change#:~:text=Floods%2C%20storms%2C%20and%20extreme%20heat,plan%20around%20a%20changing%20climate (Accessed: 29 June 2023).

Met Office, online. What is climate? Available at: https://www.metoffice.gov.uk/weather/climate/climate-explained/what-is-climate

Met Office Press Office/Dr Mark McCarthy (2022) *2022 Provisionally Warmest Year on Record for UK.* Available at: https://www.metoffice.gov.uk/about-us/press-office/news/weather-and-climate/2022/2022-provisionally-warmest-year-on-record-for-uk

Monbiot, G. (2022) This heatwave has eviscerated the idea that small changes can tackle extreme weather. Available at: https://www.theguardian.com/commentisfree/2022/jul/18/heatwave-extreme-weather-uk-climate-crisis

Ofsted (2019). *Education Inspection Framework.* Available at https://www.gov.uk/government/publications/education-inspection-framework/education-inspection-framework

Ofsted (2021a) *Research Review.* Available at: https://www.gov.uk/government/publications/research-review-series-geography/research-review-series-geography

Ofsted (2021b) Geography in outstanding primary schools. Available at: https://educationinspection.blog.gov.uk/2021/05/11/geography-in-outstanding-primary-schools/

Ofsted Research Review Geograph (2021) Available at: https://www.gov.uk/government/publications/research-review-series-geography/research-review-series-geography#forms-of-geographical-knowledge

Spielman, A. (2022) Amanda Spielman's speech at the 2022 Schools and Academies Show. Available at: https://www.gov.uk/government/speeches/amanda-spielmans-speech-at-the-2022-schools-and-academies-show

Standish, A. (2007) *Geography Used to Be about Maps in the Corruption of the Curriculum.* Edited by Whelan. London: Civitas.

Standish, A. (2009) *Global Perspectives in the Geography Curriculum: Reviewing the Moral Case for Geography.* Abingdon: Routledge.

7
EXPLORING THE HISTORY OF HUMANS AND THEIR ENVIRONMENT

KARIN DOULL

LINKS TO CORE CURRICULUM FRAMEWORK

3.2, 3.6, 4.3

SUSTAINABLE DEVELOPMENT GOALS

GOAL 4: Quality Education
GOAL 13: Climate Action
GOAL 15: Life on Land

KEY WORDS

Environmental history; ecological history; landscape; conservationists; heritage; big history

> **CHAPTER OBJECTIVES**
>
> This chapter will:
>
> - Foster curiosity about the past and how human actions have shaped the world we live in.
> - Link to current research and theory in environmental and landscape history in the primary curriculum.
> - Generate debate and discussion about environmental history to help draw parallels and conclusions about human actions, recognising both positive and negative outcomes.
> - Explore how environmental history may link to national curriculum requirements for history.
> - Provide examples and practical suggestions for investigating the impact of human activity on the landscape at different times in the past.

Introduction

Before we can consider why we might want to explore the issue of climate change through history education we need to have a firm understanding of what the subject of history seeks to do. Many have sought to define the role of history by exploring the linkage between the past, present – and even the future (Cannadine, 2002; Carr, 1964; Power, 2020). Hawkey (2018) suggests that we should focus on Carr's (1964) description of the perpetual and intertwined nature of past and present. While this relationship is clearly central it is also important to think about how we use this knowledge. A common justification for the purpose of history is that we learn lessons from it to enable us to avoid repeating mistakes. If this is so, then we clearly do not learn very well as we continue to see recurring patterns of behaviour. Perhaps it is appropriate to consider that history enables us to understand the past and how it has contributed to our present. It provides us with tools to make sense of specific issues (Cooper, 2018). Before speculating on how we can change we need to recognise how things came about (Power, 2020); to consider how the present situation has come to be (Williamson, 2018). As with all history, however, it is important to avoid applying modern moral beliefs to past contexts (Williamson, 2018). We should try to see the past through the eyes of the diverse societies within it rather than using contemporary perceptions for judgement (Jordanova, 2006). Cannadine describes this as 'time-bound preoccupations of the scholar' (2002, pviii) that can distort our understanding of past societies. It is as important to recognise how distant the past is from our thought processes as to understand how far away it is in time (Lee, 2005).

In small research project, a class of year 6 children were asked if they thought you could use history to teach about climate change. All but two children said 'yes' (11) or 'probably' (10) with one boy saying, 'not really' and one saying 'no'. Children were then asked to explain what they think history can tell us.

> *I think it can tell us how it came about, how it has grown or increased and what started it. (Girl aged 10)*
>
> *We can see what we need to change in case it happens again in case the same thing happened in the past. (Girl aged 11)*
>
> *How climate change started and how we help it. (Boy aged 11)*

These comments demonstrate children's ability to recognise how history can be used to explore past events and their relationship to the present.

History allows us to explore the complex dialectical relationships between people and their environment (Jordanova, 2006). As Sörlin and Lane suggest 'history is after all largely about societies and their decisions and concerns' (2018, p4). Central to this is a recognition that the journey from past to present to future is not an inevitable voyage of 'progress' (Fagan, 2009; Lee, 2005; Power, 2020). We need to change the perception of a future of infinite growth (McGregor et al., 2021). The history of human civilisation has always been one of progression, regression and continuity (Sheehan, 2017) thus creating a diverse ebb and flow of growth and decline. History helps us contextualise this process of transformation, identifying relevant patterns and connections (Sörlin and Lane, 2018). Both Fagan and Durrani (2021) and Diamond (2011) identify the legacy that past civilisations and their responses to climate change or environmental crisis provide, considering how this contributed to the survival of one society or the collapse of another. While we do not necessarily learn directly from the past these historical experiences are relevant (Fagan and Durrani, 2021). They can be critical for discerning strategies for managing climate change in the present and moving forward into the future (Carey, 2014, p354).

Determan suggests that 'any predictions of future trends require a *thorough understanding* of past interactions between humans and our planet' (2022, n.p.). This type of understanding necessitates critical thinking, linked to reasoned judgements and arguments (Fagan and Durrani, 2021; Jordanova, 2006). History requires us to challenge narratives and ask difficult questions while seeking evidence to support our thinking. In this, it is important that schools provide children with tools to analyse the ideas that they encounter whilst ensuring that narratives are not presented without a context (Sheehan, 2017; Sörlin and Lane, 2018). Analysis, critical thinking and evaluation are core skills within the study of history (DfE, 2013). They are essential to create an 'informed critical understanding' (DES, 1989, p3) of the issues. Misinformation, bias, personal visions, extremist views and conspiracy theories are rife on the internet and social media. They need to be exposed, debated and mediated through classroom discussion (Chapman and Hayden, 2020; Culver, 2014; DES, 1989; Determan, 2022; Power, 2020). Schools have a clear responsibility to help children interact with controversial issues to shape their understanding in safe spaces (Neil et al., 2021). Clarity of understanding is necessary to begin to formulate strategies. We would want, after all, to avoid the issue noted by Fernandez-Armesto (2002) who suggests that 'government policy [is sometimes] formulated in glaring ignorance of the past!' (2002, p150). Critical digital literacy is essential for recognising the issues that surround the history of the climate crisis.

REFLECTIVE QUESTIONS

Spend some time looking at the history of climate change on the internet or social media. What reasons are given for climate chaos and change?

How rigorous is the evidence provided to support views?

How diverse are the viewpoints presented?

Are these views very polarised or inflexible?

Could they be said to be promoting extremist views?

How could you help children build critical digital literacy to be able to navigate these sites?

Big History is a term that seeks to provide an extended context to history beyond a specific period. While it may stretch from the Big Bang to the present, it is primarily involved in placing humanity within an elongated trajectory. It is used to identify connections and trends, considering patterns across the spread of time. Within the context of the climate crisis, it links human society with wider environmental contexts (Power, 2020). It is important to recognise processes that shape history within a temporal context and to realise that changes may develop over a long period rather than be related to a specific event (Lee, 2005). Here, we might want to consider the actions of people in the past and the strategies deployed across different lived-through events (Mustapa, 1999) while considering long-term origins. In developing a historical perspective, we can enable children to move between the micro and the macro in relation to specific issues. Big history provides a map of the long-term past enabling us to create a temporal order that identifies the interrelated, but not necessarily visible, nature of previous events.

Environmental and ecological history

Environmental and ecological history focusses on the interactions between humans and their environments over a long period of time. The concept of this historical discipline developed in the 1960s and 1970s with the growing recognition of the importance of recognising human involvement in the environment. This was complimented by the development of environmental studies in primary schools in the same period (Harris, 1971). Ecological concepts and processes were used to analyse problems within past environments through the relationship of humans and other living things to their habitat. This was linked to a geographical understanding of the changing physical features of the planet. Archaeology and anthropology (study of human experiences) were also used to create an understanding of the interaction, physical and cultural, between human societies and the natural world. Within this suite of historical disciplines, we can also identify landscape history. This is very prevalent within Britain as it explores mediated or managed environments that have familiar cultural references. It explores semi-natural habitats, those created through long-term human interaction (Williamson, 2018). What is created are 'cognitive geographies of the past through relationships between people, settlement and land use' (Finch, 2008, p511).

This small island has long been settled and there is almost no inch that has not been touched by previous generations shaping, developing, redeveloping and refining the land. This interaction has produced a largely 'managed' environment in Britain.

Environmental humanities explore the outcomes of human impacts on landscapes, and we need to understand this before we can begin to consider how we might do things differently (Power, 2020). What we need to seek to do here is to identify historical perspectives between human and cultural, natural and environmental (Hawkey, 2018). We should consider how historical evidence could be used to 'establish the background and changes which had occurred over time' to provide 'knowledge and understanding of physical and human practices that interact to shape the environment' (DfES, 1984, p2). Science too is providing data about unusual climate shifts in the past which can be correlated with specific significant events (Fagan, 2009).

We describe the environment in relation to environmental history as the intersection between the natural and the human world (Mustapa, 1999). Within the natural sphere, we have the earth's physical features and processes as well as flora and fauna (non-human living beings). This physical environment is then altered by human actions and presence through farming, roads, buildings, extraction of resources and creation of communication links.

The human environment can be further sub-divided into specific categories:

- Urban areas = **built environment**
- Social institutions, political and economic systems = **social environment**

REFLECTIVE QUESTIONS

What do you know about how human beings have shaped their physical environment?

What would you describe as a 'managed environment' and does this detract from or enhance the land?

How would you describe the environment around you?

What effects do the built, social or cultural environment have on the natural and physical environment you live in?

What can past civilisations tell us about managing climate change?

Environmental history seeks to find how the environment shaped human and non-human lives and how this was in turn affected by the actions of individuals and societies. Human societies have, since their inception, been subject to stress created by factors linked to the environment. Culver suggests that 'climate is not just an environmental fact but also a cultural construction' (2014, p311) as we can appreciate societal perceptions of nature and consider links between environment and cultural characteristics (Glaken, 1967). What perceptions about nature and natural events did people in the past have and what does this tell us about their society? Inhabitants of ancient civilisations lived more closely with nature and the effects of natural phenomena had more disproportionate consequences. This relationship is reflected in the gods and goddesses they chose to oversee their lives, the gods of storms and winds, the god with the lightning rod and the goddess of fertility linked to the earth. These mythical beings were used to explain the origin of weather events such as earthquakes and floods as in the Great Deluge of Ancient Sumer.

What factors might have contributed to civilisation stress or collapse?

To be able to analyse some of the outcomes of these events, we need to identify the criteria that contributed to civilisation stress. Diamond (2011) suggests that those who inadvertently or consciously over-utilise key natural resources commit 'ecocide' as they disregard their own environmental needs. He offers eight environmental categories that contribute to societal collapse within ancient civilisations (see Figure 7.1):

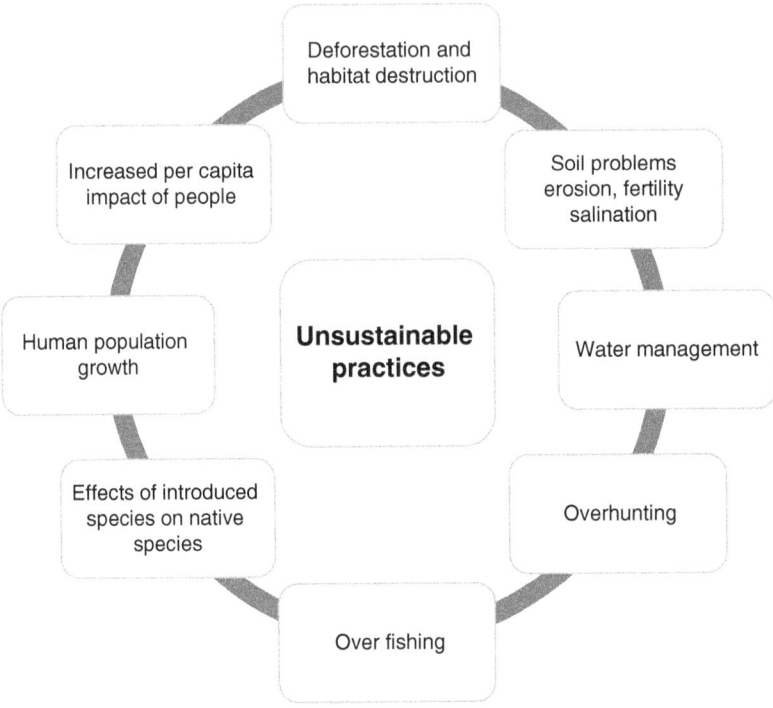

Figure 7.1 Factors that contributed to the collapse of historic civilisations (Source: From Diamond (2011, p6))

These criteria can be used to begin to explore some of the ancient civilisations and consider which were the most immediate or significant causes of decline.

When faced with societal collapse populations have a limited number of options:

- Migration – move away from the problem
- Collaboration – work together to solve the problem
- Adaptation – find ways to mitigate the problem
- Extinction – fail to take any or relevant action to allow life to continue

When civilisations are under extreme stress social disintegration is liable to occur. Populations lose trust in government and the legitimacy of religious and secular leaders, weakening the foundations of society (Fagan, 2009; Johnson, 2014) (as shown in Figure 7.2).

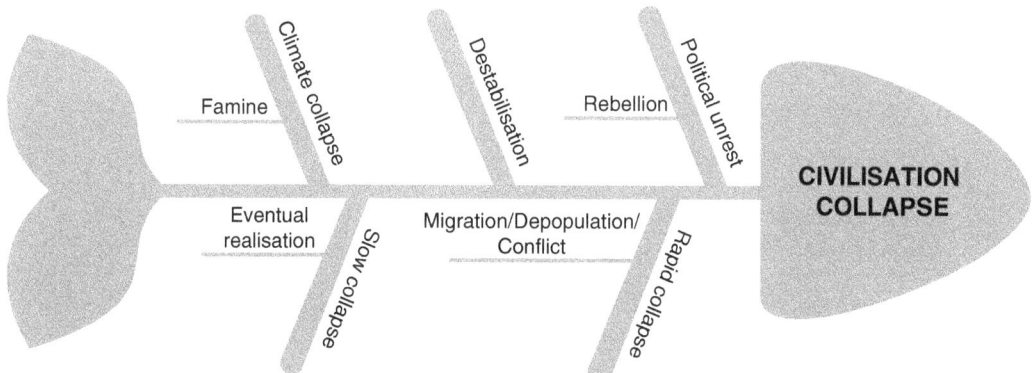

Figure 7.2   Reactions to climate crisis a (Johnson, 2014)

A historical example here would be the effects of drought on Egypt (c 2200 BC) where the Pharoah was felt to have lost ma'at or spirit of balance that held the country together. This then led to hunger, lawlessness, destruction and the collapse of the Old Kingdom.

Figure 7.3   Factors that contributed to the collapse of historic civilisations (Source: From Diamond (2011))

Environmental damage may be only one factor that leads to potential collapse.

- Climate change
    - Natural climate change (sun hotspots, change in earth's axis, movement of water/land and volcanic eruptions) could prove to be catastrophic in the immediate or longer term.

- For those with shorter lifespans or no recording systems, it was difficult to understand or manage change over a longer period.

• Friendly trade

- If a civilisation was dependent on imported trade goods, a problem in supply could leave them isolated and potentially vulnerable.

• Hostile forces

- In addition, there were always enemies, ready to take advantage of weakened societies.

• Society's responses

- The most influential factor however was always the responses that were taken by the society involved (Diamond 2011) (see Figure 7.3 above).

Considering the effects of previous climate crises and civilisation collapses will not automatically provide answers for us to navigate our current position. We can, however, investigate why some societies failed and others, perhaps at a similar point, survived. Why, for example, is the Mycenaean civilisation (c 1100s BC) destroyed by drought, civil war and marauding invaders, whilst Egypt, affected in similar ways at the same time, manages to survive – if not thrive. What actions, processes or institutions helped mitigate the problem for the Egyptians?

We cannot expect to discover strategies that are directly transferable to our current situation (Diamond, 2011; Fagan and Durrani, 2021). However, we might find some that can suggest a direction of travel.

Ancient civilisations ably demonstrated the human capacity to plan, adapt and formulate solutions to problems (Fagan and Durrani, 2021). This was often achieved through leadership and co-operation in both local and regional capacities. This is not to suggest that there was some golden utopian age when humankind lived in perfect harmony with nature. Williamson (2018) argues against the erasure of all human interaction with the natural world, suggesting that the concept of 'rewilding', for example, requires further research to judge its effectiveness. In the same way, both Fagan and Durrani (2021) and Diamond (2011) recognise that the ancestors of current Indigenous people were also guilty of environmental destruction. Perhaps the most important quality to promote natural well-being is the ability to listen to the voice of the land, and it could be strongly suggested that this is what is missing today.

REFLECTIVE QUESTIONS

Why do you think that strong, decisive leadership would be important for a society under stress?

How might this link to the possible actions that could be taken?

What considerations does this have for us today?

Would you agree with Diamond when he says, 'We can still learn from the past but only if we think carefully about its lessons? Why?'

Climate change within the primary curriculum

National curriculum

Within the current iteration of the history national curriculum, climate change and sustainability are not mentioned – however, children are expected 'know and understand the history of these islands as a coherent, chronological narrative, from the earliest times to the present day' and understand aspects of 'the nature of ancient civilisations; the expansion and dissolution of empires' (DfE, 2013, p245).

Requirements for KS1

'They should know where the people and events they study fit within a chronological framework and identify similarities and differences between ways of life in different periods' (DfE, 2013, p246). This broad canvas allows schools free reign to select significant individuals or events that may be used to help children understand the effects of climate change.

For example, the story of the volcanic explosion at Pompeii can also lead to considering what conditions in the area were like after the eruption had poisoned the air.

Requirements for KS2

Here, we expect children to continue to establish 'clear narratives within and across the periods they study. They should note connections, contrasts, and trends over time' (DfE, 2013, p246). Climate change and sustainability could be the focus for an 'aspect or theme in British history that extends pupils' chronological knowledge beyond 1066' (DfE, 2013, p248) linked to an investigation on energy use over time. In addition, the dissolution or collapse of an ancient civilisation could be considered across a range of different periods.

Local history

Local history is a key element across all phases of the curriculum and one which all should have access to. The local environment is a treasure trove that we should make automatic use of, linking wider aspects of history to our own area. No matter how bland the location, there are always historical stories to be found that demonstrate how our area has been shaped by those who lived or worked there before us.

In the classroom

Using environmental and landscape history to develop children's historical understanding

There are a number of substantive concepts that could be developed through a focus on climate change:

- Settlement – how human beings manipulate the natural environment to create appropriate living space.
- Trade – how commercial factors shape human use of the environment.
- Society – how humans create systems for living in groups.
- Power (perhaps) – the way in which control within the society is devolved.

Disciplinary concepts enable children to use historical facts and information and are key to developing historical thinking (Seixas in Clark, 2011). These should be carefully identified (see KS1 activity).

Using fieldwork and the outside environment

We should make use of the outdoor environment with children:

'Blending subject specific and context specific experiences in the outdoor environment supports children… to acquire deeper meaning and motivation' (Learning through Landscapes, 2022, pxi). A Local History unit should involve fieldwork in the physical environment rather than just using solely class-based materials (Cooper, 2013; Dixon and Hales, 2014; Doull et al., 2019). In practical outdoor investigations we link children to their area and allow them to physically explore their past. We should also take children to museums and heritage sites to help visualise the past through the rich range of resources at the museum (Doull et al., 2019) Interaction with practical activities or authentic artefacts heightens children's understanding of a civilisation.

Ideas for practical activities

Sustainability

> **ACTIVITY – EARLY YEARS**
>
> Start with the children's own experiences, thinking about what they had as babies and what happens to things we don't want or that we grow out of. You might also want to consider why we keep old things even when they are broken or worn.
>
> What do we do with our old stuff?
>
> Think about things that we had but no longer use - what do we keep, what do we do with the rest?
>
> You might start by talking about clothes or objects the children had as babies.
>
> What happened to their buggy or baby clothes?
>
> Visit a charity shop to talk about how we might recycle and reuse.
>
> Set up a charity shop - swap centre within the interactive home corner.

ACTIVITY – KEY STAGE 1 – FOOD STORIES

Select a product, on a timeline show when it entered British food history – Here you can ask questions such as where did it originate; how far did it and does it travel; how did it get to this place in the past and now; why was it brought to this country?

Think here about migration history perhaps or about the food that was imported into Britain at different times.

Create a class display and timeline with all the information.

ACTIVITY – KEY STAGE 2 – MAKE DO AND MEND

Look at government information sheets and posters from WW2.

What were the aims of these? Why might these ideas still be useful?

Investigate a material that is part of an everyday product, where does it come from, what is its useful lifespan, what happens to it when it is finished, was this different in the past, are there lessons we can adapt or learn from this? Where do the components of our mobile phones come from for example or consider the production of cheap clothing.

Make a book or poster from recycled materials to record the investigation.

Local and oral history

ACTIVITY – KEY STAGE 1 – INTERVIEW OLDER RESIDENTS

- How has our area changed over time (for better or worse)?
  Make a picture display of the changes to our place and speech bubble key quotes from visitors.
- How much green space do we have (link to Octavia Hill)?
  Design a 2D or 3D community garden or quiet space.

ACTIVITY – KEY STAGE 2 – PERSONAL EXPERIENCE OF SEVERE WEATHER EVENTS

Find some images of severe weather events, including one that you have experience of if possible, and share the experience, e.g. Hurricane of 1987, the drought of 2022, Cumbrian floods of 2009

Get children to talk about their experiences. Research one or more of these with additional sources.

(Continued)

Create and film a news report.

How might this event link to climate change?

ACTIVITY – KEY STAGE 1 – SIGNIFICANT INDIVIDUALS

The focus here is understanding the concept of 'significance'. You may want to use a set of criteria such as those of Christine Counsell or Geoffrey Partington (https://holocaustmusic.ort.org/fileadmin/user_upload/_imported/fileadmin/downloads/criteria_of_significance.pdf) to help children come to a conclusion about the significance of an individual or event. Use a picturebook to introduce the person or topic. You can find an interesting range of possible stories here: https://www.amightygirl.com/mighty-girl-picks/top-children-s-books-on-the-environment?p=2.

We can use these picturebooks to consider a range of conservation issues and the actions of 'Earth Heroes':

- Protecting trees, tree growing and reforestation
- Collecting and reusing rubbish
- Protecting special places
- Investigating and understanding nature

Use the book to introduce your focus but supplement it with additional tasks that develop historical thinking. Make use of images, photos and film with documents and artefacts to provide resources for generating historical questions.

- Chronology – identify the individual within a historical perspective.
- Causality – give reasons why they acted as they did and what effect their actions had.
- Change and continuity – link to other activists. How did their work change things?
- Historical interpretation – how are their stories presented – are there other versions or views?
- Characteristic features – how do they represent their time?
- Significance – what makes them significant (using criteria)?

Aani and the tree huggers by Jeannine Atkins

This is the story of the Chipko movement in the 1970s in India. A women's movement that developed spontaneously to protect the trees in their environment. Deforestation had affected the lives of women in the villages who relied on the trees for food and firewood. It had also caused soil erosion and landslides. Women and children hugged or encircled the trees to stop them from being cut down. After reading the story and looking at some photos and newspaper reports, discuss what the women wanted to achieve and why they were prepared to act this way.

Follow this up with a freeze frame or drama activity examples can be seen in Figures 7.4 and 7.5.

7 Exploring the history of humans and their environment

(Continued)

Figure 7.4   Children hugging trees

Figure 7.5   Saving the trees – Reconstructing an original photograph

ACTIVITY – KEY STAGE 2 – ALPHONSE THE CAMEL AND FRANK THE CAMEL KILLER (CHAPMAN, 2003)

In this activity, the story of Alphonse the camel (https://www.youtube.com/watch?v=J3wHpw7V2gw) is used to help children consider cause and effect in ancient civilisations

This same activity can be used across several different units to consider why civilisations might have failed or collapsed such as the Shang Dynasty, Indus Valley, Maya, and Britain after the Roman legions left. This could be the final session of a series of lessons on the chosen period.

Indus Valley Civilisation

First look at the video or tell the tale of Alphonse the camel.

Provide an information sheet with background detailing the fall of your chosen civilisation This should have information related to the factors that created the issue such as the lack of rain and erosion creating salination in the soil that led to the failure of crops. You will need to help children understand how these things arose and how they would affect a civilisation.

Discuss then consider possible factors that might lead to collapse (see Figure 7.1). I would provide these as labelled bags where the children have to select what is or is not appropriate.

(Continued)

- Children first sort the factors and decide which might apply discarding those that don't.
- Next prioritise categories, discussing as a group and agreeing on top three.
- Load up Alphonse by sticking bundles (water problems/famine) onto a picture of a camel.
- Compare the loads within the different groups. Is there any consensus? Which is the straw that broke the back?
- Use the results of the discussion to create a class matrix to show what were the consequences of these issues and how they might have contributed to the fall of the civilisation.

(Wondershare Edrawmind is a useful app for creating simple timelines and matrix.) An example of children's responses can be seen in Figure 7.6.

Figure 7.6   Factors contributing to the fall of Indus Valley Civilisation

CHAPTER SUMMARY

This chapter has placed sustainability and climate change within a historical context. It defined environmental history and considered why this is a useful discipline with which to explore the effect of climate in the past. It has provided a series of activities, across the primary age phases, to explore different elements of sustainability or climate change through an historical lens.

THANKS

With many thanks to Andrew and Heidi Simpson and Ichthys class at Arundel Church of England Primary School.

Further reading and resources

https://www.nationaltrust.org.uk/who-we-are/about-us/about-the-national-trust-today
The National Trust started in 1895 by Octavia Hill, Canon Hardwicke Rawnsley and Robert Hunter as the 'National Trust for Places of Historic Interest or Natural Beauty'. The idea was to preserve paces and provide access for a wide range of people. It is Europe's biggest conservation charity. It looks after coastline, historic sites, countryside and green space. Find out if there is a National Trust site near you.

'Saving the Countryside: The Story of Beatrix Potter and Peter Rabbit' by Linda Marshall. Beatrix Potter was a supporter who donated land and farms to the National Trust. To explore this organisation with KS 1 you could use this picturebook.

https://www.npg.org.uk/learning/digital/family-activities-playful-portraits/octavia-hill
The National Portrait Gallery has a good resource for Octavia Hill linked to the importance of gardens, particularly community gardens. I think the idea of a garden in a box would be very successful.

References

Cannadine, D. (ed.) (2002) *What Is History Now?* Basingstoke: Palgrave McMillan.

Carey, M. (2014) Science, models and historians: towards a critical climate history. *Environmental History*, 19(2): 354–364.

Carr, E. H. (1964) *What Is History?* London: Penguin.

Chapman, A. (2003) Camels, diamonds and counterfactuals. *Teaching History*, 112: 46–54.

Chapman, A. and Haydn, T. (2020) History education in changing and challenging times. *History Education Research Journal*, 17(1): 1–4.

Cooper, H. (2013) *Teaching History Creatively*. Abingdon: Routledge.

Cooper, H. (2018) *History 5–11: A Guide for Teachers*. Abingdon: Routledge.

Culver, L. (2014) Seeing climate through culture. *Environmental History*, 19(2): 311–318.

Department of Education and Science (1989) *Environmental Education from 5-16 (No 13) Curriculum Matters: an HMI Series*. London: HMSO.

Determan, J. M. (2022) Tracking climate change through environmental history. July 16 Al-Fanar Media.

Diamond, J. (2011) *Collapse*. London: Penguin.

Dixon, L. and Hales, A. (2014) *Bringing History Alive through People and Places: A Guide for Primary Teachers*. Abingdon: Routledge.

Doull, K., Russell, C. and Hales, A. (2019) *Mastering Primary History*. London: Bloomsbury.

DFE (2013) *National Primary Curriculum* (History Programmes of Study). Available at: https://assets.publishing.service.gov.uk/government/uploads/system/uploads/attachment_data/file/239035/PRIMARY_national_curriculum_-_History.pdf

DFES (1984) *Environmental Education from 5–16* (Curriculum Matters 13). Available at: http://www.educationengland.org.uk/documents/hmi-curricmatters/environmental.html

Fagan, B. (2009) *Floods, Famines and Emperors: El Niño and the Fate of Civilisations*. New York: Basic Books.

Fagan, B. and Durrani, N. (2021) *Climate Chaos: Lessons of Survival from Our Ancestors*. New York: Hachette Book Group.

Fernandez-Armesto, F. (2002) Epilogue: what is history now? In D. Cannadine (ed.), *What Is History Now?* Basingstoke: Palgrave McMillan.

Finch, J. (2008) Three men in a boat: biographies and narratives in the historic landscape. *Landscape Research*, 33(5): 511–530.

Glaken, C. (1967) *Traces on the Rhodian Shor. Nature and Culture in Western Thought from Ancient Time to the End of the Nineteenth Century*. Berkley: University of California Publication.

Harris, M. (1971) *Environmental Studies Wallop Schools'*. Council Publication.

Hawkey, K. (2018) Moving Forward, Looking Back – historical perspective, Big History and the rebirth of the "longue durée": time to develop our scale hopping muscles. *Teaching History*, 40–46.

Johnson, S. (2014) When good climates go bad: pivot phases, extreme events, and the opportunities for climate history, *Environmental History* 19(2): 329–337.

Jordanova, L., (2006) *History in Practice*. London: Bloomsbury.

Learning Through Landscapes. (2022) *Teaching the Primary Curriculum Outdoors*. London: Corwin.

Lee, P. (2005) Putting principles into practice: understanding history. In S. Donavon and J. Bansford (eds.), *How Students Learn: History, Mathematics and Science in the Classroom*. Washington: National Academies Press, pp31–74

McGregor, H., Pind, J. and Karn, S. (2021) A "wicked problem": rethinking history in the Anthropocene, rethinking history. *The Journal of Theory and Practice*, 25(4): 483–507.

Mustapa, A. (1999) *Social, Environmental and Scientific Education, (History Primary School Curriculum) Curaclam na Bunscoile*. Dublin: Government Publications.

Neil, C. et al. (2021) What for the future of Learning from the past? Exploring the implications of the compulsory Aotearoa New Zealand histories curriculum. *New Zealand Annual Review of Education*, 27: 5–24.

Power, A. (2020) *Climate in the History Curriculum*. 15th October. Available at: https://blog.royalhistsoc.org/2020/10/13/climate-in-the-history-curriculum

Sörlin, S. and Lane, M. (2018) Historicizing climate change-engaging new approaches to climate history. *Climate Change*, 151: 1–13.

Seixas, P. (2011) Assessment of historical thinking. In P. Clarke (ed.), *New Possibilities for the Past: Shaping History Education in Canada*. Vancouver: UBC Press, pp139–154

Sheehan, M. (2017) History's distinctive contribution to critical citizenship: reflections on chapters by Rick Rogers, Rachel Foster and Ellen Buxton. In C. Counsell, K. Burn and A. Chapman (eds.), *Masterclass in History Education: Transforming Teaching and Learning*, London: Bloomsbury, pp217–221.

Williamson, T. (2018) Historical perspective on wildlife and the environment in England: how natural is natural? In *2018 Historical Society Colin Mathew Memorial Lecture*. 17 October. Available at: https://www.gresham.ac.uk/watch-now/historical-wildlife-environment-england

8
LEARNING TO CARE ABOUT THE ENVIRONMENT THROUGH PICTUREBOOKS

VERITY JONES

LINKS TO CORE CURRICULUM FRAMEWORK

5.2

SUSTAINABLE DEVELOPMENT GOALS

GOAL 13: Climate Action

KEY WORDS

Picturebooks: fiction; climate change; plants; drought; hope

> **CHAPTER OBJECTIVES**
>
> This chapter will:
>
> - Identify why picturebooks are a useful tool to engage children in climate change and sustainable education.
> - Recognise the need for hopeful pedagogies that support children in navigating their emotional responses to climate change and sustainability.
> - Introduce key lenses through which to analyse picturebooks for use in teaching climate change and sustainability themes.
> - Demonstrate how a free children's picture e-book might be used to explore drought.

Introduction

We develop our relationship with and for the environment during childhood, however, connecting with the environment is increasingly difficult. There has been an incremental decline in children's physical activity and individual mobility over the last three decades (Balmford et al., 2002; Witten et al., 2019) with a wide public rhetoric that childhood is becoming 'de-naturalised' (Taylor, 2013). The opportunity to be outside was curtailed by restrictions on freedom of movement during the coronavirus disease 2019 (COVID-19) pandemic (albeit temporarily) and re-engagement with outdoor space has been slow to reoccur for all. This detachment is echoed by Barkham's (2020) book *Wild Child*, which argues that we are raising a generation alienated from nature. Disengagement with the environment is further expounded by some curriculums. For example, the primary National Curriculum of England (DfE, 2013) only expects children to be taken out of the classroom for geography fieldwork – an activity that the school's inspectorate (OFSTED) notes, many schools do not do (Freeland, 2021). Merleau Ponty (2012) points out that if we are to form relationships with the environment then having time outside is essential – not just as one-off activities, but building a relationship with the outdoors over time to form a habit. However, within our current social and educational systems, children can find it increasingly difficult to develop such habits and therefore are at risk of not being able to engage as critical citizens for a sustainable future. This situation provides the context for this chapter where I argue that carefully selected picturebooks can offer teachers opportunities to support children in developing skills and learning explicit rules through characters and settings that inform a child's understanding of and for the environment at a time of climate and ecological emergency.

> **REFLECTIVE QUESTIONS**
>
> How has your engagement with the environment changed over your life course?
>
> What have been the opportunities and barriers to getting outside?
>
> Are these different for children today?
>
> Are they different for children in different geographical locations or different socio-economic contexts?

How can books support eco-emotional responses through hope and action?

Young people today will be the generation most affected by climate change. Those leaving UK primary schools in the summer of 2023 will be 18 years old by 2030. This is the year that the 169 targets for the Sustainable Development Goals (UN, 2015) are set to be met; when we, as a global community of the United Nations will have (hopefully) mitigated many of the world's most pressing problems. The 11-year olds of 2023 will be voters by 2030. Yet, there is evidence that many children and young people already feel let down and even betrayed by national and global government responses to climate (in) action (Hickman et al., 2021) with children reporting feeling sad, angry, anxious, powerless and guilty for the state of the world (Jones and Whitehouse, 2022). When working with children, we need to be sensitive to how the climate and ecological emergency is impacting the well-being of children in our care. Choosing the right books to share is part of this care package. After all, we don't want to incite further sadness, anger, anxiety, powerlessness and a sense of guilt by choosing inappropriate texts and/ or not supporting meaningful discussion and reflection.

Choosing the right picturebook is not always easy. Boggs et al. (2016) warn against using just any book with a climate theme. They suggest that climate fiction should be based on scientific knowledge that is presented sensitively. Yet fiction is by its very nature imaginative and not necessarily accurate in its representation of scientific concepts. Picturebooks offer the added dimension of illustration where scientific concepts may not only be presented in text but also in illustration; each needing to be decoded. On this point, I think it is worth taking a moment to reflect on the presentation of scientific concepts associated with plants in picturebooks.

REFLECTIVE QUESTIONS

Grab a few picturebooks and flick through them. How are plants represented? Are they used to create a landscape or are they a character in the story? Are they positioned as useful? Are plant products important to the story and how are they used?

Plants are essential to the health of people and the planet and due to deforestation, intensive agriculture and climate change, the extinction of plant species is increasing. Plants provide us with air, shelter, medicine, food, building materials and fabric – the list goes on. Being with plants has also been seen to improve well-being (Larson et al., 2015). Yet plants are often a backdrop rather than a central character with explicit scientific concepts attached to the narrative of eco-literacy.

Nicola Davies' *The Promise* and Donna Jo Napoli's *Miti Wangari: Wangari Maathai and the Trees of Kenya* offer two examples of picturebooks that position people and plants centre stage. In *The Promise*, a thief finds themselves with a bag of acorns. Having made a promise to plant them they then move from city to city, transforming grey, plantless spaces into luscious green spaces. *Miti Wangari* is based on the true story of how Kenyan women transformed the landscape by planting trees. Images in both books show the transformation of landscapes. The texts also refer to how plants are rainmakers, earth coolers and environmental balancers. These are concepts that might be overlooked, but with the critical eco-literacy eye, we can use such references to consider the scientific concepts that these books touch upon.

While scientific accuracy may be important as a tool to unpack concepts around climate, Crandon et al. (2022) argue that we should choose our sustainable themed books by the actions that are embedded in the narrative – as it is through positive action that children can relate to, that may help reduce negative eco-responses. If a child sees a character switching off a light, or recycling, they may feel empowered to do it themselves – but be warned …

A warning on the hero narrative

Positive action is important in eco-literature if we are to provide role models for our young readers to be inspired by. However, positive actions tend to suggest we need a hero in our stories. The hero is a familiar character to children. Whether it's J. K. Rowling's Harry Potter fighting the dark wizards or Roald Dahl's Matilda outsmarting Miss Trunchbull, the lead protagonist often has the ability to put right the wrongs of (usually) adults. A similar trope can be seen in children's eco-fiction. Dr Seuss' *The Lorax* is a useful example: A boy listens to the story of how the Once-ler created a fabric (called a Thneed) from the Truffula trees. The demand for Thneed grew and the trees were destroyed for profit by the greedy industrial tycoons. As the boy listens to the story the overarching message becomes clear – unless someone cares for the environment it cannot improve. The task of planting the last Truffula seed lies with the boy. The child is being positioned as the one responsible for addressing the issues of overconsumption and climate change through his actions alone. Hope lies in the individual child's hands with the weight of responsibility resting on their shoulders. Such a scenario can feel overwhelming for some children and rather than provide a positive role model, may instead leave young people feeling helpless.

REFLECTIVE QUESTIONS

What children's literature can you identify where a young hero is faced with a task that undoes the wrongs of adults?

What effect does this have on your young readers?

Let's compare *The Lorax* to *Rocket Says Clean Up!* by Nathan Bryon and illustrated by Dapo Adeola. Whilst visiting her Grandparents on holiday, Rocket leads the way to educating people on a beach about plastic pollution. The story provides a positive representation of a Black, female protagonist and her family, as well as framing the improvement of the environment through action as a community (in a similar way to Miti Wangara who plants tress with the help of other women in the community). While Rocket sees the problem of plastic pollution and raises her concerns, it is with the help of Grandpa and the 'Clean Up Crew' that change can happen and be celebrated. Unlike The Lorax, the state of the world is not framed as a failure of stewardship by adults and does not vilify industry in an oversimplified narrative. Hope is found in a community of action.

Hope is essential and should be a core theme in any of the books a teacher uses (Scoffham, 2021; Tapia-Fonllem et al., 2013). Hopeful narratives of climate fiction allow children to practice creating worlds, the future worlds that they desire, in their imagination. These worlds then provide pathways to allow children to recruit ideas and actions that are able to alter their lived worlds. Put simply, if a picturebook is hopeful then it can potentially be effective at empowering children to act for the environment, but without the weight of responsibility that it is their job and their job alone to fix the problems.

Using picturebooks in the classroom: A case study for teaching about extreme weather

When it comes to the consequences of the climate and ecological emergency one of the most familiar images children refer to is the melting of the icecaps due to global warming (Jones and Whitehouse, 2022): Images of polar bears (often with their babies) stranded on decreasingly smaller icebergs surrounded by a warming ocean. One book that takes this image is Jean Craighead George and Wendell Minor's *'The Last Polar Bear'* where the children of Alaska learn about how to help polar bears adapt to a changing world. Whilst this may be useful for a study of contrasting places in geography, the purpose of the sustainable education element of using this book should be considered in relation to your own context. Books that explore contexts unfamiliar to children (such as in the Arctic) may create a feeling of distance from the problem of climate change. Children may consider this to be a problem they have no connection with. Finding texts that are locally based on your setting, or speak to the cultural context of your pupils, might be more useful.

In the classroom

In this section, I will consider drought as the extreme weather condition I want to explore. This will serve as an example of how we might draw on events close to home to teach about the climate emergency, through picturebooks.

REFLECTIVE QUESTIONS

What extreme weather events are you familiar with, whether first hand or through the news? Can you match the extreme weather event with a children's book?

Is the book:

- Set in a similar place to your setting?
- Are there any scientific concepts being presented (either overtly or covertly)?
- Is there a hero to the story and how are they represented?
- Are there any positive actions in the story children in your class could learn from?
- Is the story framed around hope?
- Are there creative ways in which the story could be used in class?

Using these questions as a critical literacy guide, I will consider drought as my chosen extreme weather event and how the picturebook *DRY, the Diary of a Water Superhero* supports climate education and sustainable practices (see information about a free version of this book in the Further Reading and Resources section).

Is the book set in a similar place to your setting?

As I live in the UK, I will take this place as my context for teaching. This means I would be looking for a story that resonates with the lived experiences of the children in my class. Drought in the UK may seem to some an absurd idea as many consider these shores as wet and rainy with an abundant water supply (Weitkamp et al., 2020). Droughts in the UK are seen as rare and infrequent risks – a public perception that is reinforced by the media who tend to present positive elements of 'good' weather when extended heat and lack of rain are experienced. However, the risk of drought in the UK – and globally – is growing. Drought is something that young people are likely to increasingly experience over the coming decades and 2022 saw the highest average temperatures recorded in England to date. It is a slow, hidden and uncertain threat with diverse impacts that affect local communities in different ways. *DRY: The Diary of a Water Superhero* is a book that explores drought.

What are the scientific concepts in the book relating to drought?

Wilhite and Glantz (1985) identify different types of drought e.g. meteorological (rainfall) drought, agricultural (soil moisture) drought, hydrological (river) drought and water supply drought – each type is indicated in the story and each type of drought manifests itself in site-specific impacts on humans and non-humans (including companion animals and wild animals). The book was informed by a four-year research project called DRY (Drought Risk and You) – funded by the National Environment Research Council Drought and Water Scarcity Programme. This project aimed to bring together scientists and communities around seven river catchments across the UK (see McEwan and Blake, 2019 for more information). The evidence gathered by the DRY project provided insight into a series of common misconceptions relating to drought that were then embedded into the picturebook.

PAUSE FOR THOUGHT

Misconceptions

Identifying misconceptions is important but often difficult if, as a teacher, you don't have a secure subject knowledge base. Referring to research-informed practice is one way of supporting quality learning and minimising misconceptions.

A useful place to start thinking about misconceptions is to reflect on what you know about the theme and what the children in your class know. What misunderstandings might they have about rain, water supply and water usage in the UK? How are you going to fact check? If there are misconceptions how might these impinge on children's future preparedness and action in the face of climate change?

For example, some of the misconceptions identified by the DRY research included:

- Water from taps is free, with no cost associated with it.
- There is no shortage of water in the UK.
- The UK never has droughts.
- You only get droughts in the summer.
- If it rains, a drought ends.
- Rain is bad.
- Wildlife can always find water.
- You can save water by drinking less.

If these misconceptions are not challenged then children (and adults) will not consider the environmental, financial and health implications of using water when it is a limited resource (see Jones et al., 2020 for more discussion on this). The Teacher Guide to the book (see free link below). Provides a list of misconceptions for pupils to discuss. This is a useful start to a lesson, or recap of what's been learned. Listing the common misconceptions and then asking whether pupils agree, disagree or don't know immediately makes for discussion and a point of assessment for learning that can inform later input. Don't forget to ask why pupils agree or disagree with statements - this will unpack how secure children are and where their sources of knowledge are coming from.

Is there a hero to the story and how are they represented?

The storyline of the book, written as a young girl's diary, runs over the course of an academic year in a UK city. It tells how an ordinary Year 6 schoolgirl (10–11 years old) transforms into a water superhero when a dry summer and winter with little rainfall leads to drought. Readers watch as the girl shares a new-found understanding and respect for water with her family and how they start to change their lifestyle habits together. The impact of the girl's passion for greater sustainable use of water is then extended into her school and community as the drought progresses.

Are there any positive actions you can take to reduce the impact of drought and promote water citizenship?

Throughout the story, actions are all relatable to children, from reusing water bottles and finishing off meals, to switching off the taps when you clean your teeth and reducing the time in the shower. The message is one of personal agency that when combined can make a difference. Through the narrative, visual clues and activities presented, we see how water practices can be changed at home and in the community. Don't forget that children in your class may have similar or different water practices at home that could be discussed. Linking water to cultural practices can be a great way of celebrating different lived experiences and learning from each other.

Is the story framed around hope?

The story aims to explore the agency of young citizens – but this is not represented as an easy journey and the protagonist has obstacles to overcome and people to work with. The emotions children feel as they read the book have been mapped (see Jones et al., 2020). Feelings of anger, despair and guilt that many children report feeling when faced with issues relating to sustainability and climate change were also reported by young readers when reading the first part of the story. However, pupils reflected that they felt more hopeful as the story unfolds because people began to listen to each other and act together.

Are there creative ways in which the story could be used in class?

Creativity offers an important role in any classroom exploring issues of sustainability – and a different set of skills that can engage and enable learners to think differently. The learner can have a conversation with the self, through the development of a creative piece, before sharing it with others. In this way, creativity can be soothing to the distracted mind and offer an alternative way of communication. Creativity can take many forms in the classroom when exploring Dry: The Diary of a Water Superhero. Here, I provide three examples that you can try.

The story refers to plants throughout (in illustration and text), not least in the allotment of the protagonist's grandfather. Invite learners to explore the work of botanical artists such as German herbalist Leonhart Fuchs, 19th century traveller and painter Marianne North or the most famous Chinese painter of flowers Xu Xi (Hsü His). Children could observe plants in your classroom, playground or local area over different seasons and record how they change with access to water. Observational drawings and techniques using different mediums (pencil, watercolour and collage) could be explored. Skills from observational drawings could then be extended to combine imagination with plant adaptation to design a new, drought resistant plant.

Poetry is a fantastic genre to explore sustainability through. In Amy Lowell's poem Bath, beautiful imagery of taking a bath on a hot, sunny day is presented to the reader. Pupils can delight in the language and free verse with none of the usual grammatical rules. They can reflect on the pros and cons of taking baths at times of water insecurity, and then develop new poems inspired by taking showers or having a bath in a drought (with only an inch of water). Encourage the children to think about what would be the same and different relating to what they see, hear, smell and taste. Poems could be performed to other groups and extended into music if they were set to a beat or accompaniment on tuned or untuned instruments.

Music has a history of bringing people together, especially around social movements. At the end of Dry: The Diary of a Water Superhero, the whole community is working together to reduce the water they use. Combining the theme of sustainability and music can be a fun and empowering way of working with children. Learning new songs, finding more out about lyrics, or how they may have been used for protest, and (re)writing new versions are creative, engaging ways of learning. A few songs to consider sharing, learning, performing or adapting could include Humming House's 'Young Enough to Try', Coldplay's 'Paradise, Louis Armstrong's 'What a Wonderful World' and 'Love Song to the Earth' by various artists including Paul McCartney, Jon Bon Jovi and Leona Lewis.

> **CHAPTER SUMMARY**
>
> The Sustainable Development Goals note that we need to take urgent action to mitigate climate change and its impacts. By 2030, drought is estimated to displace 700 million people and we need to improve education relating to people's capacity to both adapt to and reduce the impact of extreme weather events. This is but one of the many impacts of climate change that children are and will have to make sense of. In this chapter, I have looked at how and why picturebooks are a useful tool to engage children in such education and highlighted the need to support children in navigating their emotional responses to climate change and sustainability. Issues around sustainability are, by their very nature, complex and messy. Choosing the right picturebooks to support learning in your classroom can be similarly difficult. When identifying books, I urge you to consider the setting, how scientific concepts are presented and heroes represented, how mitigation to crises and hope are framed, and how science and creative thinking can be embedded. Using these lenses through which to analyse picturebooks will allow for deeper understanding of the issues and sensitivity to children's responses.

Further reading and resources

Useful resources to support learning about drought in the UK.
- E-copy of DRY: the diary of a water superhero https://issuu.com/uwebristol/docs/dry_the_diary_of_a_water_superhero

- Link to free teacher guide https://dryutility.info/wp-content/uploads/2020/01/DRY-book-Teachers-Notes-FINAL-E-VERSION.pdf

Greater preparedness in the face of the climate and ecological emergency will support children in navigating these challenging times.

References

Balmford, A., Clegg, L., Coulson, T. and Taylor, J. (2002) Why conservationists should heed Pokemon. *Science, (American Association for the Advancement of Science)*, 295(5564): 2367.

Barkham, P. (2020) Wild Child: coming home to nature. *Granta*.

Boggs, G. L., Wilson, N. S., Ackland, R. T., Danna, S. and Grant, K. B. (2016). Beyond the Lorax: examining children's books on climate change. *The Reading Teacher*, 69(6): 665–675.

Bryon, N. and Adeola, D. (2020) *Rocket Says Clean Up*. London: Penguin Random House Children's UK.

Craighead George, J. and Minor, W. (2014) *The Last Polar Bear*. New York: Harper Collins.

Crandon, T. J., Scott, J. G., Charlson, F. J. and Thomas, F. J. (2022) A social–ecological perspective on climate anxiety in children and adolescents. *Nature Climate Change*, 12: 123–131. https://doi.org/10.1038/s41558-021-01251-y

Davies, N. (2013) *The Promise*. London: Walker Books.

Department for Education (2013) *The National Curriculum in England: Key Stages 1 and 2 Framework Document*. Available at: https://www.gov.uk/government/publications/national-curriculum-in-england-primary-curriculum

Freeland, I. (2021) Geography in outstanding primary schools. Available at: https://educationinspection.blog.gov.uk/2021/05/11/geography-in-outstanding-primary-schools/ (Accessed: 28 December 2022).

Hickman, C., Marks, E., Pihkala, P., Clayton, S., Lewandowski, R. E., Mayall, E. E., Wray, B., Mellor, C. and van Susteren, L. (2021). Climate anxiety in children and young people and their beliefs about government responses to climate change: a global survey. *Lancet Planet Health*, 5: e863–873. https://doi.org/10.1016/S2542-5196(21)00278-3

Jo Napoli, D. and Nelson K. (2017) *Miti Wangari: Wangari Maathai*. New York: Simon and Schuster.

Jones, V., Whitehouse, S., McEwan, L., Williams, S. and Gorell Barnes, L. (2020) Promoting water efficiency and hydrocitizenship in young people's learning about drought risk in a temperate maritime country. *Water*. https://doi.org/10.3390/w13182599

Jones, V. and Whitehouse, S. (2022). 'It makes me angry. REALLY angry': exploring emotional responses to climate change education. *Journal of Social Science Education*, 20(4): 93–120. https://doi.org/10.11576/jsse-4551

Larson, L., Stedman, R., Cooper, C. and Decker, D. (2015) Understanding the multi-dimensional structure of pro-environmental behaviour. *Journal of Environmental Psychology*, 34(4): 411–424.

McEwan, L. and Blake, B. (2019) (Un)natural Drought. *Environmental Scientist*, 28(4): 40–45

Merleau-Ponty, M. (2012) *Phenomenology of Perception*. Abingdon: Routledge.

Scoffham, S. (2021). Finding hope at a time of crisis. *Primary Geography Spring*, 104: 8–9.

Seuss, D. (2012) *The Lorax*. London: Harper Collins.

Tapia-Fonllem, C., Corral-Verdugo, V., Fraijo-Sing, B. and Durón-Ramos, M. F. (2013). Assessing sustainable behavior and its correlates: a measure of pro-ecological, frugal, altruistic and equitable actions. *Sustainability*, 5(2): 711–723.

Taylor, A. (2013) *Reconfiguring the Natures of Childhood*. Abingdon: Rourtledge.

United Nations (2015) *Transforming Our World: The 2030 Agenda for Sustainable Development*. UN publishing.

Weitkamp, E., McEwen, L. J. and Ramirez, P. (2020) Communicating the hidden: towards a framework for drought risk communication in maritime climates. *Climatic Change*, 163: 831–850.

Wilhite, D. A. and Glantz, M. H. (1985) Understanding: the drought phenomenon: the role of definitions. *Water International*, 10(3): 111–120.

Witten, K., Kearns, R., Carrol P. and Asiasiga, L. (2019) Children's everyday encounters and affective relations with place. *Social and Cultural Geography*, 20(9): 1233–1250.

9
EDUCATION FOR SUSTAINABLE DEVELOPMENT THROUGH ART: PROJECT CARE

EMESE HALL

LINKS TO CORE CONTENT FRAMEWORK

1.2, 8.3

SUSTAINABLE DEVELOPMENT GOALS

GOAL 17: Partnerships to achieve the Goal.

KEY WORDS

Sustainability; Education for Sustainable Development (ESD); Issues-Based Art Education (IBAE); With, About, In and Through (WAIT) model; Professional Learning Community (PLC)

CHAPTER OBJECTIVES

This chapter will:

- Define what is meant by 'education for sustainable development' (ESD) with particular reference to the 17 Sustainable Development Goals (SDGs), drawn from the United Nations 2030 Agenda for Sustainable Development (UNESCO, 2017).
- Explain the curriculum potential of Issues-Based Art Education (IBAE) linked to learning with, about, in and through art - the WAIT model (Lindström, 2012).
- Describe an ERASMUS+ research project that investigated art as a vehicle for ESD in primary schools in Cyprus, Greece, Malta and England - *Art Education in New Times: Connecting Art with Real Life Issues* (CARE).
- Share research findings from Project CARE and consider the implications of the research for fostering ESD through art in UK primary schools, as well as within initial teacher education and professional development contexts.

Introduction

This chapter will draw upon a recent Erasmus+ funded research study (ref: 2019-1-CY01-KA203-058258) to illustrate the potential of art education as a vehicle for developing ESD in primary schools. *Art Education in New Times: Connecting Art with REal Life Issues* (CARE) involved research partners in Cyprus, Greece, Malta and England, as well as a critical friend team in Germany. Whilst some of the partners designed and delivered training to experienced teachers, our research participants in the UK were trainee teachers – people like you, new to teaching.

Various definitions of ESD exist, and this example is taken from our CARE training guide:

ESD enables learners to develop the knowledge, skills, attitudes and values required to become active participants, individually and collectively, in decision-making processes, both at local and global levels that will improve the quality of life of present and future generations (Vella et al., 2022, p10).

Given the significance of ESD – its relevance to everyone and everything – it is notable that teaching and learning considerations about sustainability are not currently included in the National Curriculum in England (DfE, 2013) nor the Core Content Framework for teacher training (DfE, 2019). This is especially concerning given the urgent nature of the global environment and climate crisis. However, encouragingly, there are groups arguing for these omissions to be rectified. The fact that ESD is not receiving sufficient attention in primary schools was one of the rationales for the CARE research, and demonstrating how art education can help in the development of ESD highlights the relevance of art education to children's wider learning.

There are several ways through which we can engage children in artistic processes to explore current issues, such as sustainability and the climate crisis. You might be aware of the distinction between learning *in* and learning *through* art. Briefly, learning *in* art is subject-specific learning, and *through* is non-subject-specific learning. For example, one exciting way of learning through art is to draw upon issues of relevance across the broader curriculum – this is called IBAE. Project CARE used IBAE approaches to develop children's knowledge and understanding of sustainability issues. Moving on, I will provide further explanation about Project CARE.

Setting Project CARE in context

In this section, I will expand on some of the topics signposted in the introduction. Firstly, we briefly consider the UNESCO (2017) SDGs; then, we look at some of the opportunities of IBAE; next, we turn to the WAIT model (Lindström, 2012), and finally, Project CARE is described in further detail.

The UNESCO SDGs and their relevance to art education

Because one of art's main purposes is to communicate, art education is an excellent vehicle for helping children make sense of important issues. Sharing artworks with children opens many possibilities: we might ask children to consider what they can see and what they think it might mean, but it is also enlightening to learn about the artists' intentions. Let us consider the following observation:

While the relationship between sustainability and art goes back several centuries, contemporary artistic practices tend to focus more explicitly on topical concerns related to social justice and ecological issues. Many of the 17 SDGs listed by UNESCO are frequently alluded to in the work of artists around the world today (Vella et al., 2022, p11).

We want our art teaching to be relevant to the 21st century and building children's awareness of contemporary art is an effective way to develop ESD. UNESCO's (2017) 17 SDGs, which address economic, social, environmental and cultural considerations (sometimes these are known as the four 'pillars' of sustainability). Within Project CARE, we identified a range of contemporary artworks that linked to one or more of the SDGs and shared these as teaching resources for the research participants to use with their classes. Local issues were considered alongside global concerns, as well as artists working in a variety of styles and media. The artworks offered a clear and tangible focus with which to discuss the related sustainability issues, making the teaching of complex issues much easier. You can find all the focus artworks, with guidance notes, on the CARE website (see further reading and resources section).

REFLECTIVE QUESTION

UNESCO's SDGs are equally important in ensuring a sustainable future for everyone but is there one that resonates with you in particular? If so, why might that be?

Some opportunities of IBAE

ESD and IBAE are complementary. Awareness of some of the opportunities of IBAE can aid you in planning an issue-based art activity, lesson or project.

Robinson and Robinson (2022) suggest that education should equip children with the ability to engage in personal, cultural, economic and social challenges, and this argument aligns with the four pillars of ESD. One of the biggest opportunities of IBAE is that you can link your art planning to other subjects and strengthen children's learning in a holistic sense. Guidance from Ofsted (2023) recommends that teachers select, 'age-appropriate content that explores how thinkers have drawn attention to aspects of art that shape the stories humans tell through art ("art histories"), including their perspectives on social, political and moral issues'. For instance, the issue of protecting animals and their habitats is explored through *The Wild Escape* project, a collaboration involving many UK-based cultural partners (see https://thewildescape.org.uk/). This idea of stories through art demonstrates how artistic learning should be about not only making art but also the critical and cultural dimensions of the discipline (Eisner, 1972).

In selecting age-appropriate content, Chang et al. (2012) suggests some useful questions for you to answer: 'Why is the issue important? Why is the issue controversial? How is the issue relevant to education? In what way can the issue be explored thoroughly?' (2012, p22). Discussing these questions with more experienced colleagues would be beneficial, alongside a review of existing curriculum content, such as topics explored in Personal Social and Health Education (PSHE). Elsewhere (Hall, 2022), I have written about the potential of IBAE with reference to the usefulness of Lindström's (2012) four-way learning model. I will explain and discuss this model in the next section.

PAUSE FOR THOUGHT

The InSEA (2022) publication, *Climate Literacy for Art Educators*, offers an inspiring collection of project reports from a range of different countries: https://www.insea.org/wp-content/uploads/2023/03/IMAG_issue_13_final_doi.pdf.

Introduction to the WAIT model

I have long admired Lindström's (2012) four-way learning model, which has a great potential to support holistic art planning. This model effectively illustrates how art is a rich area of learning, with multiple dimensions; it prompts an understanding of art education that goes far beyond the stereotype of 'drawing and painting' because art is so much more than a practical subject (Eisner, 1972). Encouragingly, Lindström's model is given a good level of attention in Ofsted's (2023) research review for art and design, which should mean that it is likely to influence practice in schools. I refer to this as the WAIT model (With, About, In and Through). Although I cannot take any credit for the ideas encapsulated in

Lindström's model, I do think my catchy acronym is helpful to you. Further, as I have explained before, there is also some useful advice in the word WAIT because 'rushing to implement IBAE without careful forethought would be a mistake' (Hall, 2022, p85). All issues should be approached with due care and attention.

> **REFLECTIVE QUESTION**
>
> What do you already know about the different ways a teacher might position themselves in relation to students when teaching art? Have you considered a multi-dimensional approach towards planning art lessons?

Here is simple overview of the distinction between each of the four ways of learning as proposed by Lindström:

Learning *with* art:

- Integrated/interdisciplinary/cross-curricular learning
- Teacher as advisor
- 'Are works of art used to illuminate ethical or political questions?' (Lindström, 2012, p177)

Learning *about* art:

- Covers art education basics, key knowledge and skills
- Teacher as an instructor
- 'Are detailed criteria specifying what you should do and know established in advance?' (Lindström, 2012, p177)

Learning *in* art:

- Exploring and experimenting
- Teacher as facilitator
- 'Does the assignment allow for different solutions?' (Lindström, 2012, p177)

Learning *through* art:

- 'Thinking dispositions' (Lindström, 2012, p170)
- Teacher as educator
- 'Is reflection on your own or in small groups an important element of the course?' (Lindström, 2012, p177)

Returning to Vella et al.'s (2022, p10) definition of ESD, which refers to 'knowledge, skills, attitudes and values', we can summarise the following broad learning aims: Learning *with* art covers relevant interdisciplinary knowledge about sustainability issues, be these economic, social, environmental or cultural; learning *about* art covers knowledge about artists, craftspeople and designers who address sustainability issues in their work either via subject focus, materials or processes; learning *in* art covers the skills of practical making, which should also include knowledge of the sustainability of materials (e.g. materials' origins, biodegradability/recyclability etc.); and learning *through* art covers the fostering of attitudes and values that can are in tune with addressing sustainability issues. From this list, you can see that the WAIT model accommodates all applicable ESD considerations, maximising learning possibilities.

PAUSE FOR THOUGHT

It is important for all teachers to be aware of this recent research summary: Ofsted (2023) *Research Review Series: Art and Design* – see: https://www.gov.uk/government/publications/research-review-series-art-and-design.

Project CARE in more detail

This section concentrates on describing the rationale for Project CARE, its aims, organisation/research design and some findings. The principal aim, as already stated, was to illustrate the potential of art education as a vehicle for developing ESD in primary schools.

CARE comprised six stages. Firstly, we undertook a review of the (then) current situation regarding art education and ESD in our respective countries, drawing on literature and interview evidence. Secondly, we designed local (country-specific) training programmes that offered a minimum of 15 hours learning input shaped by the teacher competencies, shown in Figure 9.1. As the project took place during the global COVID-19 pandemic, the training programmes were delivered online – this was the third stage, involving the participation of self-nominated teachers and trainee teachers. On completion of the programme, we gathered evidence of impact via questionnaires and interviews. The fourth phase of the study involved the participants designing, delivering and evaluating schemes of work in schools, which linked art and ESD. These activities provided case studies of classroom practice. An assessment of the PLCs formed through the project was stage five. Finally, we brought together all of the findings in dissemination events and a handbook for teachers. Further information can be found on the project website (see further reading and resources section).

At the start of the project, most of our participant teachers, both experienced and the trainees, were interested in art education but they mostly had limited understanding and experience of ESD. However, crucially, they believed in the importance of teaching children about real-life issues and were keen to explore the creative possibilities offered by ESD-infused art teaching. The learning

Figure 9.1   Framework of ESD-enhanced art teacher competences (Pavlou and Kadji-Beltran, 2021)

content in the training programmes for Project CARE was organised around six 'Big Ideas': the public, ecological literacy, compassion, diversity, conservation and change, and regeneration (Vella et al., 2022, p58). Some programmes involved participants collaboratively planning units of work whilst others, such as ours in England, saved this as an option for the next stage. Overall, the local training programmes were positively received, with knowledge gains reported in both ESD and art education, as well as enhanced confidence in bringing these two areas together in the classroom. Some participants noted time limitations (e.g. personally too busy) as a barrier to engagement, but this is where the online nature of the training resources was beneficial, as content could be flexibly accessed and revisited.

From the large number of participants (111) that engaged in the training programmes, a smaller number (73) chose to deliver art and ESD projects in their schools as part of the CARE research. However, many teachers said they planned to apply their new learning in different ways outside of the research project. Indeed, some keen participants were implementing new ideas into their practice during the training programme! Informed by our six UK participants' classroom projects, in the next section, I will share some inspiration for your own practice.

In the classroom

Here, I will provide a range of practical ideas for ESD through art in the classroom, considering different age phases. Some of these ideas will be drawn from the Project CARE research and others will be new suggestions. Broader implications for schools, Initial Teacher Education (ITE) and Continuing Professional Development (CPD) will also be shared. To begin, I will offer a case study from Project CARE.

CASE STUDY: 'COUNTRY TOWN: NOW AND FUTURE'

The Project CARE case study is taken from Bella's teaching. Bella was on placement in a Year 4 class (ages 8-9) of 32 pupils. Her project, 'Country Town: Now and Future', was taught in the summer term over four lessons and an artist-led workshop day. Drawing on the issue of planned development of the school's town, her learning themes covered: ecological literacy, conservation and change, regeneration, responsible consumption and production, and having a voice. The project required the children to challenge some of their existing assumptions: Bella wanted the children to explore a local issue to understand that sustainability was relevant to their home context and not only distant places. The art lessons were linked to history and geography. Maps were given a lot of attention as well as a range of relevant artworks and stories. Promoting empathy, Bella asked the children to carefully consider the perspectives of different groups on the town's planned development. During the artist-led workshop day, children collaborated to make sculptures from repurposed materials, representing the groups of insects and wildlife, children and families, farmers and businesses. Children not only learnt about sustainability issues but Bella's project also developed their understanding of how art can be defined. For example, one child commented: 'I hadn't thought about art as a message before'. and another remarked: 'I like art. Usually when I do art I think of buying things and this makes me feel a bit, like, guilty. This is a way of doing art without buying stuff, which is better for the planet...I think that's really good. I can do art without feeling bad'. The CARE training programme assisted Bella in creating an effective and affective project as seen in Figure 9.2.

Figure 9.2 Bella's CARE project: Outcomes from the artist workshop

Examples of classroom activities: CARE and beyond

Below is a small selection of art activities that you could try in school. They are listed as suitable for a specific age range, but some activities could be adapted for learners in other year groups if appropriate pedagogy is adopted. Please be aware that the activities should be linked to clear learning intentions that are applicable to your class and your school's planned art curriculum coverage (e.g. as specified in a subject curriculum map); they should also be contextualised, especially if you want to meaningfully address ESD. For each example, I give a link to one of UNESCO's (2017) SDGs, recognising that others SDG links may be applicable. Also highlighted is a suggested learning intention from the National Society for Education in Art and Design's (NSEAD, 2014) curriculum guidance which details expectations for generating ideas, making and evaluating, and knowledge and understanding. Finally, bear in mind that you can usefully consider Lindström's (2012) WAIT model in planning a sequence of lessons to ensure that ESD dimensions are suitably covered in addition to art-specific learning considerations.

ACTIVITY – EARLY YEARS

Food collage: provide children with a large selection of printed images of different foods (e.g. from magazines and newspapers) to make a collage of all the foods they enjoy – this can be connected to SDG 3: good health and well-being. As an individual or collaborative activity, this should involve lots of discussion. You can consider healthy options as well as food that is less healthy but makes us happy! Children could also make their own food drawings to include in the collage or draw directly on to the collage. This activity relates closely to learning about physical development (diet). In terms of generating ideas, this activity could address the EYFS/Year R learning objective to: 'work purposefully responding to colours, shapes, materials etc' (NSEAD, 2014, p7).

ACTIVITY – KEY STAGE 1

Artwork analysis: compare and contrast two artworks (e.g. sculptures) made from natural and man-made materials – this can be connected to SDG 12: responsible production and consumption. Regarding subject matter, the artworks could specially address one or more sustainability themes, but this is not essential. Images of the artworks could be labelled with key words (e.g. via sticky notes), and scientific knowledge could be addressed regarding classification of materials. In terms of knowledge and understanding, this activity could address the Year 1 learning objective to know: 'how to recognise and describe some simple characteristics of different kinds of art, craft and design' (NSEAD, 2014, p7).

ACTIVITY – LOWER KEY STAGE 2

Peaceful painting: using sketchbook research, ask children to work towards creating a painting that conveys an atmosphere of peace – this can be connected to SDG 17: peace, justice and strong

(Continued)

institutions. They can experiment with colour mixing and colour combinations, drawing inspiration from different artworks including, as contrast, those that focus on conflict. Symbolic forms could be investigated, or a fully abstract approach taken. Cross-curricular links could be made to religious education (RE) and history as well as PSHE. In terms of making, this activity could address the year 3 learning objective to 'develop practical skills by experimenting with and testing the qualities of a range of different materials and techniques' (NSEAD, 2014, p8).

ACTIVITY – UPPER KEY STAGE 2

Anthotypes: making photographs using different coloured plant juices (e.g. beetroot, spinach, raspberries etc.) - this can be connected to SDG 15: life on land. There is a similarity in approach to making cyanotypes, another form of camera-free photography (see: https://theartyteacher.com/exploring-cyanotype/), but anthotypes use plants rather than chemicals. This is an activity best done in the summer as you need bright sunlight to make effective images. There are excellent science connections to be made! Working in pairs or small groups is recommended as it is a lengthy process from start to finish, and the learning opportunities are very much in the processes involved. In terms of making, this activity could address the Year 5 learning objective to: 'confidently investigate and exploit the potential of new and unfamiliar materials' (NSEAD, 2014, p9). You may find this clear guidance a useful starting point https://www.hw.ac.uk/documents/Post-13-Light-Patterning_Anthotypes_Printing-with-.pdf.

Implications for schools, ITE and CPD

Schools may have existing schemes of work for art which could be enhanced with consideration of relevant issues via UNESCO's (2017) Global Goals. This would be a worthwhile review task for the art co-ordinator in your school, and equally applies to commercial schemes, where sustainability issues might not be covered. The training programmes that we developed in each CARE partner country were bespoke for our local contexts but based on the CARE training guide (Vella et al., 2021). Those working in ITE can usefully consult the guide to identify some key content to include in their art education provision. In terms of CPD, the same advice applies. Any one of the CARE publications (available on the research website) could be read and discussed to inform teachers' professional learning; there are six 'intellectual outputs', but they do not need to be read in order.

REFLECTIVE QUESTION

What local issues are relevant to your school community? Would any of these be suitable to explore through an art lesson or project? How might you go about this, and could you collaborate with any local organisations or action groups?

CHAPTER SUMMARY

All 17 of the UNESCO Global Goals are of relevance to this chapter and Project CARE. However, I would identify SDG 17 as especially applicable because this concerns partnerships for the goals. Teaching is a social endeavour – we need to have strong communication skills and be able to collaborate, both with colleagues in school and within other partnerships. A key contributor to the success of Project CARE was due to each partner working in a team, drawing on everyone's respective strengths and expertise. We developed different approaches to creating PLCs involving the research participants at a local level, with one large PLC involving all research partners. Importantly, we all shared the same values. Every school has its own values, and you could use these values as a great starting point to explore ESD through art in your own school.

Further reading and resources

Project CARE website: http://care.frederick.ac.cy

Here you will find a wealth of information and resources about the CARE project, including the artist templates from each of the partner countries. In the 'intellectual output' section, report 4 (*Children and teachers at work: Facing sustainability challenges through the visual arts*) provides many more case studies.

Art2030 website: https://www.art2030.org/

In their own words, 'ART 2030 works with art as the key to achieve the UN Global Goals by opening people's hearts, minds and imagination – to inspire action for a healthy and sustainable future'. There is a wide range of contemporary art examples here that you can draw inspiration from for your art and ESD teaching.

References

Chang, E., Lim, M. and Kim, M. (2012) Three approaches to teaching art methods courses: child art, visual culture, and issues-based art education. *Art Education*, 65(3): 17–24.

DfE (2013) *National Curriculum*. Available at: https://www.gov.uk/government/collections/national-curriculum (Accessed: 09 March 2023).

DfE (2019) *Initial Teacher Training (ITT): Core Content Framework*. Available at: https://www.gov.uk/government/publications/initial-teacher-training-itt-core-content-framework (Accessed: 11 May 2023).

Eisner, E. (1972) *Educating Artistic Vision*. New York: Macmillan.

Hall, E. (2022) Issues-based art education and its usefulness to primary teachers. In V. Pavlou (ed.), *Visual Art Education in New Times: Connecting Art with REal Life Issues (CARE) – Handbook for Teachers*. Nicosia: Frederick University, pp81–88.

Lindström, L. (2012) Aesthetic learning about, in, with and through the arts: a curriculum study. *International Journal of Art and Design Education*, 31(2): 166–179.

NSEAD (2014) The national curriculum for art and design guidance: EYFS, primary, KS1-2. Available at: https://www.nsead.org/files/8608849141653ba98fcb20e1e196289e.pdf (Accessed: 15 April 2023).

Ofsted (2023) *Research Review Series: Art and Design*. Available at: https://www.gov.uk/government/publications/research-review-series-art-and-design (Accessed: 23 February 2023).

Pavlou, V. and Kadji-Beltran, C. (2021) Enhancing Arts Education with Education for Sustainable Development Competences: A Proposed Framework for Visual Arts Education Educators. In E. Wagner, C. Svendler Nielsen, L. Veloso, A. Suominen and N. Pachova (eds.), *Arts, Sustainability and Education. Yearbook of the European Network of Observatories in the Field of Arts and Cultural Education (ENO)*. Springer. https://doi.org/10.1007/978-981-16-3452-9_11

Robinson, K. and Robinson, K. (2022) *Imagine if: Creating a Future for Us All*. Dublin: Penguin.

UNESCO (2017) *UNESCO Moving Forward: The 2030 Agenda for Sustainable Development*. Available at: https://unesdoc.unesco.org/ark:/48223/pf0000247785/PDF/247785eng.pdf.multi (Accessed: 28 March 2022).

Vella et al. (2021) *Conducting Participatory Arts Projects: A Practical Toolkit*. Available at https://www.researchgate.net/publication/347694725_Conducting_Participatory_Arts_Projects_A_Practical_Toolkit

Vella, R., Caruana, C., Gatt, I. and Zammit, C. (2022) Part I: the guide. In R. Vella (ed.), *Integrating Principles of Education for Sustainable Development into Visual Arts Education in Teacher Education Programmes*. Nicosia: Frederick University, pp9–48.

10
RELIGIOUS EDUCATION AND SUSTAINABLE LIVING

SUSIE TOWNSEND

LINKS TO CORE CONTENT FRAMEWORK

1.2, 1.5, 2.1, 3.6, 4.7

SUSTAINABLE DEVELOPMENT GOALS

GOAL 4: Quality Education
GOAL 13: Climate Action
GOAL 16: Peace and Justice Strong Institutions
GOAL 17: Partnerships to achieve the Goal

KEY WORDS

LDC – Least Developed Country; GNH – Gross National Happiness; sustainable tourism; carbon neutral; Net zero carbon; high-value low-impact tourism; stewardship; Indigenous religious beliefs

> **CHAPTER OBJECTIVES**
>
> This chapter will:
>
> - Understand the nature of sustainability and consider how far different religions support this approach.
> - Consider the role of religious groups in actively promoting sustainability.
> - Explore activities in the classroom that can be used when teaching religious education.
> - View sustainability in action with a focus on the Kingdom of Bhutan.

Introduction

'The earth does not belong to man; man belongs to the earth. All things are connected like blood that unites us all. Man does not weave the web of life; he is merely a strand in it. Whatever he does to the web he does to himself' Chief Seattle 1854 Speech, Seattle

When does religion hit the headlines in the media today? The image of a suicide bomber immediately springs to mind, an explosion in the street, shootings by someone of one religion against those of another. There are few conflicts in the world today that do not have a religious dimension. But this is not the purpose of religion, nor what is written in the religious texts. Religion for most people is about their own spiritual identity and core beliefs and revolves around learning to live a good life – not the stuff that is ever deemed newsworthy! Religions are predominantly about providing a code for living with ourselves, each other, and the world around us. Having a set of beliefs is not always related to the idea of a deity and children need to consider other sets of beliefs too such as humanism, but what they all have in common is this shared set of values about how we should live. Environmentalism is not defined as a religion, but it is a belief that the natural world should be protected from harm from human activity and an approach to achieving that is **sustainability**. Thus, the path to sustainability also outlines ways to live that will change our relationship with the world.

Michael Crichton, science fiction writer of books such as Jurassic Park and climate change sceptic, famously remarked in 2003 that environmentalism was the 'religion of choice for urban atheists'. Although his speech was a satirical attack on the concept of climate change the quote above has resonance. There are clear links between religion and sustainability which will be explored in this chapter.

Having considered what is meant by sustainability and how religious leaders hope to support the sustainable development goals (SDGs), the focus of this chapter will move to consider what is actually written in the sacred texts of some of the major religions. In what way do they support, or question the SDGs and how might their teachings influence the debate? It will conclude with strategies to use in the classroom to engage children in these key discussions and help them establish their own emerging beliefs about how to create a balance in life. This is their future, and they need to understand that everyone's voice should be heard, and all can take actions that have an impact.

What do we mean by sustainability?

For the purposes of this chapter, the focus will be on the different elements that form part of sustainability as a concept. There is a range of models that demonstrate this, but the model below (see Figure 10.1) considers four key aspects of sustainability and then links those to the United Nations' (UN) SDG.

This is an example of a possible model and is discussed when considering classroom activities below. There are many sustainability models but this one seemed to highlight a core element of religion – the importance of culture and beliefs. Our sense of identity and our belief systems, whatever they may be, are arguably what makes us human and helps us to come to terms with ourselves and our place in the world.

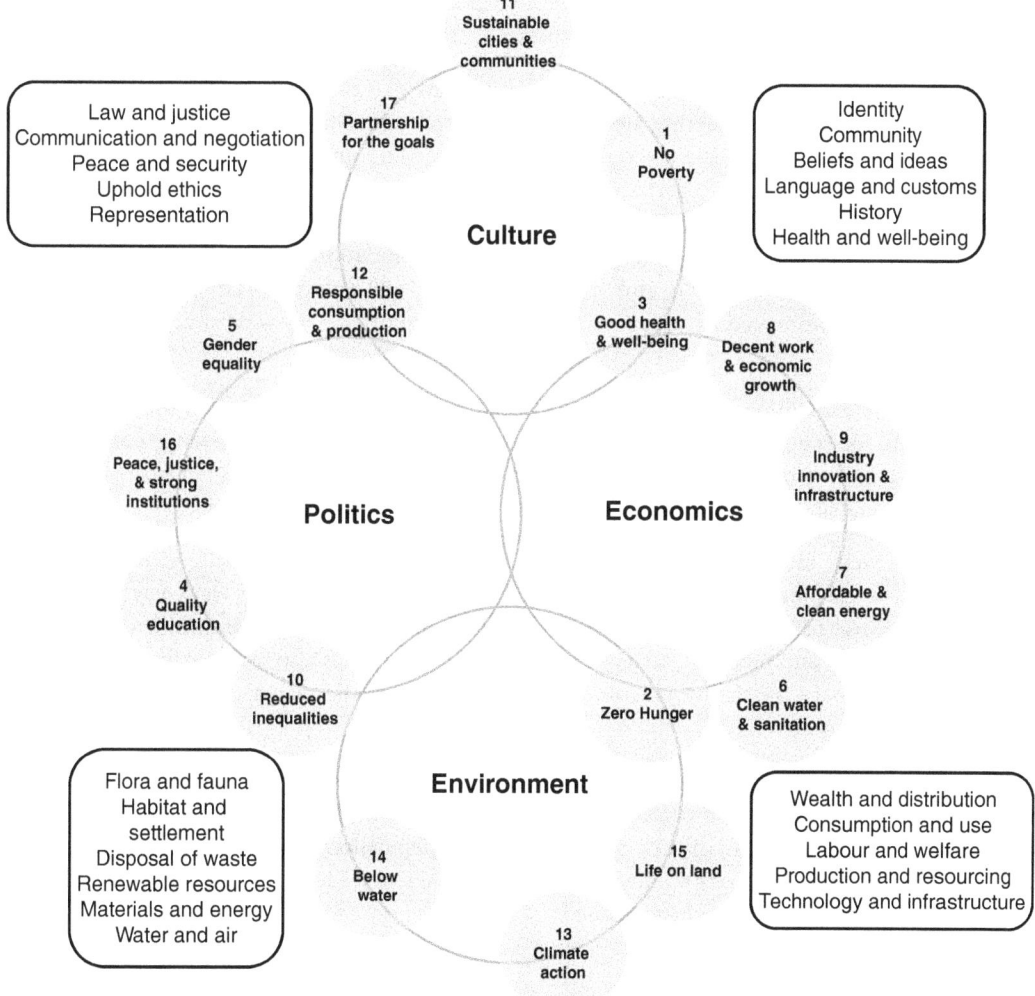

Figure 10.1   Map of Sustainable Development Goals

The SDGs have been included in the diagram, but the point of these circles is to understand that although some SDGs are more appropriate for different aspects of life, the majority are goals that can apply to all four aspects of the model. It is the balance between all four that is important, so that, for example, economic development is not at the expense of cultural political and environmental needs.

What is religion's role in sustainability?

As the United Nations states, 'Sustainable development is the development that meets the needs of the present, without compromising the ability of future generations to meet their own needs' (UN, 1987). Religious beliefs can both support this view through their teachings but also hold back sustainable development, and it is important for children to explore these ideas.

In 2008, the UN announced the Faith for Earth Initiative which acknowledged the important part that religion can play in supporting sustainable development. The vision of this initiative is 'A world where everything is in balance', and the aim 'to leave no one behind' is a constant phrase. Its three goals are to encourage partnership between Faith faith-based organisations (FBOs), to invest in 'green' approaches and to build knowledge support systems. Many religious leaders are embracing this work and are actively promoting sustainable approaches within their communities. Ethics underpins the SDGs and from as early as 1988 the importance of a sustainable lifestyle was being promoted by religious leaders who supported a view of shared global ethics (Sachs, 2014).

There are however dissenting voices. Fourteen per cent to 16% of the population of the United States are evangelicals, for example, and although there is evidence that many younger evangelicals recognise the science related to climate change there are still a significant number of Christian evangelicals who consider this liberal and 'leftie' propaganda designed to damage economic stability.

Other religious views can also affect the strive for balance. Religions have differing views about birth control and their teachings influence millions of people. Using contraceptives is viewed as 'intrinsically evil by the Catholic Church and is supported by the commandment to "be fruitful and increase in number; fill the earth and subdue it." (Genesis 1:28) Family planning is also frowned upon'. In fact it is asserted by some that Christianity sanctioned the destruction of the planet through such ideology. (White cited in Narayanan, 2013).

With 80 billion people on the planet and the population continuing to rise, unwanted pregnancies and large families will accelerate the degradation of the environment and climate change and increase overconsumption. According to the UN, 80% of the world's population is affiliated with religion, so it is essential that there is a desire for a unified approach from religious leaders and that the impact religious beliefs can have on sustainability is recognised.

These are key questions to discuss but it is also important for children to see for themselves what the actual teachings of the religions say about human beings and their relationship with each other and their environment. What the texts state may help them view the planet in a different way and consider how they might support a more symbiotic approach to living.

Religious teachings about the environment

The Indigenous peoples of the world have remained the closest in touch with the natural world around them and their understanding of the need for balance and their awareness of the impact of human, or anthropogenic activity, on the planet is evident. This is guided very much by their spiritual beliefs.

An example might be to look at the beliefs of the Native Americans. They hunted the buffalo but showed sacred respect for it. They used all parts of the animal and only took enough for their needs so that the herds were not reduced. They believed that no one owned land but that places were sacred where their ancestors were buried and that they were just guardians of the land during their lifetime.

All other religious teachings show the importance of respecting their environment and also advise on other subjects such as how to be wise with money, to give generously to those in need, to support each other and their community and not to waste precious resources. It is clear to see how many of the SDGs fit into the teachings and traditions of religious values.

An example of some of these values is shown in the Jewish story about Honi and the Carob Tree, which is often told on the New Year of the Tree when young trees are planted. You can find more about this story in the Further Reading and Resources section of this chapter.

This importance of trees is seen in the Torah as it mentions that even in wartime, they must not cut down fruit trees no matter that they might feed the enemy. There is also a reference to 'whoever breaks vessels or tears garments, or destroys a building, or clogs up a fountain, or destroys food violates the prohibition of bal tash'chit'(Kiddushin 32a) showing the importance of not wasting resources.

The idea of stewardship is seen across different religious beliefs. This is the view that we are looking after the world around us for future generations. Most consider that the world is a precious gift from God and that we should show our gratitude.

The Bible refers to the importance of looking after the land: 'You shall not pollute the land in which you live, for blood pollutes the land, and no atonement can be made for the land for the blood that is shed in it, except by the blood of the one who shed it. You shall not defile the land in which you live' (Numbers 35:33)

Islam continues this theme. 'Thus, we have made you trustees (khulafaa) on the earth after them, to see how you would act' (Qur'an 10:14). This is a key text in the Qur'an showing the importance of stewardship. As with the Jewish Torah, there are comments about conserving resources as well. 'O Children of Adam, dress well whenever you are at worship, and eat and drink [as We have permitted] but do not be extravagant (Mizan): God does not like extravagant people' (Quran 7:31).

The first precept in Buddhism is to abstain from taking life of living forms and many Buddhists are pacifists and also vegetarians. This idea is based on the notion of loving-kindness. As a result, the concept of nature and its importance permeates through Buddhist teaching and is linked to the well-being of humans and the interconnection between humans and the natural world.

To Hindus, there is no distinction between the Divine and nature – they are the same. The many Gods demonstrate different aspects of life, and the Gods often take animal form. All life is sacred and as with the Native Americans they may eat meat, although many don't, but they respect the animal. Some animals such as monkeys and cows are not eaten and are revered.

Finally, Jainism is seen by many as the religion, which has the environment at the heart of their beliefs. The supreme principle of Jainism is non-violence (ahimsa) and they are vegetarian. Often Jain priests brush the floor in front of them so that they do not knowingly kill insects and wear mouth coverings to stop them from accidentally inhaling small creatures.

These are just a few examples, and the religious texts give views on issues related to the other circles of the sustainability diagram above (Figure 10.1). These could be collated together to show the core similarities between the religions on how we should live our lives and how closely the guidance links to sustainable ways of living. The case study on Bhutan shows how religious guidance can dictate government policy.

REFLECTIVE QUESTIONS

How do religions position themselves on the ecological question?

How can they make a significant contribution to the view of sustainability?

In what ways might religion exacerbate issues of climate change?

CASE STUDY – RELIGION IN ACTION

The Kingdom of Bhutan

Hidden away between India and China, on the South slopes of the Himalayas this remote country, with a population of less than a million, did not open its borders to tourism until 1974 and has remained mainly isolated from the rest of the world until the last 20 years. The former King abdicated in favour of his son, Jigme Khesar Namgyel Wangchuck when he changed the political system to a democracy in 2008. The present King has been committed to sustainable development with a focus on maintaining traditional culture and beliefs. The country has a democratic constitutional monarchy, and the King is the Head of State and has heavily invested in projects to bring about environmental, social and economic development for his country. Almost 90% of the population are Buddhist and the values of the religion underpin the policies that the government has made. A key Buddhist perspective is that there should be a return to a more simple lifestyle and they assert that there is a fundamental need to refocus our lives away from consumerism and to look inwards through mindfulness and compassion as a way to view the outer world (Habito, 2007).

Bhutan is still one of the least developed countries (LDCs) in the world. The UN is supporting all 45 countries recognised as LDC in order 'to accelerate sustainable development in the places where international assistance is needed the most' (UN conference, 2023). It is expected that Bhutan will move off this register by the end of 2023 and will no longer fit the criteria of an LDC due to the changes that have taken place in the country.

The progress towards meeting the SDGs has been impressive. It is the only country in the world which is carbon neutral. Sixty per cent of the land must be covered with the forest at any time in an attempt to avoid deforestation. As a result, the forests act as a giant carbon sink which absorbs carbon dioxide produced by using firewood and industrial development.

> There are so many interesting aspects to Bhutan's drive to sustainability. They have banned the use of plastics and biodegradable products or materials such as jute. They have also banned tobacco in public areas including streets and it is not produced in the country. As part of their religious beliefs, they do not kill animals or birds and in fact, anyone caught killing an endangered bird such as the black-necked crane would be imprisoned. Laws against homosexuality have been overturned and women have always had equal status within communities. In relation to economic development, they have focussed on sustainable tourism by following the premise of 'high-value low-impact tourism'. Each tourist must pay 200$ a day to stay in the country and has to use tour companies. In this way, the number of tourists is reduced but the income from each is high. The aim is to bring money into the country without destroying the environment or the traditions and beliefs of the population.
>
> In harmony with their religious beliefs Bhutan is the only country to use Gross National Happiness (GNH) as a measure of economic and moral progress, with its four pillars of good governance, sustainable socio-economic development, cultural preservation and environmental conservation.
>
> Bhutan is a real example of how religious belief and sustainability can go hand in hand and provides an excellent case study to discuss in class.

In the classroom

RE lessons should be the place for discussion and debate and both really require careful planning by the teacher to make them successful and children need to have good subject knowledge of the content for there to be deep learning. In addition, RE is about teaching sensitive and controversial subjects; children will have different views about environmentalism, climate change, sustainability and religion. Beliefs are personal and therefore it is essential that the classroom environment is a 'safe space' where they can air their views, whatever they may be without fear of ridicule or censure. Some children may be very anxious about the future, or they may be from a background where climate change is not accepted so discussion must be open and allow for differing views to be aired. Key elements of a successful debate are that children learn how to listen to each other with respect and tolerance, to use evidence to justify their views and to be prepared to change their perceptions based on the arguments. This is what education is all about!

Activities to develop subject knowledge

Children need to have a good understanding of the broad spread of sustainability goals and what they might look like in action. The activities that have been suggested above are aimed at upper KS2 children but there are many ways that you can integrate RE and sustainability into your teaching at KS1 or lower KS2.

ACTIVITY – DEVELOPING SUBJECT KNOWLEDGE 1

Print and cut out the elements of the diagram in Figure 10.1, and give these to the children and ask them to reconfigure these into their own diagram. Present this as a puzzle and they could work in pairs or threes to decide how they might fit them together. They could then add to this by brainstorming what ways they could practically implement some of those goals and add them to the diagram on post-its. Or they could create a 3D object such as a flower - what would they put as the roots, the leaves, the flowers - what would each section represent? They all need to understand what the terms mean and be able to explain them.

Having established what might be meant by sustainability in terms of RE, they now need to explore different religions to see how they relate to the circles that they have created above. Using different colours for different religions they can link the religion, for example Islam, to the relevant circles and find a small quote to demonstrate its connection.

They could create a visual to represent each religion - a symbol that sums up their view about the natural world around them, the economy, and the social and cultural dimensions of sustainability. It is probably wise not to give the groups one religion each as you want them to really recognise similarities and differences in approach to these four fundamental pillars or circles.

It is important that they understand that not everything a religion believes may support sustainability. You could have statements from different religions around the class. For example, views from some Evangelical Christians denying climate change or Catholic belief that there should be no contraception. Why might these views go against sustainability?

ACTIVITY – DEVELOPING SUBJECT KNOWLEDGE 2

The unsung heroes of sustainability are the Indigenous people of the world - living in places such as the Brazilian rainforest, the Prairies, the Australian outback and the frozen North - The Native Americans, Yanomami, Aborigines and Sami to name just a few. An investigation about these people and their ways of life could be structured to be appropriate across the Key Stages. Children will love to find out about their way of life through enquiry-based learning.

What key questions would they want to ask?

They could make dioramas showing the landscape and the homes that the people live in and their way of life, or they could make their own version of an Indigenous community home in the roleplay area or outside.

How are their ways of life sustainable?

What do they believe?

And how do their beliefs affect the way that they interact with their environment?

This can then move into an investigation of their present-day fights to protect the land and their way of life. Read about the Yanomami tribe in the article linked in the Further Reading and Resources section.

ACTIVITY – ENCOURAGE DEBATE AND CRITICAL THINKING

Problem solving is a really good way for children to consider the issues having got a secure understanding of what is meant by sustainability and how religious beliefs may support this.

A scenario could be set up: There is a need for more cattle in an area as they can be sold as meat at a high price but there is not enough land and the area available is rainforest. An Indigenous tribe live in the area and are poor so they would be given some money for the land. There is a demand from consumers for the beef to make more fast-food takeaways. What are the issues and how might they resolve them? They could take on different roles.

The case study on Bhutan could be launched by setting the scene - a small unnamed mountainous but beautiful country. Simple way of life, very traditional but poor. No money for education or health care. You could put in lots more detail here. In their groups, they can think about what would they do to try and improve life for people. Once they have come up with ideas, they would then need to think about how they could do this in a sustainable way - considering getting a balance between all four pillars, or circles of sustainability.

This could then lead to an investigation about Bhutan itself and finding out the ways in which they have approached this.

When considering Bhutan, they could create their own tourism brochure, find out about Buddhism, and do a version of the eight-fold path towards sustainability or create a collage about Bhutan grouping images according to the circles that they link to.

The GNH register is an interesting idea to explore-what makes the children happy? What criteria would they have to make a judgment about GNH. You can then share the Bhutanese GNH criteria. Do they match theirs? How do they fit into Buddhist beliefs? Would the children now change their criteria? They could create a class GNH register.

Debate is so important in this topic, and it is easy to focus on countries far away. They should be able to make connections to life in their community today. What can the children do to make a difference? What beliefs do they hold?

Again, you can create a subject for debate – maybe about their local area. Or they could consider what local religions might do to support their area in terms of sustainability. You might have a more philosophical debate – what is the point of looking after the environment? Climate change is just a myth – discuss. Or they could consider which religions they feel most support environmentalism and why.

When organising a debate make sure that all are involved in some capacity. It may be that you give them a stance that they have to justify – each group might plan their opening speech and then the debate could widen and someone else could do a closing speech. Or you might have one spokesperson for each group and the others pass them written points that they have researched for them to use to support their argument. You could also have some who are reporters who are listening out for the best point or the best delivery of a speech. Children could also 'cross the floor' in other words, if they felt that the arguments were particularly strong in another group, they could change their allegiance. Another way to organise a debate is in table groups. This can be less daunting for many, and they can gain confidence in speaking in front of a smaller number of people. Each table could have a large dice with questions on four of the six sides. They roll the dice to decide which question they are going to answer and then have some time to find evidence both for and against before starting the debate. The two blank sides are for them to decide as a group on two other questions that would like to consider.

Of course, you need to set up expectations before any debate of this nature but involve the children in deciding what the golden rules for debate might be as it helps them understand the need to have such rules of behaviour. Discussion is a fundamental aspect of an RE lesson. When considering sustainability as a set of beliefs it encourages children to know and understand different religions, apply, and interpret views in the context of their own experiences and lives and evaluate and analyse their findings. Most importantly of all they will be exploring a topic that all of us must engage with.

CHAPTER SUMMARY

This chapter has sought to explore the way that religious beliefs can both support, and detract, from a sustainable approach to living. It has considered the importance of including sustainability as a set of fundamental beliefs within RE lessons providing children the opportunity to debate what the UN has described as 'the defining crisis of our time'. It is essential that our children are educated about what is happening and how we can all make a difference. The use of a case study such as Bhutan can help children to understand some of the issues, and possible solutions, in creating a sustainable way of living that will hopefully lead to a GNH measure for all of us.

We are all visitors to this time, this place. We are just passing through. Our purpose here is to observe, to learn, to grow, to love… and then we return home.

Australian Aboriginal saying

Further reading and resources

Honi and the Carob Tree

Read the story here: https://www.emanuelnyc.org/2021/01/25/the-story-of-honi-and-the-carob-tree/

Or watch this animation of the story here: https://www.youtube.com/watch?v=6Lge_gzF95E

In the amazon rainforest, an indigenous tribe fights for survival (2022) OHCHR. Available at: https://www.ohchr.org/en/stories/2022/08/amazon-rainforest-indigenous-tribe-fights-survival (Accessed: 29 June 2023).

Berry, E. (2014) Religion and sustainability in global civil society. some basic findings from Rio+20. *Worldviews: Global Religions, Culture, and Ecology*, 18(3): 269–288.

Moss, F. (2021) Investigating RE and the environment. RE Today.
Power Bratton, S. (2020) *Religion and the Environment*. Abingdon: Routledge.

UN (2016) Environment, Religion and Culture in the context of the 2030 agenda for sustainable development. https://wedocs.unep.org/bitstream/handle/20.500.11822/8696/-Environment,_religion_and_culture_in_the_context_of_the_2030_agenda_for_sustainable_development-2016Environment,_religion_and_culture_in_the_context_.pdf?sequence=2&amp%3BisAllowed=

UN (2012) Report of the United Nations Conference on Sustainable Development. Available at: http://www.un.org/ga/search/view_doc.asp?symbol=A/CONF.216/16&Lang=E

UN (2015) Transforming Our World: The 2030 Agenda for Sustainable Development. Resolution adopted by the General Assembly on 25 September 2015. Reference (A/70/L.1). Available at: http://sustainabledevelopment.un.org/post2015/transformingourworld

World Council of Churches (2015) Statement from Religious Leaders for the Upcoming COP21 United Nations Climate Change Conference. Paris. December 2015. Available at: https://www.oikoumene.org/en/resources/documents/wccprogrammes/diakonia/climate-change/statement-from-religious-leaders-for-theupcoming-cop21

References

Habito, R. L. F. (2007). Environment or earth sangha: Buddhist perspectives on our global ecological well-being. *Contemporary Buddhism*, *8*(2): 131–147.

Narayanan, Y. (2013) Religion and sustainable development: analysing the connections. *Sustainable Development*, *21*(2): 131–139.

Sachs, J. D. (2014) Sustainable development goals for a new era. *Horizons*, *1*: 106–119.

United Nation (1987) *Brundtland Report, Our Common Future*. Available at: https://www.brundtland.co.za/2022/08/03/brundtland-report-1987-our-common-future/

UN (2023) *United Nations Conference on the Least Developed Countries*. https://www.unep.org/events/conference/5th-united-nations-conference-least-developed-countries-ldc5#:~:text=The%20Fifth%20United%20Nations%20Conference,progress%20on%20the%20road%20to

11

UNDERSTANDING OUR WORLD CHALLENGES THROUGH MATHEMATICS

KARIN DOULL AND SUSAN OGIER WITH TANYA BASTIAN

LINKS TO CORE CONTENT FRAMEWORK

1.3, 3.6, 4.3

SUSTAINABLE DEVELOPMENT GOALS

GOAL 4: Quality Education
GOAL 13: Climate Action

KEY WORDS

Technonature; Critical Maths Education (CME); formatting; modelling; problem-solving; investigation; algorithm; statistics; data; super wicked problems

11 Understanding our world challenges through mathematics

CHAPTER OBJECTIVES

This chapter will:

- Consider the importance of locating mathematics in a real-world context.
- Examine what is meant by modelling and statistics in primary mathematics and their relevance as tools for understanding climate change.
- Apply data handling techniques to help children understand climate change.
- Explore the role of critical thinking in mathematics.
- Suggest problem-solving practical investigations to explore models that present climate changes.

Introduction

As the effects of climate change become more evident, and the need for us all to rethink how we live our lives in a more sustainable way becomes ever more apparent with each passing year, this could be a good time to take a critical look at how maths is taught in primary education and what we can do to help children understand how to use their mathematical knowledge. Mathematics is forefronted as a 'core' area of learning in the 2013 iteration of the national curriculum (DfE, 2013), and indeed no one will dispute that numeracy is a key skill in every area of our lives. What could be disputed, however, is children's understanding of the practical application of mathematics in how they view the world, its problems (our problems), and how maths skills can be used to resolve or mitigate against those very problems. Incredibly, not only our world but our whole universe is built and exists as a huge mathematical equation – filled with patterns, symmetry and geometric design (Lewis, 2014). These designs are present in every tiny insect, every feather of a bird, every leaf on a plant, every ripple on a stream and in our own DNA. What a fascinating concept to explore with your class! In this chapter, we shall look at ways in which you can help the children you teach to become more understanding of why we study mathematics, and how we might apply key mathematical principles to understand and improve the world around us. We shall look at literacies needed to utilise mathematical concepts to prepare children for their futures in a world that we cannot yet imagine – a world where artificial intelligence (AI) might become one – or even two – steps ahead of humanity. We will examine the value of data collection and think about how we can teach children to use data to make predictions and models for the future. This is a maths chapter with a difference: we are not going to tell you how to teach national curriculum mathematics! Rather, we are going to help you think about why children need to be numerate, the relevance of maths in every aspect of how we live, and how they will be able to apply their knowledge to their real lives in the future and encourage hope and resourcefulness for generations to come.

Numeracy: Maths in a real-world context

I wonder if you asked children in your class why they are learning maths – what would they say? Perhaps they might feel that it is important so that they get a good job one day, or maybe they will think that they do this just so that they can pass a test. Misconceptions around maths are abundant! School maths often seems to be mostly about following a formula and getting the sums right – learning by rote and practising until perfect. The sheer weight of statutory content in the English primary national curriculum means that it can become rather difficult for teachers to inject a sense of enjoyment and relevance as they concentrate their efforts on coverage. In our everyday lives, however, we use mathematics all of the time, and sometimes this is, indeed, made easier by having the ability to calculate quickly and being in the position of having deeply embedded knowledge such that we can easily and quickly draw on our maths learning (e.g. by having our times-tables at the tip of our tongue).

This begs the question of why maths is taught in such an isolated way in schools. Jain (2022) argues that this is an outdated mode that is not good enough for the challenges that today's children will face in the future. She suggests that teaching mathematics as a stand-alone subject does not give us the chance to 'allow the deep understanding and connectivity that is needed between areas of knowledge and does not allow children to go with their curiosity and to develop a true appreciation and comprehension of the world around them' (2022, p194). It is a false view of mathematics that we are promoting by focussing solely on content without context. Connectivity is a vitally important concept here. In relation to our focus on developing children's understanding of the climate emergency and sustainable living – making links between our actions as a species and what is happening in the natural world is a first step towards achieving that understanding. Jain argues for a more balanced approach that is about situating mathematics in the real world so that it becomes a meaningful learning experience for all children. In providing a high-quality mathematics education for the future, she says, 'we have the opportunity to reconsider and reimagine how we teach mathematics – to move away from the process-driven discrete teaching which has been developed to fulfil a need that was present in the past but is no longer the case for the new landscape in which we find ourselves' (2022, p194).

REFLECTIVE QUESTIONS

Where do you see a place for mathematics in teaching young children about the climate crisis and sustainable living?

Do you plan interdisciplinary projects for your class to promote the practical application of mathematical concepts?

In order to promote a more practical and engaging approach to teaching mathematics, we need to help children see and understand its relevance in our everyday activities. There seems little time for this view in the English version of the national curriculum, so let's take a look at another model of a national curriculum from within the UK and see if there is anything useful that we could adopt. The Welsh curriculum aims to enable learners who are ambitious and capable; healthy and confident individuals; enterprising and creative contributors; and ethical and informed citizens (Welsh Gov, 2015). The discipline focus for mathematics keeps these aims at its heart by encouraging an understanding of maths as a language that crosses cultures and communities, and where learning is focussed on connectedness, whether that is through real-life scenarios or in cross-curricular project work. Teachers are granted autonomy to design their own curriculum to inspire and make learning meaningful, and they use the guidance provided for this. Therefore, it is easier to relate mathematical learning to topics of current interest or to explore contemporary issues.

> **PAUSE FOR THOUGHT**
>
> Have a look at the Welsh guidance for Mathematics and Numeracy here: https://hwb.gov.wales/curriculum-for-wales/mathematics-and-numeracy/
>
> Compare it to the English curriculum for mathematics here: https://assets.publishing.service.gov.uk/government/uploads/system/uploads/attachment_data/file/335158/PRIMARY_national_curriculum_-_Mathematics_220714.pdf
>
> How can you develop your maths lessons to increase a sense of connectivity with children's current lives and with their futures?

Early years and maths

Another key difference between the two curricula is the lack of prescription for children aged seven and under, making the Welsh curriculum more in line with European countries, where children do not start formal schooling until this age. In the crucial early years, children's mathematical development happens through playful interactions with others, whether at home with parents or in the early education setting. Mathematical concepts are bound together with lived experiences and make sense *because* of those lived experiences. Taylor (2013) acknowledges that children need to develop an enjoyment of learning in the subject area and that this can be achieved by ensuring topics are related to children's interests and by providing practical opportunities to come across mathematical problems to solve. For example, she suggests using the outdoors, nature and the built environment to create a space for observational work and exploration of topical themes mathematically. Language, and thus engaging in dialogue using mathematical and environmental vocabulary, is key. Children will accrue positive dispositions and attitudes towards maths learning and the environment through their interactions with others. This presents us with a sound basis for developing mathematical literacy around climate change and living sustainably as children move up and onwards through school.

Exploring concepts of mathematical literacy, criticality and climate change

Mathematical representations and models are used daily to organise information (Barwell, 2013; Halliwell and Ng, 2022). Mathematics is seen as a global language that communicates in a rational, logical and neutral form (Barwell, 2013; Haylock and Manning, 2019; Le Roux Brown et al., 2022; Skovsmose, 2014). Haylock and Manning reflect that 'many everyday transactions and real-life problems – and most forms of employment – require confidence and competence in a range of basic skills' (2019, p1). As we have already established – there is no life without mathematics. Mathematics engenders all areas of learning, and since recent times technology further allows us to create sophisticated data and models that shape the world – and this is now the world that children inhabit. English and Mulligan (2013) observe how even young children today are exposed to computer technology and social media, and so have access to a range of data formats. Skovsmose suggests that we live in *'technonature'*, where we no longer live in nature itself, but in an environment that is 'reconstructed by means of technology' (2014, p340).

> **REFLECTIVE QUESTIONS**
>
> Think about how different occupations use mathematics or list the different ways in which you use maths on a daily basis.
>
> Do you agree with Skovsmose's description of technonature? Does this relate to your life?
>
> Are there any places where you do not think this description applies?

How can we use the concept of *technonature* to understand the climate?

It is difficult to say anything very specific about climate change or even be sure that climate change is occurring without mathematics.

(Barwell, 2013, p28)

Here, Barwell highlights the essential role that mathematics has in presenting and shaping understanding of climate change. If Barwell suggests mathematics is integral to considering climate change, just what role does the subject play? Statistical data are used to illustrate the findings of scientists in relation to weather and climate events, melting glaciers, rising temperatures and other evidence of climate change. It is important to consider carefully how this information is both created and used. Graphs and charts provide quantitative but not qualitative data. We may be given information about a specific phenomenon but not on how that affects the people of the area concerned (Barwell, 2013). This means that social dimensions of that information, which can highlight inequality are not so accessible (Abtahi et al., 2017; Hunter, 2022). In order to recognise the effect that is being produced by the statistics we need to be able to critically interrogate the data (Halliwell and Ng, 2022; Skovsmose, 2014; Stefferson, 2021).

Critical mathematics education

Skovsmose (2014) recognises the ethical aspect of mathematics teaching. With criticality can also come an appreciation of social justice that asks us to know that maths is not neutral. Mathematical data are created by humans who select what to include or ignore. We are often not aware of how and by whom this information is generated (Barwell, 2013; Skovsmose, 2014; Stefferson, 2021). The objective of the evidence often seems to be aligned with the political and social concerns of first-world organisations, ignoring the needs of those most affected by the issues. Values influence data use and so also detract from the view of mathematics as neutral (Stefferson, 2021). Barwell (2013) calls this function of mathematics to influence society 'formatting' through the selection and application of statistical information to make decisions that affect our lives, economically, politically and socially. Algorithms are created about which we have little knowledge or control. This is why we need to develop a critical appreciation of mathematical data, particularly such as is used in contested or controversial episodes, such as the COVID-19 pandemic or climate changes. As teachers, we must help children to question information rather than simply accept it. We need to move beyond the *instrumental* appreciation of maths, which is tied to performing successfully, to a recognition of the importance of *relational* understanding with a focus on developing a deeper conception of mathematical thinking (Ernest et al., 2016).

REFLECTIVE QUESTIONS

How do you see maths education and mathematics? Does it have an ethical element or is it rational, logical and neutral? Why do you think this?

How might mathematics format our lives without our knowledge?

What is mathematical literacy?

Mathematical literacy relates to the ability to use maths confidently and effectively. Fuertes et al. (2022) describe this as an amalgam of knowledge, skill and attitude: identifying the problem; selecting the correct tools to complete it; and attacking the problem with resilience. In order to do this, we need to ensure that we encourage problem-solving and critical thinking. Recent teaching strategies have begun to include the use of dialogue with additional challenges provided through more open-ended tasks. It is important that these should be related to real-world questions with authentic data (Halliwell and Ng, 2020). While we know that children respond with engagement and interest to such problems, we need to ensure that we are not merely using the problem to test mathematical knowledge. The focus is on the application of the maths to resolve the issue. In this, we have to balance both the maths and the real-world questions, which can be complicated. Steffeson (2021) talks about weak and strong questions. In a weak question such as 'Counting Pip the Penguin's Fish' (Twinkl, n.d.), the link to the climate change is tenuous at best. A strong question would look at how diminishing fish stocks might impact penguins – see more on this in the Further Reading and Resources section.

Barwell (2013) and Jones et al. (2000) suggest that we should consider a process in compiling mathematical responses to climate change:

- Description – identification of the relevant maths to be used.
- Prediction – critical application of mathematical knowledge and skills.
- Communication – presentation of the conclusions drawn.

Of course, we cannot expect primary children to discuss explicitly social justice and critical thinking. We can give them tools to ask the right questions, so they interrogate rather than accept the data. We can also encourage them to consider not just the information but what that data means for the planet (see Biodiversity Stripes activity in Section 2 of this chapter).

Wicked problems (Rittel and Weber, 1973) and *Super Wicked problems* (Aud et al., 2021) are terms for specific types of mathematical and scientific issues. The complexity of these problems requires interdisciplinary thinking and learning as highlighted earlier in the text. The terms are explained in Table 11.1 below.

Table 11.1 Wicked and super wicked problems

Wicked problem	Super wicked problem
A problem that is difficult or impossible to solve because of its complex and interconnected nature (IDF, n.d.)	Includes all the elements of wicked problems but also has additional constraints
No endpoint	Time is running out
No immediate test of potential solutions	No central authority to deal with issue
No opportunity to learn by trial and error	Those causing the problem want to sort it
Little opportunity to be wrong	Policies irrationally discount the future with weak commitments that keep getting pushed off as future needs

It is clear to see why climate change is designated a super wicked problem. It is also a potentially political issue which, however, might cause teachers to be wary of considering it within their classroom. School policies, parent voice, complexity, and lack of time and resources all make it a difficult topic to approach with primary children. Mathematical literacy provides children with agency and critical thinking allows them to ask the questions that require answering. We also know that climate change is a question children want to become involved with.

In the classroom

In this section, we shall look at ways that you can connect learning in mathematics to learning about the environment, the climate emergency and living sustainably. We shall begin by looking at a case study, which explains simple ways to develop mathematical learning through real-life themes. We then suggest some activities for you to try in the classroom.

> **CASE STUDY**
>
> Tanya Bastian, Year 2 teacher, mathematician and subject leader in a South-West London primary school, gives us an insight into how maths can underpin an emerging understanding of environmental concerns in the following case study:

Mathematics plays a pivotal role in our everyday lives, extending far beyond the confines of the classroom. Its positive impact can be observed in a number of real-life scenarios, enhancing our understanding, problem-solving abilities and decision-making skills. Connecting mathematics to real-life situations will allow pupils to understand the practical applications and relevance of the subject. By incorporating situations and examples from our everyday lives, teachers can demonstrate how mathematics is intertwined with the world around us. This approach is the best way to motivate students by showing them how maths can be useful, relevant and applicable in their daily lives. By encouraging pupils to embrace the positive uses of mathematics, they can navigate the complexities of the modern world and make informed decisions that impact our lives for the better. Using mathematics to teach pupils about climate change and sustainability will ensure that they develop a comprehensive understanding of the issues and are equipped with the necessary tools to contribute to positive change.

Here are some ways in which mathematics can enhance the teaching of climate change and sustainability in your school and classroom:

Data analysis

Mathematics provides the foundations for analysing and interpreting all kinds of data, which is crucial for understanding climate change. Students can analyse and explore temperature trends, carbon dioxide levels and other environmental data. They can discuss and present their findings on trends, patterns and the implications of climate change. Pupils can also exercise skills such as reading and interpreting graphs, calculating averages (mode, median, mean and range) and making predictions. Opportunities to build their own mathematical models to represent various aspects of climate change and sustainability can be easily incorporated within a classroom setting. This can be adapted appropriately for a range of year groups using a variety of models such as pictograms, bar graphs, line graphs and pie charts. By engaging in accurate data sets, pupils can develop a data-driven understanding of climate change and its impact.

Energy efficiency and renewable energy

Pupils can use mathematics to explore energy efficiency and the importance of conserving energy. They can explore and discuss real-world scenarios, such as comparing the energy consumption of different light bulbs or appliances. Mathematical challenges can be implemented by asking pupils to investigate and compare energy usage and costs, deepening their understanding of the environmental benefits of using energy-efficient technologies. Additionally, pupils can explore renewable energy sources and make calculations related to solar or wind power generation, such as estimating energy output or analysing cost-effectiveness.

Carbon footprints

Mathematics enables pupils to calculate and compare carbon footprints; they can explore how various human activities contribute to greenhouse gas emissions. Pupils can research and calculate the carbon footprint of different everyday actions, such as energy consumption, food habits or transportation choices. As a result, pupils will have a clear understanding of the environmental impact of different choices, and this will encourage them to adopt sustainable practices that will tackle the climate crisis in the future.

Population growth and resource consumption

Pupils can use mathematical models to understand and demonstrate how population growth affects the demand for food, water and energy. They can explore mathematical concepts such as exponential growth, probability, ratio and proportion to understand the impact of populations on the environment. This will also enable them to evaluate the likelihood and potential consequences of different climate scenarios, fostering a more informed approach to climate change mitigation.

Waste management and recycling

In society today, it is imperative that pupils are aware of waste management and the importance of recycling. Engaging in investigations involving calculating recycling rates and waste reduction percentages can deepen pupils' understanding of the scale of waste and its environmental consequences.

Economic analysis

Economics plays a crucial role in both understanding and addressing sustainability and climate change. Pupils can investigate and evaluate the economic feasibility of renewable energy projects such as sustainable transport systems and new and upcoming environmental initiatives. Pupils will be well-equipped in facing challenges associated with sustainability.

Integrating mathematics into climate change and sustainability education allows pupils to develop a deeper and more practical understanding of these topics. It makes concepts less abstract and more relevant, empowering students to address climate change and enabling them to make informed decisions and take action for a sustainable future.

11 Understanding our world challenges through mathematics

ACTIVITY – BIODIVERSITY STRIPES

This activity combines maths, english, science and art focussing on helping children to recognise the decline in nature within the British Isles. This decline is represented not only in the habitat and species loss but also within personal experiences of the natural world.

- Investigate the Biodiversity Stripes website: https://biodiversitystripes.info/global
- Go to the *Nature* tab. This shows the decline of the use of the word 'nature' since the 1880s. It also shows the increase in the usage of the word 'me' since 1990s.
- Discuss with children what that might mean.
- Ask: how many children have watched a TV programme about nature, accessed the CBBC Newsround Nature channel or read a book about nature this week?

The Oxford Dictionary began removing words linked to nature and replacing them with technological words.

Introduce children to the book, *Lost Words* by Robert MacFarlene and Jackie Morris: https://www.johnmuirtrust.org/john-muir-award/ideas-and-resources/literacy-and-nature/the-lost-words

a. Select a series of words linked to nature. Ask children if they think they know these words, then ask them to define them.
b. Ask children to think of three other words related to nature that they know. Are there any common words? Which ones stand out? Are there any misconceptions?
c. Create a class Wordle with these.
d. Record this information using data handling (graphs/pie charts/pictograms).

ACTIVITY HOW MANY BIRDS?

Visit the Birds Trust for Ornithology website: https://www.bto.org/our-science/case-studies/garden-birdwatch-and-our-garden-and-urban-bird-research

Look at the chart showing sightings of garden birds from 1995 to 2019.

Make a chart to show patterns of rise or fall. For example, look for birds that have stayed the same gone up less/more than five points, or gone down by less/more than five points.

Look at data collected by RSPB, Big Garden Bird Watch: https://www.rspb.org.uk/get-involved/activities/birdwatch/

Discuss the different types of data – encourage children to be thoughtful and critical in their discussion.

Create your own bird survey! Publish your data on the school newsletter or website.

ACTIVITY – CLIMATE STRIPES

This activity allows children to engage with authentic real-life data related to warming temperatures.

Visit Climate Stripes website: https://showyourstripes.info/s/globe

Go to *Global region* and 'the Labelled Stripes' tab. Explain to children that this is a representation of aggregated temperature data across the globe from 1860 (the beginning of the industrial age) to present. Each stripe represents one year.

a. What do children think the colours mean (blue/cold, red/hot)?
b. What do children think this shows about world temperatures? This period comes after such anomalies as the medieval warm period or the little ice age.

Go to tab: *Bars with Scale* - this will show the same data but in a different representation. Which do children prefer and why? Can they use mathematical vocabulary in their response?

Split your class into groups and give each group a region to look at using *Bars with Scale*. Ask each group to look at four specific dates (1910/1939/1989/2010) for their area and categorise them (very light blue/red, light blue/red, blue/red, mid blue/red, dark blue/red, very dark blue/red)

Use information to create graphs or other data representations with the data they have collected.

As a class, monitor temperature readings at a regular time each day over a period of time and create your own class 'stripes' chart.

CHAPTER SUMMARY

In this chapter, we have considered the concept of mathematics as being central to our very existence, and how we can teach children of primary school age to understand its relevance in the everyday. We have critiqued the perception that maths is learned purely in order to progress well in education or in the world of work and have argued that numeracy should be grounded within real-world issues and problems in order to make it relevant for children of all ages. We have suggested a range of activities and themes for you to try in the classroom to inspire the children you teach to become mathematically literate, and to help them understand how they can be part of the resolution of the climate crisis.

Further reading and resources

https://friendoftheearth.org/conservation-project/save-the-penguins/

Read more about the Save the Penguins campaign at friendoftheearth.org.

https://ltl.org.uk/resources/maths-outdoors-in-early-years/
This free download from Learning Through Landscapes is full of ideas on how to engage children in mathematical thinking within the natural world.

https://playofthewild.com/2020/09/14/outdoor-maths-activities-ks2-teaching-maths-outside/
At KS1 and 2, here are some ideas from Play of the Wild.

https://www.nspcc.org.uk/globalassets/documents/fundraising/number-day/number-day-resources-2020/ns012_mot_fibonacci_numbers_worksheet_ks2_aw.pdf
Explore Fibonacci numbers with this simple worksheet from NSPCC.

https://www.mathsisfun.com/numbers/fibonacci-sequence.html
…and here from Maths is fun!

References

Abtahi, Y., Gøtze, P., Stefferson, L., Hauge, K. H. and Barwell, R. (2017) Teaching climate change in mathematics classrooms: an ethical responsibility. *Philosophy of Mathematics Education Journal*, *32*: 1–18.

Aud, G., Berstein, S., Cashore, B. and Levin, K. (2021) Managing pandemics as super wicked problems: lessons from and for COVID-19 and climate crisis. *Policy Sciences*, *54*: 707–728.

Barwell, R., (2013) Mathematics and politics, Climate change in the mathematics classroom 27–37. In D. Leslie and H. Mendick (eds.), *Debates in Mathematics Education*. Abingdon: Routledge.

DfE (2013) *Mathematics Programmes of Study KS1 and 2*. Available at: https://assets.publishing.service.gov.uk/government/uploads/system/uploads/attachment_data/file/335158/PRIMARY_national_curriculum_-_Mathematics_220714.pdf

English, P. and Mulligan, T. (2013) *Reconceptualising Early Mathematics Learning*. London: Springer.

Ernest, P. et al. (2016) *The Philosophy of Maths Education*. Cham: Springer International Publishing AG.

Fuertes-Prieto, M. et al. (2022) Using mathematics to teach climate change to pre-service teachers: is knowledge enough? *European Journal of Teaching and Education*, *4*(3): 49–55.

Halliwell, T. and Ng, O. T. (2022) Imaging possibilities: innovating mathematics (teacher) education for sustainable futures. *Research in Mathematics Education*, *24*(2): 128–149.

Haylock, D. and Manning, R. (2019) *Mathematics Explained for Primary Teachers*, 6th edition. London: Sage.

Hunter, J. (2022) Challenging and disrupting deficit discourses in mathematics: positioning young and diverse learners to document and share their mathematical funds of knowledge. *Research in Mathematics Education*, *24*(2): 187–201.

Interaction Design Foundation (n.d.) *What Are Wicked Problems?* Available at: https://www.interaction-design.org/literature/topics/wicked-problems

Jain, P. (2022) Balancing the equation. In S. Ogier (ed.), *A Broad and Balanced Curriculum in Primary Schools*, 2nd edition. London: Sage, pp187–199.

Jones, G. et al. (2000) A framework for characterising students' statistical thinking. *Mathematical Thinking and Learning, 2*: 269–308.

Le Roux Brown, K., Coles, A., Halliwell, T. and Ng, O. T. (2022) Editorial for Special Issue on innovating mathematics in precarious times. *Research in Mathematics Education, 24*(2): 117–127.

Lewis, T. (2014) *What's the Universe Made of? Math, Says Scientist*. Live Science. Available at: https://www.livescience.com/42839-the-universe-is-math.html

Rittel, H. and Webber, M. (1973) Dilemmas in the general theory of planning. *Policy Sciences, 4*(2): 155–169.

Skovsmose, O. (2014) *Critique as Uncertainty*. Charlotte: Information New Age Publishing.

Stefferson, L. (2021) *Critical Mathematics Education and Climate Change: A Teaching and Research Partnership in Lower Secondary Schools*. Thesis. Available at: https://www.reseachgate.net/publications/348882267 (Accessed: 3 June 2023).

Taylor, H. (2013) How children learn mathematics and the implications for teaching. In H. Taylo and A. Harris (eds.), *Learning and Teaching Mathematics 0-8*. London: Sage, pp3–18.

Welsh Gov (2015) *The Four Purposes of the Curriculum for Wales*. Available at: https://www.gov.wales/sites/default/files/publications/2018-03/the-four-purposes-of-the-curriculum-for-wales.pdf

12
EXPLORING OUR WORLD THROUGH MUSIC AND SOUND

LINKS TO CORE CONTENT FRAMEWORK

1.1, 1.2, 4.3, 4.4

SUSTAINABLE DEVELOPMENT GOALS

GOAL 3: Good Health and Well-being
GOAL 4: Quality Education
GOAL 13: Climate Action
GOAL 17: Partnerships to Achieve the Goal

PART 1: SOUND ENVIRONMENTS

ALASTAIR GREIG

> **KEY WORDS**
>
> Patterns; dynamics; timbre; texture; sound worlds; recycled materials; aural memory

> **CHAPTER OBJECTIVES**
>
> This chapter will:
>
> - Widen participation in creative music making.
> - Celebrate music's diversity and discover connections with children's lives.
> - Encourage a playful attitude with sound.
> - Develop teacher confidence in the subject and expand possibilities.
> - Listen objectively to a variety of sounds within nature.

Introduction

Anyone fortunate enough to have witnessed a solar eclipse will tell you how eerie the world becomes with the sudden absence of bird song. Equally reassuring is its return upon the reintroduction of light. As the sounds of nature became much more audible during the lockdown of 2020, due to reduced air and road traffic, this taught us all how important our local sonic environment is, and we must endeavour to sustain these areas for nature's music makers to thrive. There is no sound without nature – the naturalist Rachel Carson warned us of the consequences of taking nature for granted many years ago - and here we are, with many species on the edge of extinction because we have not heeded these messages. Their sound is life – and it is up to us to make sure we appreciate and look after it.

Creative music making should be part of every child's experience in primary school, but many teachers approach the subject with apprehension. One of the aims of this chapter is to offer an alternative approach which *all* can facilitate regardless of previous musical experience or available resources. I hope to point you toward answering a few common questions:

- When children make their own music what should we be listening for?
- How do we encourage musical creativity through engaging with natural sounds?
- How do we listen? Subjectively or objectively?

Playing with sound

As sound is one of the main components of music, the other being silence, it is imperative that all of us understand how breaking music excerpts into smaller sonic elements will enable all pupils to engage in musical creativity and understand the importance of their own sound worlds. This is not as complex as it may appear but does necessitate listening objectively.

A resource on our doorstep

We all agree that preserving our environments for wildlife, flora and fauna is a crucial part of controlling climate change and, of course, this means that the sonic environment will remain audible. To encourage the development of a *critical, thinking ear*, we must raise awareness of what constitutes the sound world around us. We are surrounded by noise: technology has given us a range of personal devices that emit sound, such as our mobile phones, and we can often block out natural sounds by using earphones. We can distinguish between all kinds of sound, but how many times do we stop, put down the phone and just listen? Not all the sounds will be beautiful, some may even be unpleasant, but they are part of the texture of your sound world, and it is a resource that changes on a daily basis. All we have to do is take time and listen.

REFLECTIVE QUESTION

Get up very early one morning, make a cup of tea, wrap yourself in a blanket and open your window or go outside. Spend time LISTENING. What do you hear? Hopefully, you will hear nature's orchestra: the dawn chorus. How does this sound make you feel? Make a recording of the birdsong and play it for the children in your class for a moment of mindfulness at some point during the school day.

Getting started: The elements of music

The following example, showing the **elements of music**, outlines a simple compositional process that we can all follow, and indicates where and when the pupils will be exploring different components of sound:

- Dynamics-quiet and loud
- Duration-long and short
- Pitch-high or low
- Silence
- Tempo-fast and slow
- Texture-how many sounds
- Timbre-quality of sound

What is in the National Curriculum?

The three pillars of the National Curriculum for Music are listening, performing and composing and the aim is to integrate them. The process above does just that without the teacher having to demonstrate any musical skills of their own, but this does require an understanding of how music is assembled through exploring and manipulating the elements as listed.

Throughout the centuries composers have been fascinated with the natural sound world and in the 20th century several key historical figures made this the centre of their compositional world. The French composer, Olivier Messiaen, notated bird songs from around the globe and in works such as 'Catalogue des Oiseaux', 'Le Merle noir' and 'Oiseaux Exotiques' incorporated the transcribed melodies of birdsong into the fabric of the music.

The American composer, John Cage, took the opposite view. '4' 33' is a three-movement piece consisting of silence from the performer. The 'music' comes from the audience's tense breathing, the concert halls creak and groan, and sounds are heard from outside, in fact, anything at all is part of this performance. As I mentioned before, objectivity is the key. These examples obviously link with the national curriculum (NC) requirement that all pupils should:

> *perform, listen to, review and evaluate music across a range of historical periods, genres, styles and traditions, including the works of the great composers and musicians.*
>
> (DfE, 2013)

But who decides which genres, which style? What we are looking for are the ideas behind the music and how can we apply them appropriately in our classroom?

A simple listening activity is a catalyst for creative music making, exploring and discussing the local environment, working together and recreating their experience with their own compositional choices.

Imagine if all the year groups participated in this activity, created and performed their pieces for each other during the course of the school year. We would hear how they perceive the change in sounds from season to season, and it would heighten the importance of this unique resource, *their* sound worlds.

In the classroom

Simple steps-listening and creativity

Explore the sound around the school, and take your pupils on a sound walk. Make frequent stops and listen to all the sounds you can hear, natural and mechanical. Document by creating a sound map, and digitally record sounds as you walk along, including footsteps and talking. Do our sounds have an impact on the environment? Can we sense vibrations as our sounds move in the air and through the earth?

> *This simple activity develops the ability to distinguish sounds and vibrations; how they are combined; how loud or quiet; how high or low; long or short and so on. In other words, you are thinking about the elements, in this case texture, timbre, pitch, dynamics, duration.*

Once back in the classroom, it is time to explore and analyse. You will need a variety of sound-producing objects, some of which may be standard classroom percussion, and some may be part of your Junk Percussion set, which we will return to later.

The sounds you hear act as your primary resource for music making. At first, allow your pupils time and space to try to recreate the sounds they heard on the walk with the sonic resources available. This develops not only listening skills through comparing and analysing (*timbre*) and aural memory (*duration and structure*) but also promotes discussion on sound and begins to acquire an appropriate music-based vocabulary that extends beyond like and dislike.

The sound map that was created as you walked becomes a sound indicator:

- Where and when did you hear the sounds (*structure*)
- How many sounds (*texture*)
- High or low (*pitch*)
- Loud or quiet (*dynamics*)
- What kind of sound (*timbre*)

The map becomes a music score and it's a simple way to introduce the purpose of notation, a visual representation of sound.

The class then can recreate the sound walk but with the objects and follow the score (map) and refine and create their own piece of music.

The combined sounds may not be to everyone's taste but that is not the point. The process is the important aspect to focus on, the output will be raw, rough, and seemingly chaotic but this is how children develop their own critical ear and begin to understand how music works for them. Listen to how they use their instruments, combine them, and choose how to proceed.

That is the essence of composition.

Adapting this for the differing key stages would be relatively straightforward and here are a few suggestions:

ACTIVITY EARLY YEARS

- Outdoor listening for learning
- Recalling sounds and recreating using percussion instruments
- Combining two or more sounds
- Ordering sounds

If this simple activity could be integrated into the monthly plan one would, perhaps, be able to observe the development of listening skills which may have a much greater impact all round.

ACTIVITY KEY STAGE 1

- Simple sound maps
- Discussing sounds and developing vocabulary
- Exploring and comparing timbre (sounds)
- Recalling sounds (aural memory)
- Developing performing skills (more instruments and Junk Percussion)
- Understanding the principles of notation (sound represented in visual form)
- Creating a whole class composition

ACTIVITY KEY STAGE 2

- More complex sound maps
- Applying musical vocabulary
- Exploring timbre, texture, pitch, duration, dynamics and tempo
- Developing notational skills
- Discussing different sound environments
- Human impact upon the sound worlds
- Creating their own pieces in groups
- Developing performing skills
- Decision-making and problem-solving
- Using digital recording devices
- Music technology

Were this to become part of every primary school's curriculum we could create an online soundscape of our United Kingdom, as heard through the ears and minds of our pupils. Send sonic postcards (recordings of the pieces created and 'the walk') to schools in different parts of the nation or beyond. Perhaps I am getting beyond myself, but the potential is there.

Percussion with recycled materials

Every child in school should have access to a wide variety of pitched and non-pitched percussion instruments and be able to create music on a regular basis. I used the word *should* with good reason, as we all know that instruments cost money and budgets will always be tight. Creating unique sound objects through using recycled materials would add to the timbral possibilities for children to explore and create with. This method is not new and here is a brief overview of several genres of music, how they developed, why they sound as they do and how we can learn from their resourcefulness.

Tri-ni-dad and To-ba-go steel pans

The original instruments were disused oil drums, pans and lids! This provides children with an example of how an entire musical culture began with recycling. I am not proposing that all teachers should now try to appropriate 'Yellow Bird' on their Junk Percussion. In fact, I do not advocate any form of imitation at all. The evolution of this musical genre demonstrates why the music sounds as it does, provokes questions beyond the subject and gives one permission to allow the time and space for pupils to create with the sounds they can find. For this, all one needs are a few simple rhythmic patterns.

A simple starting point would be to clap the syllables of *Tri-ni-dad* followed by *To-ba-go*. The emphasis I leave to you, but as long as you repeat the patterns these then become your starting points, and the pupils begin to use rhythmic **ostinati** (repeated patterns).

Here you are exploring duration which includes rhythm, pattern and so on. Split the class into two groups and clap the two patterns at the same time (texture). As this repeats, you will find that the pattern fits into a cycle of beats but, as a group, this can happen naturally as there may be only one way for all to clap the rhythms.

These patterns become the building blocks as you can encourage the class to think of more Caribbean countries and transform these into ostinati. Add them to the existing patterns and let the children play with the sounds.

Transform the clapping patterns by allowing the class to explore your collection of Junk Percussion, using them to change the timbre, texture, dynamics, duration and tempo of their music. The next stage would be to give them a simple structure, such as ternary form (*verse-chorus-verse*), also referred to as A B A. Given that the group consists of five children, the resultant composition could resemble the example in Figure 12.1:

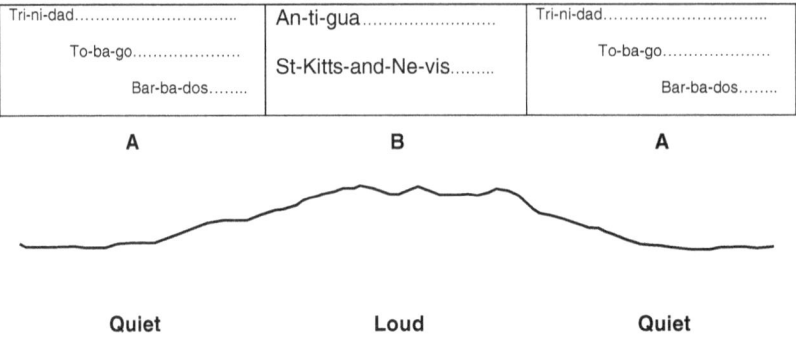

Figure 12.1   Ternary form as a three-part pattern

The group then can add more sounds if they wish, with or without a pattern, thus playing with texture, timbre, dynamics, rhythm and developing their aural memory, performance and notational skills and, of course, listening to each other. One could turn this into a class piece by adding groups together, one at a time, creating their own recycled musical sounds.

Let's now look at some other examples of resourceful and sustainable ways to make musical sounds, from indigenous cultures around the world.

Music from Bougainville, Papua New Guinea

Watch Bamboo Music in Tangari Village, Bougainville, Papua New Guinea

https://www.youtube.com/watch?v=jhh-y4feRcw

Musicians from this part of the world perform on hollowed-out tubes using small paddles. Applying the compositional process outlined above one could use the same plan but be specific about the type of object (i.e. hollow). The timbre changes instantly and should provoke the discussion about why music sounds the way it does because of where it comes from. Timbreor instruments may change, but there is more that unites all of our music making. Commonalities include employing patterns, using dynamics, working within structures and experimenting with textures to give but a few. One of the key points in working in this way is to enable children to understand more about how music works, not emotionally, but objectively and then developing the confidence to play, experiment, collaborate and create.

Women's Water Music: Vanuatu

Watch the women performing Water Music here: https://www.youtube.com/watch?v=vUUVEvffzSI

When there are few objects with which to create sound, nature offers other natural resources for us to explore. The women of Vanuatu, an island in the South Pacific Ocean, use the water in their local river to create sound. This music created by the women is directly related to the environment and to their own lives. How can we start to connect children to nature in our own environments? What sounds can we find that define *our* environment? Can we use them in a respectful and sustainable way?

A very important point to remember, do not play any of the music to the children before beginning any creative music lesson as it will quickly turn into a re-creative/imitative session, the antithesis of our aim. The most appropriate time for listening to the music would always be at the very end of the process, once all pieces had been created, performed and evaluated. The listening audience then will use their direct musical experience to inform their critical ear. They will be able to make a connection and understand a little more about why the music sounds as it does but without subjectivity.

I would recommend that all staff involved become immersed in whatever music you are planning to explore during planning and understand the need for objectivity. The plan is for the teacher to set the parameters, provide simple material, encourage experimentation and understand how music is constructed by allowing the pupils to play with the elements of sound.

CHAPTER SUMMARY

Music can be accessible for all if we change our perception of what we hear. If we can encourage children to listen objectively and process the sounds for themselves, make what they will with them and create their own music, they will develop an insight into how music works and apply that, perhaps, when they listen. Align that with the formulation of a widening vocabulary to define what they hear and move way beyond the subjective. These are just a few examples of music that offer you much more than would at first appear.

I hope that this is your own starting point and that you will go on to discover your own musical resource bank. Do not choose a piece because you like it, make an informed decision based on what you can hear after several times. Find a pattern, listen to the texture, distinguish between timbres, uncover the structure, be aware of dynamic changes and apply your understanding of the elements as you plan your child-centred, creative music-making activities.

Further reading and resources

These examples are from the output of John Cage. The first piece is all about the sounds one can hear when the music stops, and the second explores the sound of water. Could your pupils go and record what happens in the water tray in Reception? Could that provide a resource to create a piece with?

John Cage

4′33″
https://www.youtube.com/watch?v=AWVUp12XPpU

Water Walk
https://www.youtube.com/watch?v=v-h-M0UWxDA

Olivier Messiaen, Oiseaux Exotiques
https://www.youtube.com/watch?v=lmjETPAkF70

Le Merle Noir
https://www.youtube.com/watch?v=A_oVkSExZvA

The Australian Digeridoo provides a way to connect us, but also remains unique as a sound, it helps to explain why the environment is connected to sound and to our celebration of this. I prepare for this by creating a graphic score which explores the sustained drone of the didgeridoo, the movement of the male voice and the rhythm sticks. Listen closely and you will hear what I mean but remain objective, this is a very useful piece. Do not play this to your class first, only when they have completed their own response via your graphic score.

Saltwater Dusty Legune & Campbell Allenbar

https://www.youtube.com/watch?v=g95WNDmBdf4

https://www.youtube.com/watch?v=yG9ZX1FS20A

PART 2: CONNECTING CHILDREN TO THE ENVIRONMENT THROUGH MUSIC

HELEN MEAD, SARAH LLOYD AND JON AUDAIN

KEY WORDS

Connection; collaboration; awareness; creativity; engagement

CHAPTER OBJECTIVES

This chapter will:
- Appreciate how music connects us to our environment.
- Consider further the links between music, issues of climate change and sustainability.
- Understand how these issues are reflected in classroom practice.

Introduction

Music is a connector. It connects us to memories, people, moments and emotions. Music is universal – every culture on the planet uses music to communicate, celebrate and connect. This connection is something we can engage with when looking at climate change and sustainability education. A personal connection and an awareness of the environment and its natural world can lead to our young people developing a personal sense of responsibility for it.

Through music, we can connect ourselves to a larger entity. From lullabies and nursery rhymes in early childhood to music at weddings, funerals and live performances, music plays a vital role in the lives of most human beings. As young adults our taste in music can form the backbone of our identity, fashion choices and friendship groups.

We are living in a time when the impact of human actions on the environment is a very real and sometimes overwhelming issue for our young people (Jones and Whitehouse, 2022) and this can lead to them having to contend with anxiety.

> *Watching our natural world change, sometimes combined with feeling personal guilt or witnessing climate indifference and elected powers failing to act with the pace required, can evoke a variety of emotions, from anger and frustration to dread, powerlessness and hopelessness. It can be uncomfortable, overwhelming and paralysing.*
>
> (Wright and Osterloff, 2022, online)

As teachers, we need to support our children to connect with the emotions that learning about climate change can bring, and music is a tool with which to do this.

Through music, we can connect to those around us. When we make music with others, endorphins are released, and a sense of social bonding is created. Think about an energetic concert or festival, the audience moving in sync with the rhythm, singing together. To make changes to our environmental impact we need to work together towards a common goal, whether that be at a class, school, local or global community level.

Through music, we can connect to the world we are living in. From indigenous cultures, to popular music and classical genres, musicians have taken inspiration from the natural world. In an increasingly tech-based, fast-paced world, our young people can feel disconnected and isolated from nature. Listening and responding to music inspired by the natural world can bring children to connect with what is around them. It is only through this that an understanding of the issues of climate change and sustainability can have meaning to the individual.

REFLECTIVE QUESTIONS

- What music has importance in your life?
- Are there songs or pieces of music that connect you to a certain place, time or person?
- What music affects your mood? Does it make you cry or energise you?

Music has been and continues to be a powerful voice for expressing ideas, whether that be in classical works, protest songs or performance pieces. Through music we can help young people to connect with the natural world to express their emotions and find their voice. Music can become the 'golden thread' to weave through learning about sustainability and climate change. '*Through music, we can connect with our science, math, and even history counterparts to contribute to the narrative on nature and effectively promote change…*' (Lawler, 2019, n.p.). In this chapter, we shall offer a range of practical examples to engage children with learning about the environmental crisis through key musical themes. We will explore how music can help children connect to their own emotions, how it can raise their awareness of the world they are living in and how music can be a creative tool to express issues around environmental awareness and sustainability.

Musical activities for the classroom to promote sustainability and an awareness of climate change

ACTIVITY – MUSIC FOR CONNECTION 1 – EXPLORE HOW MUSIC CAN MAKE CHILDREN FEEL

Choose three contrasting pieces of music, one which you think may be calming, one which might create an energetic response, and one which may make the children feel happy, or even laugh!

Encourage children to relax and focus on their personal responses to the pieces. Invite children to connect to their physical response to the music using prompts such as: notice how you are breathing during this piece; notice if your body wants to move or remain still; do you notice a change in your heart rate?

Allow children to verbalise their responses and use this emotional connectivity during discussion on climate change.

Once you know the pieces that your children connect with and how they make them feel, play different pieces at different points throughout the day, when you want to energise or calm your children. It is important to note that until we share music with children, we don't know what will over-excite the nervous system or shift a mood, so the child becomes disengaged. Be aware of how you choose music for listening and well-being with children. Music can bring with it an emotional memory, so it can be helpful to use music that the children may be unfamiliar with. A good place to start can be with music from a third culture - one from which neither you nor the child belong.

Create a drawn response to a piece by taking a pencil for a walk. Use different colours and line styles in response to the music. For example, there might be a long smooth meandering line for a slow, calm piece, using greens and yellows to colour and draw whilst listening.

ACTIVITY – MUSIC FOR CONNECTION 2 – USE SINGING TO SUPPORT EMOTIONAL WELL-BEING

Singing is a fantastic way to create a general feeling of connection between your children and by its very nature create a sense of increased community and belonging. It is an inclusive activity which will improve mental health, social skills and self-confidence and allow your children to communicate in an expressive way. Singing improves children's mood with the release of positive neurochemicals such as endorphins and a reduction in the stress hormone (Keeler et al., 2015).

(Continued)

Unite your children as a class and harness the power of singing to support their emotional well-being and social closeness. Depending on the age of your children this might be singing a known song together such as a song from a current film/musical or chart hit.

ACTIVITY – MUSIC FOR AWARENESS 1 – USE SINGING AS A TOOL TO TEACH ABOUT CLIMATE CHANGE AND SUSTAINABILITY

In addition to supporting well-being, singing is a great way to raise awareness and engage with issues surrounding climate change and sustainability. You will find a wealth of songs and musicals around these themes. Creating performance opportunities that tackle environmental issues can be a simple concert or assembly to friends and parents, or on a larger scale a musical production where ticket sales could raise money towards an environmental cause. Coming together as a group or class can develop a sense of community and teamwork as well as communicate important messages about environmental awareness.

The offer of commercial packages for school productions is forever changing, and some will require purchasing to use with your children, but the powerful content and lyrics will support discussions and further aid understanding around the issues. Three examples are:

- 'Eddie the Penguin Saves the World' (https://www.outoftheark.co.uk) is a fantastic musical for children aged 4-8. Eddie discovers his world is changing, the ice is melting and goes on a mission to save the planet.
- 'Plastic Pirates' (https://www.theschoolmusicalscompany.com) for Key Stage 2 children considers the effects of plastic in the sea.
- 'The Big Green Adventure' (https://www.edgyproductions.com) encourages children to look at how fragile the planet is and what we can do about it.

Musicals and song banks from Fischy Music (https://www.fischy.com) and Sing Up (https://www.singup.org) will support whole school-themed weeks and aid focus for discussion in class. Although these resources need purchasing you will find songs such as 'One World' free from Portsmouth Music Hub's Song Source (https://www.portsmouthmusichub.org/songsource).

Singing is a fantastic way to raise awareness not only with the children but with the wider school community and can have a very powerful impact.

Indigenous music

Singing traditions are an integral part of the spiritual health of the ecosystem and the means by which biocultural knowledge is carried on over many generations and through shifting social and ecological contexts.

(Curran et al., 2019, p354)

It is vital that we support our young people to become 'global citizens' developing their knowledge of cultures around the world. The importance of the voice of indigenous people is slowly being recognised with twenty-eight indigenous representatives being invited to take part in decision-making and discussions at the UN Climate Change Conference, COP26.

Since the beginning of human interaction, stories, music, and song have been used to pass knowledge from generation to generation. Colonisation, the slave trade and past governments' laws and sanctions have played a huge role in the loss of indigenous songs and the vital knowledge and understanding of the natural world that they carry.

For many generations, indigenous cultures have lived alongside and in-harmony with the natural world around them. The knowledge of ancestors was passed down through song allowing this harmony to continue and be passed on. For example, the totemic songs of Aboriginal women in interior Australia were a rich source of knowledge of edible seeds. These seeds once played an important role in sustaining the people of this area. The songs and their performances showed techniques for seed production and made connections to the habitat and religion of the area (Fernandez-Llamazares and Lepofsky, 2019).

Connecting young people to the music of indigenous cultures will allow them to see how past generations have lived with the natural world and appreciate the importance of keeping this connection alive. This could also form part of a geographical study of another country, adding to the children's ability to personally connect with another country and culture. Allow the young people time to reflect on how we can learn from these indigenous cultures and their attitudes to the natural world.

ACTIVITY – MUSIC FOR AWARENESS 2 – EXPLORE INDIGENOUS AUSTRALIAN (ABORIGINAL) – SONGLINES

Share the meaning and context of 'songlines'. The video 'What are songlines?' This short video (can also guide your explanation: https://youtu.be/kVOG-RKTFlo. Discuss how these songlines are reflected in Aboriginal art. Explore the symbols in the art. What might they represent?

Listen to some examples of Aboriginal songlines and explore how sounds on the didgeridoo represent different animals.

Listen also to modern indigenous Australian artists such as Emily Wurramara. Children may spot connections to the natural world in her song 'Black Smoke'. https://www.youtube.com/watch?v=Z_PUJ2S4uww

Children could compose their own songline-inspired music, creating a 'map' of an imaginary journey through the Australian outback, or creating a musical journey through their local landscape.

> **REFLECTIVE QUESTIONS**
>
> - What can we learn about environmental awareness from the music of indigenous cultures?
> - How does the music of the cultures show a connection to the environment around them?

Classical music

Themes of nature can be found throughout many musical genres, none more so than classical music. The natural world is an infinite source of inspiration for many composers and through these pieces of music and the narrative they tell, children could be inspired and encouraged to tell nature's story through their own musical compositions.

> **ACTIVITY – MUSIC FOR CREATIVITY 1**
> **EXPLORE CLASSICAL MUSIC INSPIRED BY NATURE**
>
> ### Vivaldi's four seasons
>
> This piece of baroque music was composed by the Italian, Antonio Vivaldi in 1723. Each movement, written for strings, depicts a season of the year.
>
> Listen to each of the four movements and ask the children to make observations on the changes in the music and how they relate to the changes in the seasons. Invite the children to connect with the environment around them. Go outside and observe the sensations of the weather – what do they feel, hear and see. How might this translate into a musical piece? Try taking musical instruments outside and making the music there.
>
> ### Beethoven's Symphony No. 6 'Pastoral'
>
> Composed in 1808, Beethoven's Pastoral Symphony takes us on a journey from the city to the countryside. The five movements are entitled 'Joyful feelings upon arriving in the country', 'By the Brook', 'Peasant Merrymaking', 'The Thunderstorm' and 'The shepherd's song after the Storm'.
>
> Use this music to connect children to their own emotions when going into nature, compose their own music to portray a thunderstorm and even try a simple folk dance.
>
> This musical connection to the natural world is not just confined to the past. Contemporary composers and performers are addressing the issues of climate change with increasing urgency, adding a musical voice to the issues at hand. In 2016, Italian composer and pianist, Ludovico Einaudi, collaborated with Greenpeace to create a visually and aurally compelling performance. A film was made of him performing his minimalist composition, **'Elegy for the Artic'** on a specially built 'iceberg' while huge chunks of ice fell from the glacier behind him. American composer, John Luther Adams won the Pulitzer Prize for Music for his orchestral piece **'Become Ocean'** (2014). The piece immerses the listener in a sound world inspired by the oceans, evoking the melting of the ice caps and rising sea levels.

ACTIVITY – MUSIC FOR CREATIVITY 2 – EXPLORE COMPOSERS INSPIRED BY OUR PLANET

Explore the pieces listed above or others such as Hans Zimmer's '**Earth**' from the BBC Ten Pieces (https://www.bbc.co.uk/teach/ten-pieces/classical-music-hans-zimmer-earth/zh4k382) or pieces from **Earth Prom** 2022 (https://www.bbc.co.uk/events/ezdfbp) including **Earth Symphony** by Iain Farrington.

Create an art response to the piece. With older children this could be annotated with words to create an initial discussion.

Compose music to reflect earth: simple soundscapes describing features such as water or land moving towards creating motifs for these with older children.

Create a film by adding your images to the music using PowerPoint or iMovie.

REFLECTIVE QUESTIONS

- How can the arts play a role in changing attitudes and awareness of issues of sustainability and climate change?
- How can you plan to use the arts to promote learning about our changing climate in your school?

Popular music

The influence of pop music and pop musicians on our young people is huge. For decades musicians, performers and songwriters have used the platform of popular music to express their views and beliefs to a wide-ranging audience. Coinciding with the United Nations first ever discussion on the environment (1973), ecology and environmental issues became a topic for pop songs in the 1970s with performers such as Joni Mitchell (*Big Yellow Taxi*) and Marvin Gaye (*Mercy, Mercy Me* combining lyrical melodies and challenging lyrics to bring the issue into mainstream prominence. Performers as diverse as Billie Eilish (*All the Good Girls Go to Hell*), Michael Jackson (*Earthsong*), Metallica (*Blackened*) and Will.I.Am (*SOS Mother Nature*) have all lent their voices to the environmental cause.

ACTIVITY – MUSIC FOR ENGAGEMENT – EXPLORE LYRICS AND MUSIC VIDEOS

Explore the lyrics of some of the songs listed above with your class. Ask them to highlight the lines that stand out to them, contain imagery they like etc. Create a display of illustrated phrases taken from these songs.

(Continued)

Watch the music videos for some of these songs e.g. Earthsong (Michael Jackson) or Eyes Wide Open (Gotye). Discuss the images used and the effect it has on the person listening to the song. Children could create their own music videos, using their own artwork or photography inspired by the lyrics of the song.

ACTIVITY – MUSIC FOR COLLABORATION – EXPLORE SONGWRITING

As a class or school, choose an environmental topic to create a collaborative song. This could be as simple as turning the tap off when you're brushing your teeth (e.g. Brushing My Teeth (Barney the Dinosaur) or recycling the paper in the classroom (e.g. 3 Rs, Jack Johnson).

Once you have your topic, start with the chorus. Create a short, catchy line or two with a simple melody. Your verses could take the form of raps, created by each class in school. Create successful rap lyrics by rhyming two lines at a time (rhyming couplets) and making each line last **four** beats. Or you could use a song that already exists and re-write the lyrics to fit your topic or theme.

You can find simple backing tracks for songs online or why not commission a local musician to create the backing music for your school's environmental anthem?

REFLECTIVE QUESTIONS

- What impact will it have to involve the children in writing their own environmental songs?
- How might this be more powerful than singing a song that has been written by someone else?

The music industry

The impact of the music industry on the environment is a current hot topic and something that cannot be denied. Its production of vinyl records, CDs and merchandise creates plastic waste, with the decomposition life span of a record taking up to 1000 years (Tachev, 2022, online). Both the classical and popular music industry rely heavily on the income made from international touring, which has its own environmental impact from flying the artists across the world, to the travel of audiences, and the power required to run the venue. Even the streaming of music isn't a simple solution with data centres and cloud services needing powering and cooling. '*The carbon footprint of our gadgets, the internet and the systems supporting them account for 3.7% of global emissions. This equals the airline industry's share*'.

There is no easy solution – but an awareness of these issues and an industry-wide movement to look for solutions and make changes is what is needed, and some artists are beginning to lead the way.

The German orchestra 'Orchestra des Wandels' (https://www.orchester-des-wandels.de/#c68) aims to use different and unusual concert formats to reach people. Whilst the UK-based 'Orchestra for the Earth' (https://www.orchestrafortheearth.co.uk/) aims to inspire, educate and influence audiences through music connected with protecting our planet.

Singer Billie Eilish is one global superstar who is highlighting the issues of climate change and the music industry and is going to efforts to make a change. In June 2022, Eilish headlined 'Overheated', a six-day climate-focussed event at The O2, London. Panel discussions, presentations and keynote speakers aimed to increase awareness and spark conversation on a number of environmental issues including sustainable fashion and plant-based diets. Eilish also appears in the Overheated documentary (https://youtu.be/4suoAkkZy7c) discussing her own personal reaction to the climate emergency.

Other popular artists have also taken measures to make a change. In 2020, Massive Attack announced that their European tour would take place using train travel instead of planes. Coldplay have also made attempts to decrease the environmental impact of their tours, pledging to cut their carbon emissions by 50%, support new green technologies such as kinetic dance floors and energy-generating bikes, and to fund sustainability projects.

It is important for children to have an awareness of these issues so that the choices they make can be informed, even if, as yet, a perfect solution is not clear cut.

ACTIVITY – MUSIC FOR AWARENESS 3 – HOLD A CLASS DEBATE

This activity would suit an Upper KS2 class: As a class, research and compare the environmental impact of producing physical music recordings (for example, compact-discs (CD) or vinyl records), streaming services for music and attending live music events. Invite groups of children to present their findings and argue the case for which is the best environmental choice. Can you come to a consensus of opinion? Are there any solutions to these issues?

REFLECTIVE QUESTIONS

As a school community, consider one change you would like the music industry to make to reduce their impact on the environment e.g. ask the children to write to their favourite musician with suggestions on how they could reduce the environmental impact on their next tour.

ACTIVITY – MUSIC FOR CONNECTION 3 – TAKE MUSIC OUTSIDE

Music lessons and activities which take place outside simply feel and sound different. Take time to allow your children to experience the way sound travels and how connected they can be to their environment by simply being musical in it.

Allow the children time to explore their surroundings and find different sound makers. Once they have collected, for example, a range of sticks and conkers allow them time to develop rhythm and beats with their scavenged materials from the surroundings. Explore with recording and develop sounds. You could even try creating natural musical scores to represent their music. Use stones, sticks and leaves to represent their sounds and lay out the sound sequence on the ground.

Take your scavenged sound makers back to your classroom and create an outside music wall. Try adding different materials from inside as well – pots and pans would add a different timbre to the natural materials your children find.

CHAPTER SUMMARY

Throughout the chapter, we have shown where music can be used as a tool for **connection, collaboration, awareness, engagement** and **creativity**. we have offered ways that music can be used to spark discussion, reflection and learning around sustainability and climate change. Music has a powerful role to play in supporting our young people in their environmental journey. UNESCO's sustainable development goals provide a framework to develop children's knowledge on how to live more sustainable lives, but through music, we can help to develop the attributes needed for them to become the very best advocates of environmental change.

- We need young people to develop a **connection** to emotions and well-being that can aid the control of the anxiety and frustration environmental issues can bring.
- We need young people to be **engaged** with issues of sustainability and climate change and motivated to try to engage with changes.
- We need young people to have an **awareness** of and **connection** to the natural world, locally and globally so it brings about the sense that the choices and decisions we make personally can have an impact and importance in local and global change.

Citizens who can think **creatively** are most likely to be able to think outside the box and take risks to find alternative solutions in the future. Music is one of the highest forms of creativity. An ability to **communicate** effectively is essential for ideas and issues to be disseminated.

Through music, we can instil awareness and appreciation for the environment, promote personal responsibility, and effectively communicate the importance of taking care of the planet.

(Lawler, 2019, online)

Further reading and resources

https://www.beatgoeson.co.uk/junk-percussion-guide/
Ideas for using recycled material percussion in the classroom can be found online e.g. Ollie Tumner's Junk Percussion Guide on the Beat Goes On

https://ltl.org.uk/free-resources/
More ideas for musical activities outside can be found online e.g. Learning through Landscapes.

References

Curran, G., Barwick, L., Turpin, M., Walsh, F. and Laughren, M. (2019) Central Australian Aboriginal songs and biocultural knowledge: evidence from women's ceremonies relating to edible seeds. *Journal of Ethnobiology*, *39*(3): 354–370.

DfE (2013) *Music Programmes of Study KS1 and 2*. Available at: https://assets.publishing.service.gov.uk/government/uploads/system/uploads/attachment_data/file/239037/PRIMARY_national_curriculum_-_Music.pdf

Fernandez-Llamazares, A. and Lepofsky, D. (2019) Ethnobiology through song. *Journal of Ethnobiology*, *39*(3): 337–353. https://doi.org/10.2993/0278-0771-39.3.337

Jones, V. and Whitehouse, S. (2022) "It makes me angry. REALLY angry": exploring emotional responses to climate change education. *Journal of Social Science Education*, *20*(4): 93–120. https://doi.org/10.11576/jsse-4551

Keeler J., Roth E., Neuser B., Spitsbergen J., Waters D. and Vianney J. (2015) The neurochemistry and social flow of singing: bonding and oxytocin. *Frontiers in Human Neuroscience*, *9*(5): 18. https://doi.org/10.3389/fnhum.2015.00518

Lawler, B. (2019) Songs and science: using music as a tool to teach about climate change. June 1. Available at: https://www.alfred.com/blog/songs-and-science-using-music-tool-teach-about-climate-change/

Tachev, V. (2022) How to reduce the music industry's climate impact. 12 July 2022. Available at: https://energytracker.asia/how-to-reduce-the-music-industry-climate-impact/

Wright, S. and Osterloff, E. (2022) Eco-anxiety: how to cope at a time of climate crisis. Available at: https://www.nhm.ac.uk/discover/how-to-cope-with-eco-anxiety.html

13
PHYSICAL EDUCATION FOR SUSTAINABILITY AND WELL-BEING

ALISON MURRAY, SARAH ADAMS AND JO NUGENT

LINKS TO CORE CONTENT FRAMEWORK

1.4, 3.6, 4.1, 5.2

SUSTAINABLE DEVELOPMENT GOALS

GOAL 3: Good Health and Well-being
GOAL 4: Quality Education
GOAL 10: Reduced Inequality
GOAL 11: Sustainable Cities and Communities

KEY WORDS

Physical education; reciprocity; progression spiral; micro-adventures; Bronfenbrenner

13 Physical education for sustainability and well-being

CHAPTER OBJECTIVES

This chapter will:

- Provide means to plan for sustainability in how we experience ethical learning and teaching in physical education, using a Bronfenbrenner developmental approach.
- Introduce *The Sustainability Shell*: the concept of thinking for sustainability, through a process of ecologically focussed ethical reasoning.
- Explore physical education through the lens of The Sustainability Shell pedagogy.
- Present our 'active travel' progression spiral. as an exemplification of curriculum design which is embodied through physically active learning.

Introduction

Physical education (PE) enables children to move with confidence through the physical world and to interact effectively with each other and their environment. In this, we recognise the effect that we may be having through our actions and the choices we make. This responsibility to acknowledge our interdependence is what we might call **reciprocity**. The notion of reciprocity exemplifies awareness and willingness to give back, rather than just take (Creswell, 2013), linking to sustainable practices that can shape education and personal lives. Children need the opportunity to increase self and collective awareness of their imprint upon our environment and our world. Time needs to be given if this is to be considered in the curriculum. Curriculum time needs to be made for children to take on greater ownership of how to care for our world in meaningful and sustainable ways. The same can be said for how we go about our general everyday living, and therefore across our planned and emergent curricula as well as in extracurricular experiences. How can we make these count in relatable and tangible ways for school and community sustainable living?

This chapter shares a pragmatic means to plan, enact and recycle sustainable practices through physically active learning. PE offers practicable means to host, support and exemplify several of the sustainable global development goals. We hope that colleagues might also capture pupil interest and imagination in considering and connecting with the more subtle elements across the global sustainability goals. We are delighted to share a tangible framework to support sustainability through PE and physically active learning. We have taken our inspiration from the Fibonacci spiral as demonstrated within a conch or nautilus shell, where the original starting point expands, repeats and grows. This metaphorical shell pedagogy can wrap around your PE curricula. We have used the spiral of the shell as it symbolises how the gradations of content within the curriculum can be expanded, developed and adapted in an ecologically responsible manner (Figure 13.1).

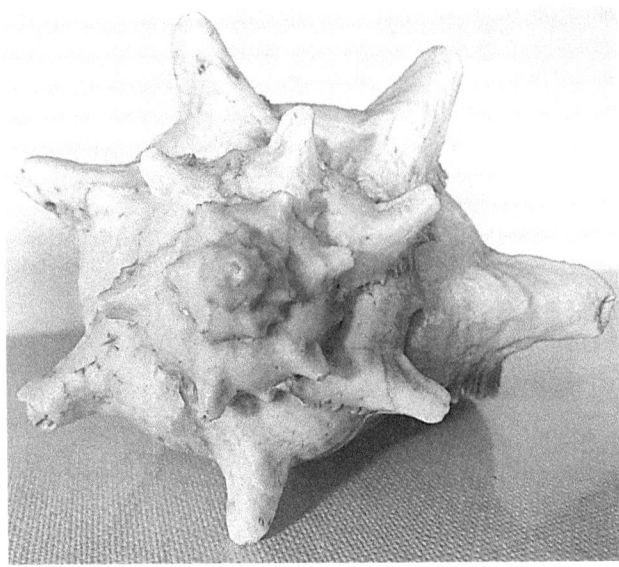

Figure 13.1   Conch shell demonstrating the Fibonacci spiral

The concept of the shell represents a transferable tool that can be implemented (and re-implemented) across a variety of contexts, to offer guidance on how content can be situated through sustainable education in a scaffolded fashion. As sustainable development is of itself, a process of constant change (Hauff, 1987), we invite colleagues to try out the suggested pedagogy and adapt this to your own particular context.

The concept of reciprocity also increases in weighting from early years, through Key Stages 1 and 2.

- At first, it is simply actively encouraging learners to think about someone else – picking up and caring for toys and resources – thinking beyond the 'me' and beyond this moment by considering environmental care.

- By Key Stage 1, this reasoning extends to consider caring for the resources and equipment and people involved in the learning experience and also doing something to add value to the sustainability of such choices for other classes for example.

- By Key Stage 2, children can ethically reason where they are learning and how to care for it of course, but also model this and transfer these principled actions back out to the home and the wider community (Figure 13.2).

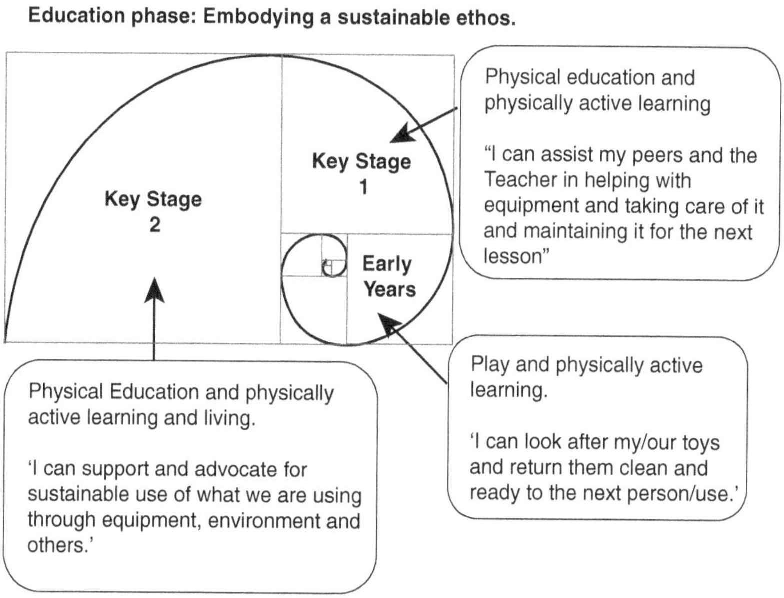

Education phase: Embodying a sustainable ethos.

Key Stage 2

Key Stage 1

Early Years

Physical education and physically active learning

"I can assist my peers and the Teacher in helping with equipment and taking care of it and maintaining it for the next lesson"

Play and physically active learning.

'I can look after my/our toys and return them clean and ready to the next person/use.'

Physical Education and physically active learning and living.

'I can support and advocate for sustainable use of what we are using through equipment, environment and others.'

Figure 13.2 Exemplification of implementing the 'shell' spiral in a PE/physically active learning setting

Sustainable ways to practise

What does sustainability mean through active learning in and around the PE curriculum?

Sustainability education needs to foster knowledge, skills, attitudes and values (UNESCO, 2014). Pupils need to garner a foundational comprehension of sustainability in order to become *sustainability literate'* (US Partnership, 2009). There are comprehensive means to encourage physical activity and to support ecological tenets through education (Baena-Morales and González-Víllora, 2022). Furthermore, explicit work to extend children's awareness of the environment and support sustainable goals is already being effectively implemented through PE (Högman et al., 2020; Lundvall and Fröberg, 2022; Pasek et al., 2022). Hence, we have potentially the perfect environment and opportunity to illuminate meaningful ways for our pupils to make sense of the global to local policies through and around school curricula and communities.

In our chapter, we have selected three aims that span the intent, implementation, and potential impact of ecological progressions. Collectively, class members can think about and target ways, for example, to:

1. interact with nature, safely abiding by the policy rules and cultural expectations of their own context.

2. interact with the environment in ways that show and share respect and value of it whilst enjoying the activity.

3. use reflection as a means to transfer and connect ideas for us to coexist as active movers within the environment.

These three aims are underpinned and influenced by Bronfenbrenner's ecological framework for human development (1977).

Bronfenbrenner's model offers an opportunity to understand a holistic approach to teaching and learning as we recognise how layers of influence shape and inform our decisions through a micro to macro level (see Figure 13.3). The important connection here is realising what might impact the choices we make in relation to respecting and interacting with our environment and responding to issues around sustainability, health and well-being. Placing the child in the centre allows us to consider potential factors that could impact changes in lifestyle that are both sustainable and have long-term benefits for the environment. Everyday practices within a primary school setting, link with the wider community, teacher knowledge and understanding of sustainability. They all contribute to, and influence, how children view and take responsibility for their interaction with the world.

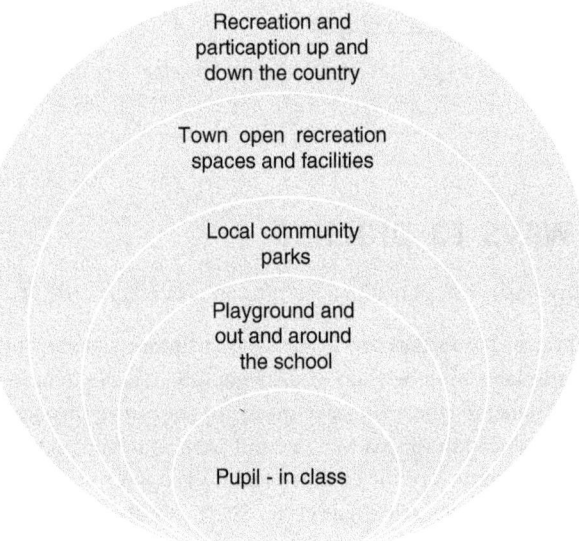

Figure 13.3 Adapted from Bronfenbrenner's ecological framework for human development (1977)

REFLECTIVE QUESTION

How might you encourage pupils to recognise how factors from their decisions and actions in the classroom can be translated to decisions and actions they take in the playground and local community? For example, thinking of sustainability principles: reduce, reuse and recycle in what ways can children care for the environment during the school day?

Pedagogical approaches

Poth argues for ethical reasoning to embody cultural awareness in our decision-making (2020). Through a Bronfenbrenner perspective, children can develop a variety of meaningful ways to develop authentic awareness about how to care for what they are using, how to care for the environment in which they are experiencing the learning, and how to participate in equitable ways.

What is vital is that children acquire competencies and confidence to explore the wider environment, to get out into nature (DfE, 2022), and to do so in ways that enable them to participate beyond curricular time. When that endeavour is sustainable, it can be revisited, and enjoyed by others. To achieve this increased involvement, we need to provide adequate time to plan how the environment may be used equitably and in a sustainable manner. In addition, we need to ensure that children share ideas through reflection, discussion and demonstration (see Figure 13.4).

The Active Travel Progression Spiral is a curriculum spiral that revisits fundamental skills needed for children to successfully engage in active movement. These basic movement skills are required to develop agility, balance, and coordination across early years (DfE, 2021), to develop and master them across Key Stage 1 and then progress into more advanced motor skills and specific sports techniques through Key Stage 2 (DfE, 2013). Explicit links as scaffolded across the development spiral will support class members to build a collective awareness of what they can do in small yet meaningful ways, as they move around the gym, the school building, the playground and out and about in the local communities.

We can extend the impact of PE learning through Bronfenbrenner's ethos, by empowering children to become agents of sustainable change and do this within a class collective, a school collective and a community collective. For example, beginning with tidying up in the classroom, moving to picking up litter around the playground, helping clean at home and extending to caring for community surroundings and taking litter home and disposing of it appropriately through recyclable ways. Ultimately, the impact of our actions will be felt by those around us and in turn, encourage others to take small meaningful actions to create a positive change for our environment.

Using and consuming equipment

The way we teach children to consume information and resources will make a significant difference in how they understand how to value materials and equipment in their own lives. This is linked to the United Nations Sustainable Development Goal (SDG) 4.7, which highlights the importance of high-quality education.

In PE that might be demonstrated as children learn more about their activity space and the environment in which they move. As awareness and opportunities for thinking about sustainability are provided, it should be possible to support children to make their own good choices. For example, in an active lesson on 'transport', pupils will be able to make equipment selections that are best suited to their ability level and meet the intended learning outcomes. Here they might make the choice between a scooter, tricycle, bicycle or other wheel-based equipment. In addition to providing the structured choice, pupils will learn to take care of and maintain the equipment in order to ensure its long-term use. It is not always possible for all schools to buy high-quality wheel-based equipment so the option of having respective schools share the cost, care, and maintenance of such pieces ensures that the opportunity can be enjoyed by several partners across the academic year. Agency might extend not only to learning how to use and care for the equipment, but in becoming part of the collective voice they will not only consider learning opportunities, they will also understand how decisions around purchasing and maintenance of the equipment are made. The PE and Sport Premium is one current lever whereby colleagues can plan for sustainable practice (rather than one-off experiences). Therefore, the implementation of how we provide our curricula offers another means to enact sustainability principles.

Implementation of PE through a sustainability lens

In addition to the pedagogic content knowledge (the 'what' is taught and 'how' it can be experienced), we must consider the equipment choices and the long-term, lasting impact they will have. By choosing and purchasing high-quality, transferable equipment, the teacher is demonstrating a consideration of the environmental impact of purchasing power. Spending more money on durable, multipurpose equipment, which is built to last beyond one school year, will contribute to less landfill waste. Sustainably principled education will encompass the protection of the environment and nature (Pasek et al., 2022). Taking time to model how to care for equipment is a modest yet pragmatic means to show the value of respecting equipment and being thoughtful about how these are acquired. Schools will design their own ecological ideas as shaped by their values, context and available learning affordances. Affordances are opportunities across your environment that offer potential for meaningful physically active learning across PE and, as a complement to your PE curriculum.

REFLECTIVE QUESTION

In what ways could you use your PE and Sport Premium to acquire equipment and or access resources that offer enduring impact potential? How might funding complement available affordances?

The sustainability of human resources cannot be underestimated. In order to ensure a high-quality PE programme, it is important to consider the individuals who work within it. If a specialist is brought in to deliver a specific sport or skill focus, it is crucial that the teacher learn from this expertise and utilise the opportunity as a means of moving their practice forward. To create a sustainable professional development cycle that notion of reciprocity could ensure that all stakeholders benefit from learning more about developmentally appropriate PE (Graham et al., 2022). They could ensure that disseminated content knowledge and experiences are accessible, engaging and reflective of the wider sustainability ethos.

Micro-adventures

In addition to the content and staffing considerations, we can think about the sustainability of experiences. Specialised off site provision can provide fantastic adventure-based learning opportunities;

however, these experiences are often costly and almost impossible to replicate in the school environment. Adopting a *micro-adventures* approach (Williams and Wainwright, 2022), where the learning takes place on the school grounds or local area, allows for the learner to develop and practise the necessary skills within an accessible environment. These learning experiences can take children beyond the traditional learning setting, into affordances that educate and prepare children to safely enjoy a natural environment by following a series of meaningfully scaffolded micro adventure progressions. For example,

- Exploring the indoor gym through imaginative adventure scenarios will allow the implementation of useful skills such as knot tying and shelter planning
- Creating an outdoor playground
- Walking or jogging in local green spaces
- Working with wheeled equipment creates an opportunity to experience the surroundings

Participating in such activities offers space for critical thinking around a key sustainability theme of health and well-being through locomotive skills. Here, we could allow children to analyse the different spaces within the school and consider how to make use of them for a variety of purposes and PE activities

Adopting strategies that necessitate thinking sustainably supports the teacher and learners in the decision-making process around choices in planning and teaching what, how, where and why. As educators and caring citizens, we all understand that when we know why we are doing something, we 'buy-in' to the decisions that are made. Ethically speaking, we need to embody that 'buy-in' for children so that their ecological awareness develops through their physically active learning. The reciprocity here is mediated through the school sustainability culture. Children are valued not just in what they do, but how they do it. Ultimately as with all PE, we hope to motivate and educate children to take more responsibility in caring for themselves, their peers, equipment and the environment across each respective context.

REFLECTIVE QUESTIONS

In what ways can we show forethought in how we plan for meaningful interactions with the environment that afford sustainable practice?

How might we facilitate a caring consumer approach as our learners participate in physically active learning?

If we can capture and nurture this through good quality education during PE lessons, our children will have experienced and seen how to be mindful when they move beyond the curriculum. Therefore, we consider the intent, implementation and potential impact of practice through a life-cycle approach, sharing ideas using ecologically applied ethical reasoning, and applying a Bronfenbrenner ethos.

Regarding enjoying and respecting the environment through physical activity, this commences from ourselves as individuals, and develops beyond:

- me-myself-and I, to
- me-myself--I-and my peers, to
- myself, peers and others

Drawing on the ecological model of human development, messages are reinforced in the way that children recognise their role and responsibilities and engage more purposefully and intentionally with sustainable living. It is the interactions with environmentally aware learning, for example through micro-adventures, which influence longer-term and wider-reaching change.

In the classroom

Enactment of the progression spiral in and beyond curricular settings

The premise for the metaphor of the shell is to provide a means for educators and pupils to position themselves within sustainable goal policy. The shell conceptualises the spiral nature of the curriculum (Bruner, 1960) and we advocate that teachers use this model when designing curriculum progression (see Figure 13.3 for our example). This means it can be recycled and renewed for the next learning content and next context. It is sustainable in terms of colleagues' time and effort and hopefully, permits the collective reasoning to build as children grow up through their school experiences.

Our chosen movement theme is 'travel', as this is a lovely entry point to sustainable practice. The topic of *travelling* can start in the early years and progress into curricular opportunities later on in a child's journey through primary school (DfE, 2013, 2021). The benefits of movement are well documented (Chaput et al., 2020). Global through national policies (WHO, 2020; NHS, n.d.) demand that all children are physically active on a daily basis. Travelling in PE educates and encourages children to value how they move in and around their immediate and extended environments.

A progression spiral trumps a sequence of lesson plans as it can be implemented in context to suit the ecology of the class set up, the school and the surrounding environment.

Our progression spirals here (Figure 13.4) uses the content of locomotor skills to represent active transport to get out and about in local communities and in outdoor green spaces. Context-wise, we might choose micro-adventures in the school gym and outdoor playground to begin with. As proficiency and understanding develop, children will be able to explore the local green space/park using these same skills demonstrating proficiency along the progression spiral.

Within the growth mindset, linked to the metaphor of learning is scaffolded and expanded so that children develop personal ownership to effect responsible change. This is experienced at the pace of each respective group/class to be accessible and to progress at a meaningful pace across the primary years. Fundamental skills as themed through an active travel spiral are exemplified in the following representation. Note: it reads from the bottom upwards.

We can reflect upon how we feel better using active travel in PE so that we share more ideas about how to enjoy active travel out of PE around school and out and about when at home.

Our group can gather and return the equipment and save our map for another PE challenge.

We can take another group through our mapped route and then talk about the health benefits in our healthy active travel.

In our group, we can practise setting up the map in the gym, or out on the playground and use equipment to show the surroundings.

In a small group, we can create a safe and healthy travel route (on a map) around the gym as representative of how to get to the closest green space e.g. park area, from school.

With my partner (or in a small group), I can place cones down to advance the pathway into a travel route. Together we can practise this and talk about the environmental advantages to using our bodies to power our travel.

Using equipment e.g. a body scooter board, a scooter and or my imagination as a car (standing inside a hula hoop), I can travel with a partner and make our own I can form a pair and make our own roadway scenario to practise coming up to a stop light, signalling and then accelerating off.

I can follow a peer through their pathway and stay behind at a safe distance such that when speeds change, both are safe and avoid colliding.

I can show a peer my travel pathway, lead then through it and explain and show where it is safe to slow down (anticipating stopping and or turning) and speed up (to move into an open space in forwards direction).

I can make a travel pathway using some of the skills I practised changing directions and controlling my speed to enter the directional change including deceleration and then acceleration out of the change (e.g. 3-5 changes using a variety of locator skills.

I can move using a variety of locomotor (travel) skills such as walking, skipping, wheeling, jogging; learner selected and directed. (n.b. learners initiate with their accessible mode of travel and progress with that).

Figure 13.4 Active travel progression spiral

Conclusion

Sustainability is achieved in a variety of ways. Not only through the practical means of buying equipment or choosing sustainable learning opportunities but also through the process of sustainable thinking. Providing learners with modelled and scaffolded opportunities to develop their ability to look beyond themselves into the wider world, we hope to empower the individual to impact positive change and make decisions with sustainability in mind. The integration of a sustainable thinking approach will add ecological value to the expected skill, competence and knowledge curriculum. The selected Sustainable Development goals for this chapter embrace and align with our pedagogical intentions by virtue of overlaying the metaphorical shell across the planned and emergent learning experience (e.g. the Active Travel Progression Spiral). Children will want to build competence and confidence in how to participate and enjoy physically active opportunities in socially just and environmentally friendly ways.

CHAPTER SUMMARY

In this chapter, we have used a pedagogical notion of all-encompassing shell to raise awareness of how to implement sustainability practices through physically active learning. Our shell draws upon an ecological model of human development in order to illuminate the power and potential of our collective practice. We have considered how children can start taking responsibility for themselves, equipment and resources. We have introduced the idea of creating micro-adventures and using these to develop children's physical development across the expanding spiral of knowledge, skills and content. This we have linked to Bronfenbrenner's ecology systems for learning about stationarity through active PE. We have concluded the chapter by providing a practical example using 'Travel' as a focus.

Further reading and resources

The association for physical education (afPE) has set out a most constructive strategy to support national policies high-quality PE, physical activity, health and sports for educational school and related environments:

The main site: https://www.afpe.org.uk/physical-education/, provides information and resources to support sustainable practices. https://www.afpe.org.uk/physical-education/afpe-strategy/.

The Youth Sports Trust also provides resources and information which support and promote sustainable practices; https://www.youthsporttrust.org/.

These next readings we recommend as comprehensive as regards the breadth and potential of a primary PE curriculum and means to plan and implement it:

- Griggs, G. and Randall, V. (2022) *An Introduction to Primary Physical Education*, 2nd edition. Routledge.
- Lynch, S., Walton-Fisette, J. L. and Luguetti, C. (2022) *Pedagogies of Social Justice in Physical Education and Youth Sport*. Routledge Focus.

References

Baena-Morales, S. and González-Víllora, S. (2022) Physical education for sustainable development goals: reflections and comments for contribution in the educational framework. *Sport, Education and Society*. https://doi.org/10.1080/13573322.2022.2045483

Bronfenbrenner, U. (1977) Toward an experimental ecology of human development. *American Psychologist*, 32(7): 513–531.

Bruner, J. (1960) *The Process of Education*. Cambridge: Harvard University Press.

Chaput, J. P., Willumsen, J., Bull, F. et al. (2020) WHO guidelines on physical activity and sedentary behaviour for children and adolescents aged 5–17 years: summary of the evidence. *International Journal of Behavioral Nutrition and Physical Activity*, 17: 141. https://doi.org/10.1186/s12966-020-01037-z

Creswell, J. W. (2013) *Research Design: Qualitative, Quantitative, and Mixed Methods Approaches*, 4th edition. London: Sage.

Department for Education (2013) *National Curriculum in England: PE Programmes of Study*. Available at: https://www.gov.uk/government/publications/national-curriculum-in-england-physical-education-programmes-of-study

Department for Education (2021) *Statutory Framework for the Early Years Foundation Stage*. Available at: https://www.gov.uk/government/publications/early-years-foundation-stage-framework--2

Department for Education (2022) *Sustainability and Climate Change Stategy*. Available at: https://www.gov.uk/government/publications/sustainability-and-climate-change-strategy/sustainability-and-climate-change-a-strategy-for-the-education-and-childrens-services-systems

Graham, G., Holt/Hale, S. A., Parker, M., Hall, T. and Patton, K. (2022) *Children Moving: A Reflective Approach to Teaching Physical Education*, 10th edition. New York: McGrawHill.

Hauff, V. (Hrsg.) (1987) *Unsere gemeinsame Zukunft: der Brundtland-Bericht der Weltkommission für Umwelt und Entwicklung. Auflage*. Greven: Eggenkamp, ISBN 978-3-923166-16-9. Available at: https://sustainabledevelopment.un.org/content/documents/5987our-common-future.pdf

Högman, J., Augustsson, C. and Hedström, P. (2020) Let's do those 60 minutes! Children's perceived landscape for daily physical activity. *Sport, Education and Society*, 25(4): 395–408. https://doi.org/10.1080/13573322.2019.1610374

Lundvall, S. and Fröberg, A. (2022) From individual to lifelong environmental processes: reframing health in physical education with the sustainable development goals. *Sport, Education and Society*. https://doi.org/10.1080/13573322.2022.2062320

NHS (n.d.) Physical activity guidelines for children and young people. Available at: https://www.nhs.uk/live-well/exercise/exercise-guidelines/physical-activity-guidelines-children-and-young-people/

Pasek, M., Bendíková, E., Kuska, M., Żukowska, H., Dróżdż, R., Olszewski-Strzyżowski, D. J., Zając, M. and Szark-Eckardt, M. (2022) Environmental knowledge of participants' outdoor and indoor physical education lessons as an example of implementing sustainable development strategies. *Sustainability*, 14(1): 544. https://doi.org/10.3390/su14010544

Poth, C. N. (2020) *Research Ethics: Little Quick Fix*. London: Sage.

United Nations Educational Scientific and Cultural Organization (UNESCO) (2014) *Roadmap for Implementing the Global Action Programme on Education for Sustainable Development.* Paris: UNESCO.

United Nations. Global Sustainable Development Report (GSDR) (2023) THE 17 GOALS | Sustainable Development (un.org).

US Partnership (2009) *Decade of Education for Sustainable Development.* United Nations Decade (2005–2014). National Council for the Social Studies. Available at: www.ncss.org

WHO (2020) *World Health Statistics: Monitoring Health for the SDGs, Sustainable development Goals.* Geneva: World Health Organization, Licence: CC BY-NC-SA 3.0 IGO. Available at: https://apps.who.int/iris/bitstream/handle/10665/332070/9789240005105-eng.pdf

Williams, A. and Wainwright, N. (2022). The role of outdoor and adventurous activities in primary education. In G. Griggs and V. Randall (eds.), *An Introduction to Primary Physical Education*, 2nd edition. Oxon: Routledge.

APPENDIX 1
A SMALL RESEARCH PROJECT: INVESTIGATING CLIMATE CHANGE AND SUSTAINABILITY WITH ICHTHYS CLASS

When considering the importance of providing environmental education for children, it seemed reasonable to ask children themselves what they felt about the issues. This small and limited research project took place with a year 6 class of 23 children in a one-form entry Church of England maintained primary school in West Sussex.

There were 12 boys and 11 girls aged between 10 and 11 years.

Children were provided with a questionnaire including multiple choice and opened responses. Mixed qualitative and quantitative questions provided a wide range of responses allowing collection of some data and analysis of children's understanding of concepts.

After completion of the questionnaire, children discussed specific vocabulary linked to climate change and sustainability and then took part in a series of activities linked to exploring history and climate change.

Climate change

Children were confident that they had encountered the term 'climate change', with 74% feeling they knew either quite a lot or something about it. Only one child (boy) knew nothing. Girls identified as more knowledgeable than boys with 90% (10) suggesting they knew either quite a lot or something compared to 58% (7) of boys. More children felt that they knew something than a lot 52% (12) > 22% (5). This suggests some experience of the concept rather than confident knowledge. Children were then asked to explain what they thought climate change meant. The class had studied a unit on orangutans and their disappearing habitat linked to palm oil production, and this may have contributed to children's understanding. All the girls and most of the boys provided reasonable answers linked to the heating of the earth, often by fossil fuel-produced gases and connected to human actions. There were some misconceptions linked to geography and weather, but children clearly had some basic understanding.

> I think climate change is a dangerous thing that is effecting our world and was made by human's actions. (Boy aged 11)

> I think climate change is about the environment and how it can infect animals and humans. (Girl aged 11)

There was one child who did not recognise climate change as man-made phenomena:

> I don't think that it is to do with CO_2 warming the earth. I think that the world is almost on a scheduled warm up cycle because we had the medieval warm period so maybe that's happening. (Boy aged 11)

Feelings and thoughts about climate change

Chosen phrase/word	Percentage	Gender
We must do something	69.5% (16)	10 girls and 6 boys
We are killing the earth	156.5% (13)	7 girls and 6 boys
I want to help	35% (8)	5 girls and 3 boys
I do not know	30% (7)	4 girls and 3 boys
I do not know what to do	26% (6)	1 girl and 5 boys
Affects everybody	22% (5)	4 girls and 1 boy
Bored	13% (3)	Boys
Worried	9% (2)	1 girl and 1 boy
Anxious	9% (2)	1 girl and 1 boy
Does not affect me	9% (2)	Boys
Not interested	4% (1)	Boy
Not something to worry about	4% (1)	Boy
Challenged	4% (1)	Girl

Some analysis

Boys seem less engaged than girls (does not affect/not interested/not something to worry/bored) – 30%.

Both boys and girls show signs of eco-anxiety (22%).

There is a clear call to take action (69.5%) from both boys and girls with 90% of girls selecting this.

Children clearly wanted some direction about how to become involved. About 35% expressed desire to help, and 69.5% believed that we must do something. However, 26% of them were unsure about what to do and expressed that they do not know what to do.

Sustainability

Children were far less confident with this area. Twelve children were unable to provide a definition (48%). Those that were provided were less precise and several focussed on animal habitat:

> *When you throw something on the ground and animals die from eating it. (Boy aged 11)*
>
> *It doesn't affect animals habitat. (Girl aged 11)*

Some linked to keeping something:

> *Renewing it again and again. (Girl aged 10)*
>
> *Use for along or forever. (Girl aged 11)*
>
> *If a plant sustains atmosphere, it keeps it alive and working. (Boy aged 11)*

Children were also asked to explain what they do to help with sustainability.

Only 10 children responded (43%) – 7 girls and 3 boys.

Responses focussed on litter/plastic/supporting bees/wind power and short showers. All of these were appropriate showing that children who answered had a sound understanding of sustainable practices.

Final thoughts

The majority of children are interested in these areas. There is some evidence of eco-anxiety. Children feel more confident in saying they have some knowledge of climate change than sustainability. They clearly want to do something but require support to explore these complex ideas.

APPENDIX 2
THE 17 SUSTAINABLE DEVELOPMENT GOALS (SDGS) TO TRANSFORM OUR WORLD

GOAL 1: No Poverty

GOAL 2: Zero Hunger

GOAL 3: Good Health and Well-being

GOAL 4: Quality Education

GOAL 5: Gender Equality

GOAL 6: Clean Water and Sanitation

GOAL 7: Affordable and Clean Energy

GOAL 8: Decent Work and Economic Growth

GOAL 9: Industry, Innovation and Infrastructure

GOAL 10: Reduced Inequality

GOAL 11: Sustainable Cities and Communities

GOAL 12: Responsible Consumption and Production

GOAL 13: Climate Action

GOAL 14: Life Below Water

GOAL 15: Life on Land

GOAL 16: Peace and Justice Strong Institutions

GOAL 17: Partnerships to achieve the Goal

Appendix 2 The 17 sustainable development goals (SDGs) to transform our world

Chapter	Links
Introduction: Teaching for Sustainable Futures	GOAL 4: https://sdgs.un.org/goals/goal4 GOAL 13: https://sdgs.un.org/goals/goal13
Chapter 1. The Personal, Social, Emotional and Citizenship Dimensions of Sustainability Education	GOAL 13: https://sdgs.un.org/goals/goal13
Chapter 2. Creating Harmony Through Curriculum Design	GOAL 4: https://sdgs.un.org/goals/goal4 GOAL 7: https://sdgs.un.org/goals/goal7 GOAL 13: https://sdgs.un.org/goals/goal13
Chapter 3. Learning to Care About Our World in the Early Years	GOAL 3: https://sdgs.un.org/goals/goal3 GOAL 4: https://sdgs.un.org/goals/goal4
Chapter 4. Becoming Conservation Champions Through Science Learning	GOAL 15: https://sdgs.un.org/goals/goal15
Chapter 5. Teaching for Sustainability Within Design and Computing Education	GOAL 14: https://sdgs.un.org/goals/goal14 GOAL 15: https://sdgs.un.org/goals/goal15
Chapter 6. Exploring the Climate in Context Through Geography	GOAL 11: https://sdgs.un.org/goals/goal11 GOAL 13: https://sdgs.un.org/goals/goal13 GOAL 15: https://sdgs.un.org/goals/goal15
Chapter 7. Exploring the History of Humans and Their Environment	GOAL 4: https://sdgs.un.org/goals/goal4 GOAL 13: https://sdgs.un.org/goals/goal13 GOAL 15: https://sdgs.un.org/goals/goal15
Chapter 8. Learning to Care About the Environment Through Picturebooks	GOAL 13: https://sdgs.un.org/goals/goal13
Chapter 9. Education for Sustainable Development Through Art: Project CARE	GOAL 17: https://sdgs.un.org/goals/goal17
Chapter 10. Religious Education and Sustainable Living	GOAL 4: https://sdgs.un.org/goals/goal4 GOAL 13: https://sdgs.un.org/goals/goal13 GOAL 16: https://sdgs.un.org/goals/goal16 GOAL 17: https://sdgs.un.org/goals/goal17
Chapter 11. Understanding Our World Challenges Through Mathematics	GOAL 4: https://sdgs.un.org/goals/goal4 GOAL 13: https://sdgs.un.org/goals/goal13
Chapter 12. Exploring Our World Through Music and Sound	GOAL 3: https://sdgs.un.org/goals/goal3 GOAL 4: https://sdgs.un.org/goals/goal4 GOAL 13: https://sdgs.un.org/goals/goal13 GOAL 17: https://sdgs.un.org/goals/goal17
Chapter 13. Physical Education for Sustainability and Well-Being	GOAL 3: https://sdgs.un.org/goals/goal3 GOAL 4: https://sdgs.un.org/goals/goal4 GOAL 10: https://sdgs.un.org/goals/goal10 GOAL 11: https://sdgs.un.org/goals/goal11

Web link to Sustainable Development Goals https://sdgs.un.org/goals

APPENDIX 3
INITIAL TEACHER TRAINING (ITT) CORE CONTENT FRAMEWORK (CCF)

Chapter	Links to the CCF
Chapter 1. The Personal, Social, Emotional and Citizenship Dimensions of Sustainability Education	1.5 A culture of mutual trust and respect supports effective relationships. 7.3 The ability to self-regulate one's emotions affects pupils' ability to learn, success in school and future lives. 7.4 Building effective relationships is easier when pupils believe that their feelings will be considered and understood.
Chapter 2. Creating Harmony Through Curriculum Design	1.1 Teachers have the ability to affect and improve the well-being, motivation and behaviour of their pupils. 3.1 A school's curriculum enables it to set out its vision for the knowledge, skills and values that its pupils will learn, encompassing the national curriculum within a coherent wider vision for successful learning. 4.6 Questioning is an essential tool for teachers; questions can be used for many purposes, including to check pupils' prior knowledge, assess understanding and break down problems. 4.7 High-quality classroom talk can support pupils to articulate key ideas, consolidate understanding and extend their vocabulary.
Chapter 3. Learning to Care About Our World in the Early Years	2.2 Prior knowledge plays an important role in how pupils learn; committing some key facts to their long-term memory is likely to help pupils learn more complex ideas. 3.1 A school's curriculum enables it to set out its vision for the knowledge, skills and values that its pupils will learn, encompassing the national curriculum within a coherent wider vision for successful learning. 4.7 High-quality classroom talk can support pupils to articulate key ideas, consolidate understanding and extend their vocabulary.

(Continued)

Chapter	Links to the CCF
Chapter 4. Becoming Conservation Champions Through Science Learning	3.3 Ensuring pupils master foundational concepts and knowledge before moving on is likely to build pupils' confidence and help them succeed. 3.6 In order for pupils to think critically, they must have a secure understanding of knowledge. 4.2 Effective teachers introduce new material in steps, explicitly linking new ideas to what has been previously studied and learned.
Chapter 5. Teaching for Sustainability Within Design and Computing Education	1.6 High-quality teaching has a long-term positive effect on pupils' life chances, particularly for children from disadvantaged backgrounds. 2.1 Learning involves a lasting change in pupils' capabilities or understanding. 3.1 A school's curriculum enables it to set out its vision for the knowledge, skills and values that its pupils will learn, encompassing the national curriculum within a coherent wider vision for successful learning. 3.2 Secure subject knowledge helps teachers to motivate pupils and teach effectively.
Chapter 6. Exploring the Climate in Context Through Geography	1.6 High-quality teaching has a long-term positive effect on pupils' life chances, particularly for children from disadvantaged backgrounds. 2.1 Learning involves a lasting change in pupils' capabilities or understanding. 3.1 A school's curriculum enables it to set out its vision for the knowledge, skills and values that its pupils will learn, encompassing the national curriculum within a coherent wider vision for successful learning. 3.2 Secure subject knowledge helps teachers to motivate pupils and teach effectively.
Chapter 7. Exploring the History of Humans and Their Environment	3.2 Secure subject knowledge helps teachers to motivate pupils and teach effectively. 3.6 In order for pupils to think critically, they must have a secure understanding of knowledge within the subject area they are being asked to think critically about. 4.3 Modelling helps pupils understand new processes and ideas; good models make abstract ideas concrete and accessible.
Chapter 8. Learning to Care About the Environment Through Picturebooks	5.2 Seeking to understand pupils' differences, including their different levels of prior knowledge and potential barriers to learning, is an essential part of teaching.
Chapter 9. Education for Sustainable Development Through Art: Project CARE	1.2 Teachers are key role models, who can influence the attitudes, values and behaviours of their pupils. 8.3 Teachers can make valuable contributions to the wider life of the school in a broad range of ways, including by supporting and developing effective professional relationships with colleagues.
Chapter 10. Religious Education and Sustainable Living	1.2 Teachers are key role models, who can influence the attitudes, values and behaviours of their pupils. 1.5 A culture of mutual trust and respect supports effective relationships.

(Continued)

(Continued)

Chapter	Links to the CCF
	2.1 Learning involves a lasting change in pupils' capabilities or understanding. 3.6 In order for pupils to think critically, they must have a secure understanding of knowledge within the subject area they are being asked to think critically about. 4.7 High-quality classroom talk can support pupils to articulate key ideas, consolidate understanding and extend their vocabulary.
Chapter 11. Understanding Our World Challenges Through Mathematics	1.3 Setting goals that challenge and stretch pupils is essential. 3.6 In order to think critically, they must have a serious understanding of knowledge within the curriculum area they are asked to think critically about. 4.3 Modelling helps pupils understand new processes and ideas; good models make abstract ideas concrete and accessible.
Chapter 12. Exploring Our World Through Music and Sound	1.1 Teachers have the ability to affect and improve the well-being, motivation and behaviour of their pupils. 1.2 Teachers are key role models, who can influence the attitudes, values and behaviours of their pupils. 4.3 Modelling helps pupils understand new processes and ideas; good models make abstract ideas concrete and accessible. 4.4 Guides, scaffolds and worked examples can help pupils apply new ideas but should be gradually removed as pupil expertise increases.
Chapter 13. Physical Education for Sustainability and Well-being	1.4 Setting clear expectations can help communicate shared values that improve classroom and school culture. 3.6 In order for pupils to think critically, they must have a secure understanding of knowledge within the subject area they are being asked to think critically about. 4.1 Effective teaching can transform pupils' knowledge, capabilities and beliefs about learning. 5.2 Seeking to understand pupil's differences, including their differing levels of prior knowledge and potential barriers to learning, is an essential part of teaching.

INDEX

A
Academics, 5, 15
Acid rain, 80
Active learning, 36
Active travel progression spiral, 179, 183 (figure)
Adaptation, 4, 96
Adeola, D., 110
Algorithms, 72, 145
Amabile, T. M., 68
Anthotypes, 126
Anthropocene, 3, 6
Archer, L., 53
Ardern, J., 63
Art Education in New Times: Connecting Art with REal Life Issues (CARE), 118
Artificial intelligence (AI), 141
ASPIRES project, 53

B
Baggaley, J., 16
Bamber, P., 34
Bamboo Music, 160
Barkham, P., 108
Barwell, R., 144–145
Become Ocean, 168
Bhutan, 134–135
Bible, 133
Big Bang, 94
Big history, 94
Bilton, H., 41
Biodiversity, 17 (table), 22–24, 29, 29 (table), 47
Biodiversity Stripes, 149
Black Lives Matter, 7
Boggs, G. L., 109
Bon Jovi, J., 114
Boyd, D., 37
Britain, 94
British Design Council (2009), 66
Bronfenbrenner's ecological framework for human development, 178, 178 (figure)
Bryon, N., 110
Buddhism, 133, 137
Built environment, 95

C
Cage, J., 156
Cannadine, D., 92
Cantell, H., 52
Canva, 73
Carbon footprints, 148
Carmi, N., 52
Carr, E. H., 92
Carson, R., 6, 154
Chang, E., 120
Charts, 144
Chawla, L., 38
Children
  as agents of change, 52
  algorithms, 72
  citizenship education, 16
  climate change, 14–15, 64
  curiosity, 39
  digital skills, 64
  ecological knowledge, 46
  engaging with water, 40, 40 (figure)
  environment, 13
  geography, 40, 40 (figure)
  history, 93, 99–100
  holistic development, 38
  hugging trees, 103 (figure)
  individual mobility, 108
  mathematics, 141
  misconceptions, 48
  motivations, 39
  music, 163–172
  to nature, 53–54
  physical activity, 108
  physical education (PE), 175
  play, 38–39
  recycling, 71
  religions, 132
  science literacy, 48
  search engines, 73
  social and emotional skills, 15–16
  sustainability, 15, 23–24, 64
  textile design, 72–73
Childs, K., 70
Chipko movement (1970), 102

Christianity, 132
Circular economy, 67
Citizen science, 54
Citizenship education, 16–17
Civilisation
  climate change, 93, 95
  environmental crisis, 93
  Indus Valley, 103–104, 104 (figure)
  Mycenaean, 98
  stress/collapse, 96–98, 96 (figure)–97 (figure)
Classical music, 168–169
Classroom, 28–30, 38
  design and computing education, 68–69
  digital tools and technologies, 64
  environment, 12–13
  geography, 83
  history, 99–100
  mathematics, 146–150
  personal development, 16–18, 17 (table)
  physical education (PE), 182–183
  picturebooks, 111–112
  religious education (RE), 135
  science learning, 54–59
  sound environments, 157–161
  sustainability, 12–13, 63, 69, 69 (table)
Climate, 78–79, 95
  anxiety, 13
  concepts, 82–83, 82 (figure)
  curriculum and, 80–82, 81 (table)
  emergency, 66, 111, 142
  fluctuations, 1
  technonature to, 144
Climate Action Award, 24
Climate change, 1, 6–7, 12–13, 16, 22, 25, 47, 64, 92, 97–98, 109, 130, 137, 141, 163, 187–188
  'bicycle' model on, 52
  children's direct and indirect experience of, 14–15
  emotions, 13
  feelings and thoughts, 188
  history, 99
  human-caused, 13
  integrating mathematics, 148
  mathematics, 143–144
  music, 165–166
  past civilisations, 95
  psychological impact of, 13
  teaching, in schools, 4–6, 5 (figure)
  weather, 82
Climate crisis, 3, 4 (figure), 13, 24, 36, 93–94, 118
  reactions to, 97 (figure)
Climate Education Bill (2023), 23–24
Climate Stripes, 150
Co-dependency of systems, 3, 3 (figure)
Communality, 39
Community, 38–39
Concept cartoons, 48
Conference of the Parties (COP), 17
Connectivity, 142
Conservation, 37, 63
  biodiversity and, 48–49, 53–54
  butterfly, 58
  practices, 46
  wildlife, 64
Continuing professional development (CPD), 5, 124, 126
Core content framework (CCF), 192–194
Coronavirus disease 2019 (COVID-19) pandemic, 108
Country Town: Now and Future, 124, 124 (figure)
CPD. *See* Continuing professional development (CPD)
Craighead George, J., 111
Crandon, T. J., 110
Creativity, 114, 157
  design thinking and, 67–68
Crichton, M., 130
Critical mathematics education, 144–145
Critical thinking, 146
Curriculum, 5–6, 8, 15
  citizenship education, 16
  climate change, 16
  community and responsibility, 17
  design and computing, 65–66
  education for sustainable development (ESD), 35 (table)
  geography, 80, 82 (figure)
  guidance, 23
  history, 99
  Issues-Based Art Education (IBAE), 119
  joined-up, 29
  physical education (PE), 175
  school vision, 36
  science model, 47
  Scotland, 37
  sequence, 49
  sustainability, 16
Curriculum for Excellence (2019), 23
Curriculum for Wales (2022), 23–24

D
Data analysis, 147
Data visualisation, 73
Davies, N., 109
Davis, J., 34
Deforestation, 3, 18, 85, 102, 109
Delgado, C., 5
Denial, 4
Design and computing education
  algorithms in a coding project, 72
  art, 70–71
  classroom, 68–69, 69 (table)
  as consumers, 66–67
  creativity and, 67–68
  in curriculum, 65–66

data visualisation, 73
parts of, 70
positive change, 67
recycled digital artefact, 71
textile design, 72–73
Design and Technology Association (DATA), 66
Design thinking, 67–68
Determan, J. M., 93
Diamond, J., 93, 96, 98
Diffey, J., 13, 15
Digimaps, 73
Digital artefacts, 70
recycled, 71
Digital literacy, 74, 93
Disciplinary knowledge, 50–52
Diversity aids understanding, 64
Dolan, A., 3–4
Dreamson, N., 35
Drought, 113
agricultural, 112
hydrological, 112
impact of, 113
meteorological, 112
water supply, 112
DRY, the Diary of a Water Superhero, 112
Durrani, N., 93, 98

E
Early Childhood Education for Sustainability (ECEfS), 35
Early years, 38, 100
food collage, 125
mathematics and, 143
play, 38–39
sound environments, 158
sustainability, 34, 37, 42
Early Years Foundation Stage (EYFS), 16, 17 (table), 35 (table)
active learning, 36
creating and thinking critically, 36
playing and exploring, 36
statutory framework, 36
Earth Prom, 169
Earth Symphony, 169
Eco-anxiety, 7, 13, 81, 189
Eco-Awakening (2021), 67
Ecocide, 96
Eco-friendly alternatives, 69, 69 (table)
Ecological history, 94–95
Ecological knowledge, 52
Economic analysis, 148
Economic influence, 3
Economist Intelligence Unit (EIU), 67
Eco-Schools programme, 37–38
Ecosia, 65
Ecosystems, 1
Education for sustainable development (ESD), 34

art teacher competences, 122, 123 (figure)
classroom, 124–126
curriculum, 35 (table)
definitions of, 118, 122
Issues-Based Art Education (IBAE), 120
pedagogy, 35 (table)
primary schools, 118
significance of, 118
WAIT model, 122
Edwards, S., 41
Egypt, drought on, 97
Eilish, B., 169, 171
Elegy for the Artic, 168
Emotional development, 15–16
Emotional well-being, 165–166
Energy efficiency, 147–148
England, 23–24, 47, 73, 79, 81, 108, 118
English, P., 144
Enquiry questions, 27 (table)
Enquiry types, 51 (table)
Environment, 16, 39–41, 53–54, 108
children, feel about, 13
damage, 97–98
disengagement, 108
education, 6
history, 94–95
music, 163–172
physical, 95
protection, 13
religious education (RE), 133–134
sound, 154–161
sustainability and, 12–13
Environmentalism, 130
ESD. See Education for sustainable development (ESD)
Ethical consumerism, 63
External activism, 15–16
Extinction Rebellion, 7
Extreme weather events, 86–87
EYFS. See Early Years Foundation Stage (EYFS)

F
Fagan, B., 93, 98
Fernandez-Armesto, F., 93
Fibonacci spiral, 175, 176 (figure)
Fishing, 47
Flynn, T., 7
Fortner, R., 5
Fuchs, L., 114
Fuertes-Prieto, M., 145

G
Gardening, 55, 58
Gaye, M., 169
Geography, 78
classroom, 83
climate and curriculum, 80–82, 81 (table)
climate concepts, 82–83, 82 (figure)

concepts and climate, 78–79
curriculum planning problems, 80
extreme weather events, 86–87
grammar of, 79
urban water cycle, 85–86
weather, 84–85, 85 (figure)
wind, 83–84
Germany, 70
Glantz, M. H., 112
Global climate summits, 2
Global warming, 1–2, 4
Google Sheets, 73
Graphs, 144
Greenhouse gases, 48
Gross National Happiness (GNH), 135, 137

H
Habitats, 57–58
Hapa Zome, 72–73
Harmony: A New Way of Looking at Our World (2010), 25
Harmony Project approach, 28, 30
Hickman, C., 13, 15–16
Hindus, 133
History, 93, 126
    civilisation, factors contribution, 96–98, 96 (figure)–97 (figure)
    classroom, 99–100
    climate change, 99
    climate crisis, 93
    ecological, 94–95
    environmental, 94–95
    human civilisation, 93
    past civilisations, 95
    practical activities, 100–104
Human world, 2–4
Hungerford, H. R., 52

I
IBAE. *See* Issues-Based Art Education (IBAE)
India, 102
Indigenous music, 166–167
Indus Valley Civilisation, 103–104, 104 (figure)
Initial teacher education (ITE), 5, 124, 126
Initial teacher training (ITT), 192–194
Insect pollinators, 49
Intensive farming, 47
Interconnectedness, 6–7, 22
    disciplinary knowledge, 51, 51 (figure)
    substantive knowledge, 51, 51 (figure)
Interdependence, 23, 30, 49
Internal activism, 15–16
Ireland, 37
Islam, 133
Issues-Based Art Education (IBAE), 119–120
ITE. *See* Initial teacher education (ITE)
Ives, C. D., 26

J
Jackson, M., 169
Jainism, 134
Jain, P., 142
Jenson, B., 6–7
Jo Napoli, D., 109
Jones, V., 145
Junk Percussion, 159

K
Kaga, I., 34
Key Stage 1 (KS1), 17 (table), 27 (table), 65
    artwork analysis, 125
    food stories, 101
    interview older residents, 101
    reciprocity, 176
    requirements for, 99
    significant individuals, 102, 103 (figure)
    sound environments, 158
Key Stage 2 (KS2), 17 (table), 27 (table)
    Alphonse the camel and Frank the camel killer, 103–104, 104 (figure)
    make do and mend, 101
    reciprocity, 176
    requirements for, 99
    severe weather events, personal experience of, 101–102
    sound environments, 158
Kiddle, 73
Kim, S., 35
Knowledge
    disciplinary, 50–52
    ecological, 52
    scientific, 48
    substantive, 48–49
Korkmaz, A., 35, 37

L
Lambert, D., 79
Lane, M., 93
The Last Polar Bear, 111
Learning, 6–7, 18, 142
    academic, 15
    citizenship education, 16
    four ways of, 121–122
    new framework for, 25–28, 27 (table)
    science, 53
    social and emotional, 15
    sustainability and nature, 30, 37
    teaching and, 25–28, 27 (table)
Least developed countries (LDCs), 134
Leger-Goodes, T., 7
Lewis, L., 114
Life cycles, 58
Lindström, L., 120
Lindström's model, 120–121
Local history, 99, 101

The Lorax, 110
Lovelock's theory of the Gaia hypothesis, 2
Lower Key stage 2, 125–126

M
Mackintosh, M., 79
Mathematics, 141
  carbon footprints, 148
  classroom, 146–150
  climate change, 143–144
  critical mathematics education, 143–145
  data analysis, 147
  early years and, 143
  economic analysis, 148
  energy efficiency, 147–148
  literacy, 143–146
  population growth, 148
  real-world context, 141–143
  renewable energy, 147–148
  resource consumption, 148
  super wicked problems, 146, 146 (table)
  technonature, 144
  waste management and recycling, 148
  wicked problems, 146, 146 (table)
McCabe, K., 83–84
McCartney, P., 114
Messiaen, O., 156
Micro-adventures, 180–182
Microplastics, 66
Microsoft Paint 3D, 71
Minor, W., 111
Mitchell, J., 169
Mitigation, 4
Miti Wangari: Wangari Maathai and the Trees of Kenya, 109
Monbiot, G., 87
Mottley, M., 63
Mulligan, T., 144
Music, 114, 163–164
  children feel, 165
  class debate, 171
  classical, 168–169
  climate change, 165–166
  collaboration, 170
  elements of, 155–156
  engagement, 169–170
  indigenous, 166–167
  indigenous Australian (Aboriginal), 167
  industry, 170–171
  outside, 172
  popular, 169–170
  singing, 165–166
  sustainability, 165–166

N
Nakate, V., 72
National curriculum (NC), 23, 25–26, 47
  art (craft) and design, 66
  cross-curricular framework, 31
  Design and Technology, 65–66
  history, 99
  mathematics, 141–142
  objectives, 30
  scientific programmes of, 52
  sound environments, 156
  weather, 82
National Society for Education on Art and Design (NSEAD), 66
Natural world, 2–4, 6, 22
Netherlands, 59
New Zealand, 5
Non-violence (ahimsa), 134
Northern Ireland, 23
NSEAD. *See* National Society for Education on Art and Design (NSEAD)
Numeracy, 141–143

O
Ofsted's Research Review (2021), 80
Oral history, 99, 101
Orchestra des Wandels, 171
Organization for Economic Co-operation and Development (OECD), 24
Ostinati, 159
Owens, P., 36
Ozone layer, 4, 80

P
PE. *See* Physical education (PE)
Pedagogy, 35 (table), 36
  approaches to, 38
  of hope, 36
  physical education (PE), 179
  playful, 41
Personal development, 15–18, 17 (table)
Personal Social and Health Education (PSHE), 120
Physical education (PE), 175
  classroom, 182–183
  micro-adventures, 180–182
  pedagogical approaches, 179
  reciprocity, 175
  sustainability, 177–178, 180
  using and consuming equipment, 179–180
Picturebooks
  classroom, 111–112
  creativity, 114
  drought, 112–113
  eco-emotional responses, 109–110
  hero narrative, 110–111
  hope, 114
  water citizenship, 113
Piktochart, 73
Play, 38–39
Playful pedagogy, 41

Poetry, 114
Ponty, M., 108
Popular music, 169–170
Population growth, 148
Pramling, I., 34
Pressoir, E., 41
Primary Science Capital Teaching Approach (PSCTA), 53
Primary science education, 47
Problem solving, 137
Project CARE, 119
  art education, 119
  case study, 124, 124 (figure)
  classroom activities, 125–126
  continuing professional development (CPD), 126
  initial teacher education (ITE), 126
  schools, 126
  stages of, 122
  UNESCO SDGs, 119
The Promise, 109
PSCTA. *See* Primary Science Capital Teaching Approach (PSCTA)

Q
Qur'an, 133

R
Rainfall, 85–86
Rawlinson, S., 4
Razzouk, R., 68
Reciprocity, 175–176
Recycling, 71, 148
Religious education (RE), 126, 130
  case study, 134–135
  classroom, 135
  debate and critical thinking, 137
  environment, 133–134
  subject knowledge, 135–136
  sustainability, 132
Renewable energy, 147–148
Resource consumption, 148
Resource depletion, 1
Rewilding concept, 71
Robinson, K., 120
Routines, 41–42
Royal Society for the Protection of Birds (RSPB), 54
Runco, M. R., 68

S
Sakamoto, S. O., 68
Schleicher, A., 24
School grounds, 54–55
Schulte, C., 70
Science capital, 53
Science learning, 46, 49
  children, as agents of change, 52
  children to nature, 53–54
  citizen science, 54
  classroom, 54–59
  disciplinary knowledge, 50–52
  evolution and inheritance, 59
  flower, in plant reproduction, 57
  gardening, 55
  habitats, 57–58
  knowledge, 48
  life cycles, 58
  nature study, 47–48, 56
  plants and seasonal changes, 56
  plants topic, 49, 50 (figure)
  policy background, 47
  Primary Science Capital Teaching Approach (PSCTA), 53
  school grounds, using, 54–55
  substantive knowledge, 48–49
  understanding, 48
Science Technology Engineering and Mathematics (STEM), 37
Scoffham, S., 4
Scotland, 23, 36–38
Self-efficacy, 25
Seuss, D., 110
Shute, V., 68
Singing, 165–166
Skamp, K., 52
Skovsmose, O., 144
Social and emotional learning, 15
Social aptitude, 15
Social development, 15–16
Social environment, 95
Social justice, 7, 16, 146
Social media, 65
Sörlin, S., 93
Sound environments, 154
  classroom, 157–161
  components of, 155–156
  creativity, 157
  early years, 158
  Key Stage 1 (KS1), 158
  Key Stage 2 (KS2), 158
  music, 155–156
  national curriculum, 156
  percussion with recycled materials, 159–161, 160 (figure)
  playing, 155
  simple steps-listening, 157
Sport Premium, 180
Standish, A., 81
Statistics, 144
Stefferson, L., 145
Stewardship, 133
Strengthening Welfare in Marine Settings Act (SWIMS Act of 2022), 4
Substantive knowledge, 48–49
Super wicked problems, 146, 146 (table)

Supportive practice, 41–42
Sustainability, 16, 25, 36–38, 63, 118, 130–132, 163, 189
  action, 27 (table)
  biodiversity, 29 (table)
  children's educational experience, 23–24
  children's voice and empowering action on, 15
  classroom issues of, 23
  creativity, 114
  early childhood education for, 34–36
  economic dimension, 37
  environment and, 12–13, 37
  history, 100
  man-made world, 63–64
  music, 165–166
  physical education (PE), 177–178, 180
  playful pedagogy for, 41
  recycling, 71
  religion's role in, 132
  sociocultural dimension, 37
  strong, 4
  teaching, in schools, 4–6, 5 (figure)
  weak, 4
Sustainable Development Goals (SDGs), 2, 37, 130
  ethics, 132
  4.7, 179
  map of, 131 (figure)
  17, 118, 190–191
Sustainable urban drainage systems, 86
Swiggle, 73

T
Taylor, H., 143
Taylor, N., 4
Teachers training, 5
Teach the Teacher campaign, 24
Technonature, 144
Textile design, 72–73
Thneed, 110
Thunberg, G., 7

U
United Kingdom (UK), 37, 159
  drought, 112
  farming, 87
  flooding, 87
  hot summer, 86
  weather, 84–85, 85 (figure)
United Nations Educational, Scientific and Cultural Organization (UNESCO), 34, 118–119, 126. *See also* Sustainable Development Goals (SDGs)
United Nations Framework Convention on Climate Change (UNFCC), 12
Upper Key Stage 2, 126
Urbanisation, 47
Urban water cycle, 85–86

V
Vella, R., 122
Virtual National Education Nature Park, 47, 54
Volk, T. L., 52

W
Wales, 23
Warwick, A., 36
Waste disposal, 1
Waste management, 148
Water Music, 160–161
Weather, 82, 84–87, 85 (figure), 111
Well-being of Future Generations Act (2015), 24
The Wellcome Trust's (2017), 47, 54
Wicked problems, 146, 146 (table)
Wild Child, 108
Wildlife conservation, 64
Wilhite, D. A., 112
Williamson, T., 98
Wind, 83–84
With, About, In and Through (WAIT) model, 120–122
World Wildlife Fund for Nature (WWF), 67

Y
Yildiz, T. G., 35, 37
Young people, 13, 22–23
  Eco-Schools programme, 37–38
  learning, 26
  music, 167
  opportunities, 24–25

Z
Zimmer, H., 169

www.ingramcontent.com/pod-product-compliance
Lightning Source LLC
Chambersburg PA
CBHW081156020426
42333CB00020B/2519